MW00623776

"From the opening section concerning the 'Missionary Call' to the closing chapter about language learning and creative access platforms, Pratt, Sills and Walters ably introduce the reader to a wide range of theories and practice in the field of world missions. Any reader contemplating missionary service and every student desiring a more complete understanding of the issues in international missions will be greatly enlightened by reading *Introduction to Global Missions*."
—**Robin Dale Hadaway**, professor of Missions and vice president for Institutional Initiatives, Midwestern Baptist Theological Seminary

"John R. W. Stott compares liberals and their productions to 'hot-air balloons' carried along by prevailing winds on the one hand, and evangelicals and their productions to 'kites' tied to Scripture on the other hand (Edward & Stott, 1988, p. 160). Truth be known, these days it is sometimes difficult to differentiate evangelical 'kites' from liberal 'hot-air balloons' because evangelicals, like liberals, become overly 'caught up' in winds of change. That's why *Introduction to Global Missions* needed to be written. And that's why it needs to be widely read and carefully studied by all believers interested in Christian mission. This is evangelical missiology at its best—contemporary and creative but tied securely to the Word of God."
—**David J. Hesselgrave**, professor emeritus of Mission, Trinity Evangelical Divinity School

"From the initial call experience to missionary service to the various strategic applications of missionary practice on the field, this book covers it all. It's a comprehensive textbook—a useful tool in helping people develop biblical foundations, theological parameters, and practical methodologies for mission advance. Beyond just compiling information, the book pulsates with passion for global mission advance. Read it and get moving!"
—**Dr. Jeff Iorg,** president, Golden Gate Seminary

"This missiology text is thoroughly engaging. I have not previously read a missiology text where the authors so consistently anticipated and answered my questions both as a teacher and a missionary practitioner. Students will love this book. There is a unique presentation of the big picture of missiology with wonderful detail in so many practical applications and gems of wisdom. This book will surely help prepare more effective missionaries and produce more excitement about missionary service. One aspect of this book that sets it apart from others is how reproducible its teachings are for those who embark on global mission work. I have used a good number of missiology texts over the years, but I have not encountered one like this. It will resonate with you and a new generation of missionaries."
—**Mark McClellan**, dean of the Herschel Hobbs College of Theology and Ministry, professor of Theology and Missions, Oklahoma Baptist University

"We are standing at the threshold of one of the greatest moments of opportunity and responsibility for the Christian Church. With the Great Commission as our charge, there has never been a greater need for a book that would introduce Christian missions in all of its fullness and urgency, and for that reason I warmly welcome *Introduction to Global Missions* by Zane Pratt, David Sills, and Jeff Walters. These three authors combine decades of experience on the mission field and thoughtful engagement with the most crucial, biblical, and theological issues of the Great Commission Challenge. This book represents the latest scholarship, the keenest biblical thinking, and a very current analysis of the challenges and opportunities we face around the world. This book is urgently important, spiritually challenging, and belongs in the hands of every gospel-minded Christian."
—**R. Albert Mohler Jr.**, president, The Southern Baptist Theological Seminary

"*Introduction to Global Missions* is a solid and comprehensive survey. It is i[d]
college or seminary class that can open a student's heart and mind to this exciting fi
glad to recommend its widest possible use."

—**Daniel L. Akin**, president, Southeastern Baptist Theological Seminary

"Zane Pratt, David Sills, and Jeff Walters have provided a top-shelf text in *Intr*
to Global Missions. The book is designed to be the perfect volume for a one-semest[e]
on global missions, and it treats very effectively the biblical, historical, cultural, and
aspects of missions."

—**Bruce Ashford**, provost and dean of faculty, Southeastern Baptist Theological [S]

"For any student interested in missions, specifically in local churches or on th
sity level, *Introduction to Global Missions* proves to be a thorough, balanced textl[
will greatly enhance one's understanding of the basics of mission work. I highly rec
this work."

—**Jeff Brawner**, chair, Department of Missions, Mid-America Baptist Theological [

"Missiology is a complex subject that cuts across a multitude of disciples. Bibl
ies, theology, anthropology, world religions, and communications theory are just a [f
topics involved. Lucidly written and up-to-date in its coverage of these topics, this
tion will undoubtedly provide students, pastors, and local church leaders a superb re
turn to in order to engage in God's global mission with knowledge and effectiveness

—**J. Scott Bridger**, Assistant Professor of World Christianity and Islamic
Criswell College

"Zane Pratt, David Sills, and Jeff Walters have provided their readers with [a
ous and well-written overview of global missions. This insightful introduction guide
through important biblical, theological, historical, and practical understandings of
Drawing upon their many years of service as missionaries and missiologists, th[e
move beyond a general overview with more specific engagement on such matters [a
anthropology, cultural understanding, and world religions, as well as practical in
regarding disciple-making and church planting. With genuine joy, I highly recomn
outstanding, thoughtfully conceived, capably researched, and highly applicable volu

—**David S. Dockery**, president, Trinity International University

"*Introduction to Global Missions* is a tool each missionary, pastor, teacher, an
leader should keep in the 'readily accessible' section of their library. In a mann[e
at once biblical and practical, theological and inspirational, the authors provide a[r
treatment of every significant aspect related to global missions. This is a book that [
the causes of the kingdom, especially those related to missions, many years into the

—**Tom Elliff**, president, International Mission Board of the Southern Baptist Co

"*Introduction to Global Missions* offers a comprehensive and contemporary m[
cal education for the classroom, as well as challenging hearts to the call of being in
God's mission. This valuable guide by three outstanding scholars provides a broad
of the biblical, historical, and cultural foundations to empower the practice of twe[r
century global missions."

—**Robert L. Gallagher**, chair and director of M.A. (Intercultural Studies), [
College Graduate School

INTRODUCTION TO
GLOBAL
MISSIONS

ZANE PRATT, M. DAVID SILLS, JEFF K. WALTERS

PUBLISHING GROUP

NASHVILLE, TENNESSEE

Introduction to Global Missions
Copyright © 2014
by Zane Pratt, M. David Sills, and Jeff K. Walters
B&H Publishing Group
Nashville, Tennessee
All rights reserved

ISBN: 978-1-4336-7875-2

Dewey Decimal Classification: 266
Subject Heading: MISSIONS—HISTORY \ MISSIONS—BIBLICAL
TEACHING \ MISSIONARIES—CALL AND TRAINING

Unless otherwise noted, all Scripture quotations marked are taken
from The Holy Bible, English Standard Version, copyright © 2001 by
Crossway Bibles, a division of Good News Publishers. Used by permission. All rights reserved.

Scripture citations marked HCSB are from the Holman Christian
Standard Bible®, copyright © 1999, 2000, 2002, 2003, 2009 by
Holman Bible Publishers. Used by permission. Holman Christian
Standard Bible®, Holman CSB®, and HCSB® are federally registered
trademarks of Holman Bible Publishers.

Scripture citations marked NASB are from the New American Standard Bible. © 1960, 1962, 1968, 1971, 1973, 1975, 1977, 1995 by The
Lockman Foundation. Used by permission.

Scripture citations marked NIV are from the HOLY BIBLE, NEW
INTERNATIONAL VERSION®, copyright © 1973, 1978, 1984, 2011 by
Biblica, Inc.® Used by permission. All rights reserved worldwide.

Printed in the United States of America
2 3 4 5 6 7 8 9 10 • 20 19 18 17 16 15

SB

CONTENTS

PREFACE

The story is not really that unusual. A missionary—whether long- or short-term—arrives on the field full of excitement and anticipation. After all, he or she is finally going to fulfill the Great Commission call to make disciples, to touch the nations, and to care for those most in need. Soon, however, the excitement begins to fade. The problem is not weak calling, lack of faith, or dearth of passion. It is a problem of knowing: how do I do what God has called me here to do among these people who need to hear the good news of Jesus Christ? The need for that knowledge is the genesis of this book.

As a carpenter seeks the best tools and a soldier the best equipment, so must a missionary, pastor, or mission team volunteer build a tool chest of effective missionary foundations and practices. The purpose of this textbook is to provide an introductory survey of the most important subjects for any missionary. We have you in mind—whether you are looking ahead to full-time missionary service for a lifetime, a pastor seeking to lead your church on mission, or a first-time, short-term missions team member. Jesus' Great Commission command to "make disciples of all nations" is for the whole church, so the whole church needs to understand the why and how of missions.

Missiology (simply, the study of missions) has traditionally been divided into four areas: biblical and theological foundations, history of missions, cultural studies, and practical strategies. We have followed the same outline for this textbook. Section 1 begins where we should always begin: with the Bible. Section 2 transitions to the historical background of twenty-first-century missions. You will see how the early church applied the Great Commission and how missionaries ever since, with varying degrees of success and faithfulness, have sought to spread the gospel and see the church multiply. All missions and evangelism takes place in culture, so section 3 considers the impact of culture on the missionary task, especially taking into consideration the major world religions. Finally, section 4 deals with the practical application of biblical truth, historical experience, and cultural interpretation to your work of global evangelization, both as individuals and as a local church.

Our prayer as you begin this study is that God will both *prepare* you for your task and *propel* you among the nations. May all the glory go to the God who has made us, who has called us, and who will do the work of salvation among those who hear.

We would like to thank some important people who have contributed to this project. Hannah Carter, David Wells, and Douglas Renfro have gone above and beyond all expectations in their hard work of encouragement, research, editing, and support. We appreciate the administration and faculty of the Billy Graham School of Missions, Evangelism, and Ministry and The Southern Baptist Theological Seminary for making it possible for us to teach this material to hundreds of God-called and gifted students. Chris Cowan and the editorial team at B&H Academic have been supportive and helpful, adding much to the value of this book.

Certainly, our wives, children, and grandchildren have been patient and have prayed faithfully for us (and for you). And we recognize the missionaries and professors on whose shoulders we stand. We would not be who we are, and this project would not ever have been completed, without any of these.

CHAPTER 1

INTRODUCTION: THE MISSIONARY CALL

As we begin our study, we are going to focus primarily on what we mean by missions and how someone can discern what God is calling him to do in missions. Clearly, God is working in his world today, and he uses churches and individual believers in the process. An introductory study of the call to missions includes understanding how it affects both individual Christians and the church.

God has called his people to join him on mission. Sometimes people ask whether there is a biblical basis for missions. Of course there is! But to state it that way minimizes the force of God's missionary heartbeat. We would prefer to state that there is a missiological basis for the Bible. Ask yourself, "If God had not revealed himself in the Bible, what could I know about God?" The answer is "little." Of course, we would know that he exists as Creator because Psalm 19:1–4 teaches that the heavens declare his glory. Paul continued this idea in Romans 1:18–20, adding that we can know about him through what is plainly revealed in creation. In the Bible we study what he has revealed about himself to know him more. We learn throughout the Bible that he wants us to make him known. We conclude that God gave us the Bible that we may know him, enter into a right relationship with him, and make him known in the world. That is what missions is: knowing him and making him known. Therefore, we should conclude that there is a missionary basis to the Bible.

Missions is clearly seen throughout God's Word. In both the Old Testament and the New Testament, God is concerned that the nations know him and worship him. Too often believers, finance committees, and pastors ask, "What is the place of missions in my life, budget, and church?" Rather, as we understand the missionary heartbeat of God, we should ask, "What is the place of my life, budget, and church in missions?" God has called his people to join him on mission in his world. What is your role in that? How would God have you to be involved?

In Romans 10:13–15, Paul stated a marvelous truth and then asked a series of defining questions to bring our question into sharper focus. He began by saying, "For everyone who calls on the name of the Lord will be saved" (HCSB). That is a beautiful truth that all Christians celebrate and depend upon for personal salvation and peace with God. However, Paul began to ask some troubling questions when we think of the vast areas of the world where Christ has not been preached in a way so that those who live there can understand. He asked, "But how can they call on Him they have not believed in? And how can they believe without hearing about Him? And how can they hear without a preacher? And how can they preach unless they are sent?" We may conclude from this that we all have a role to play—either we are goers or we are senders.

If all of us were to go, there would be no one to provide and send. If all were to stay as senders, no one would go. When the Holy Spirit told the church in Syrian Antioch to set aside Barnabas and Saul for the work he had for them to do, he did not tell the rest of the church to go as well; neither did he judge them for not being as spiritual or godly. He told them to set aside and send out the ones he was calling. We are all called to global missions if we are recipients of his saving grace, but we are not all to go. What is the level of involvement of your church, your family, or your life? Welcome to the pilgrimage to find your place in that call.

The field of missiology is growing and expanding, and because it is, many terms are being coined for increasingly specialized needs. Someone has said that words do not have meaning as much as they have usage. In the term *global missions* we mean two key ideas. While the word *global* seems clear enough, we mean more than simply "worldwide." The word *global* does include the idea of worldwide, but it also includes the idea of being fully orbed, integral, whole, and complete. There is much more to missions than merely handing an evangelistic tract to a lost person in another country. This textbook will help you explore the biblical role of believers and churches in God's plan for the world—in its fullness.

The term *missions* is another that is used in varying ways today. Some of the terms people use today—*mission, missions, missionary, missional,* and *missiology*—have a common root in the word *missio,* which derives from the Latin word *mitto,* meaning "to send." The term *missio Dei* refers to the mission of God and means all that he is doing in his world. All the church and believers do flows from God's mission and plan in his world, and what he does includes using us in his mission.

Missiologists and authors sometimes use the words *mission* and *missions* (with an *s*) synonymously. *Mission* (singular) is meant to be broader in its scope to refer to the intentional and overall purpose and goal of the church. Thus, discussions or debates about *the mission of the church* concern that which Christ has charged his church to do in the world. *Missions* (plural) refers to all the many ways that churches seek to carry out their mission in the world in actual missions efforts to reach and teach the peoples of the world for Christ's sake. However, because there is not widespread acceptance of such narrow definition, this textbook will continue the use of both terms in their traditional usages.[1]

While *missionary* basically means "one who is sent," we could describe a *missionary* as someone who intentionally crosses boundaries for the purpose of communicating the gospel to win people to Christ, discipling new believers, planting churches, training biblically qualified leaders, and ministering to the whole body of Christ in holistic ways. The boundaries that must be crossed may be linguistic, religious worldview,

---

[1] For instance, the largest mission agency in the world is the International Mission Board of the SBC, and it uses the singular. Moreover, most churches refer to their short-term efforts as mission trips, not missions trips.

geopolitical frontiers, socioeconomic, and so on. Most of the time we mean that this individual must go from one culture to another.

UNDERSTANDING THE MISSIONARY CALL[2]

Missionaries define their call to missions in terms that often seem so clear and unmistakable. They may relate a keen sense of God's presence while studying the Bible, an overwhelming awareness of the world's needs, a missions experience on the field, or even waking at night to see Jesus standing at the foot of the bed telling them to go to Africa as a missionary. In the absence of such an experience, others may excuse themselves from missions concluding that they have not yet been called. Still others ransack their Bibles looking for an undeniable teaching on the missionary call. Perhaps the confusion that surrounds the concept of the missionary call is responsible more than any other cause for people not going to the mission field. At the beginning of this textbook, we want to take a glance at the call God has used and still uses to get believers from their knees to Nigeria and from the pew to the people of Peru. Some even ask whether there is any biblical basis to a missionary call because we find no such term anywhere in the Bible.

Throughout the pages of missions history, there have been different perspectives on the missionary call. One argues against any specific call. Because the word *missionary* is not found in the Bible, and therefore there is no explicit mention of a missionary call, it is argued to be an extrabiblical and modern invention of missions speakers and mission agencies. Some individuals who hold to this viewpoint have maintained that missions as a career is a personal choice based on capabilities and desire without any divine involvement, just as one might choose to be a secretary, lawyer, or carpenter.

Another viewpoint, and one often repeated in contemporary times, is that there is indeed a call, and everyone already has it. It's called the Great Commission (Matt 28:18–20). Proponents of this view say they do not need a call because they already have a

---

[2] Portions of this chapter's exploration of the missionary call were excerpted and adapted from David Sills's previously published book, *The Missionary Call* (Chicago: Moody, 2008). It should be consulted for a far more comprehensive exploration of the missionary call.

verse. They echo the same sentiment Jim Elliot once stated: "We don't need a call, we need a kick in the pants."[3] However, Elliot also wrote a pastoral letter to his friend Pete Fleming who was struggling with whether to accompany Jim to Ecuador, telling him that if he had not heard from the Lord, Elliot had no word for him either.[4] The hurdles were too high and dangerous to go forth without God's sending.

Others argue that there is indeed a call, and it is specific to the individual. In fact, they continue, the world is so dangerous and gospel-hostile that unless you have a clear call to go, you better not try to go. However, if you have one, you had better not try to stay. Such warnings in the midst of the other positions leave many wondering what exactly they should do and how they can understand the missionary call. The paralysis of analysis sets in, resulting in the inertia of indecision and the guilt of unheeded "shoulds" and "oughts." Let's address the foundation of that paralysis before we go any further. We should be aware that there is clearly a missionary call. God has a plan for every one of our lives, and it includes some level of involvement in global missions. The question before us is how to discern what that level of involvement is for each one of us.

One bit of clarification often helps shed light on the issue, and that is the understanding of the difference between the inner and the external call. The inner call is that awareness of the great needs in the world today—spiritual and physical, real and felt. It is coupled with what the Spirit teaches us through our Bible studies, hearing sermons, and meditating on the commands of Christ. Add to that the deep longing to know about other cultures, travel internationally, learn other languages, and share Christ with people who desperately need to know of his grace and forgiveness. The seeds of these grow in the heart of the one being called and flower into a desire that consumes our days and often invades our dreams. We watch the news with new eyes and read the daily newspapers with our hearts breaking. An overwhelming yearning to spend and be spent for the advance of the gospel in another culture is difficult to describe to someone

---

[3] Elisabeth Elliot, *Shadow of the Almighty: The Life and Testament of Jim Elliot* (New York: Harper, 1958), 54.
[4] Ibid., 150.

who does not have it, but it is as real as describing to someone who has never been in love the difference between liking someone, loving someone, and being in love with someone.

In God's mercy missionaries do not pack and move to the field based on the inner call alone. God has graced us with fellow believers around us who know us well. They have watched us grow in Christ, seen us fall and rise, move up and slide back, advance and retreat in our Christian experience. They know our weaknesses and strengths, talents and gifts, and have watched us for years. The external call refers to a body of believers in close fellowship with the one called who recognizes these gifts and talents and agree in the Lord that God has prepared this person for missionary service. They lay hands on the person, ordain them or commission them, and publicly bless them to go forth to serve in this way as a missionary. The harmony of the inner and external call encourages the missionary in coming days of culture shock and difficulty when adjusting to life on the mission field.

A VARIETY OF CALLINGS

The callings in the Bible reflect numerous ways in which God has called his people. Sometimes there is a call to himself for service to God's people, calls to specific acts of service, calls to salvation, or combinations of these. For instance, in Genesis 12:1–3, God spoke to Abraham in the land of Ur and called him to leave his father's land, kin, and comfort zone to go to a place he would tell him when he arrived. That required great faith, but as is true in many occasions of Abraham's life, prompt obedience followed the call.

In Exodus 3:1–4:12, God called Moses from a burning bush both to follow him and to the specific service of leading his people out of slavery in Egypt. Just as with Abraham, this required great faith to trust in a God he could not see. Yet he obeyed and did what the Lord called him to do.

God called the prophet Jonah to serve him in a specific service that is clearly in line with that of a missionary. Indeed the familiar story throughout the entire book of Jonah details his missionary call, his disobedience to the call, and the result of his repentance of running from the call and surrendering to the will of God—the salvation of many in a hostile land. Some readers may identify with Jonah and wonder whether it is too late to repent and return to obey God's call. Leave all and return to the last clear call of God you received. He will work out the details—with or without a great fish.

Jesus called his disciples to leave their livelihoods, families, and comforts of home to follow him. He called them to salvation, to service, and to missions. In Matthew 4:17–25, Jesus clearly told Peter, Andrew, James, and John to leave all and come after him. Much more amazingly than we recognize with our modern Christian minds, they immediately obeyed, leaving father, fishing, and family behind.

One of the clearest examples of the call to salvation, service, and missions is that in the life of Paul. We see on the Damascus road that he, in the midst of a career of persecution of the church, was struck down and arrested by Jesus Christ himself. A little later he would be told all that he was to do and later still that he was to go far away to the Gentiles. Given these examples and many others, no one can deny that in the Bible God directly calls and guides his people to paths of service that he has prepared in advance for them to walk and work for them to do (Eph 2:10).

Although the Bible does not provide a definition of the missionary call, it gives us a window through which we may look to see God's desire for the nations and how he calls people to himself to carry out his desires. The biblical examples of a call are not prescriptive of how every call should be. We should not view them as precedents in order to make a checklist to compare against our own experience. Rather, the biblical examples are descriptive of what happened when God called people at various times in biblical history.

APPLYING THE MISSIONARY CALL

Once a Christian comes to acknowledge that there is a missionary call, several questions naturally follow: What does that look like applied and lived out? How specific does it have to be, and how can you know it? Where should you go? If to China, then how can you know which province? If you believe God has called you to Shanghai, are you out of God's will if you one day transition through an open door to effective service in Beijing? If

God calls you to India, is it up to you to decide where? Or is God's "where" so specific that he cares whether it is Kolkata, Mombai, or Madras? Or to which part of any of those cities?

Even after obtaining some insight into the exact "where," should you continue to wait until you have further direction on whether to work in English, Hindi, Urdu, or one of the hundreds of other languages of India, or does it matter? Should you work primarily with Muslims, Hindus, or some other religious-background population? Is it essential to know the agency you will work with before you even begin this process? Or does God simply allow you to use whichever agency best facilitates your ability to obey his call? Must you go as a missionary with your own denomination, or may you go with one of the hundreds of other sending agencies? What about the particular job assignment of your missionary career? Is God's call so specific that you must know his will about the job duties of the position you accept?

You can see that the questions could be never ending and all of incredible significance. Finding God's will in the missionary call is sometimes difficult, but the angst of trying to discern and follow God's will does not go away once you come to a place of surrender and acceptance of the general call. For the rest of the missionary's life, decisions must be made about where to live, where to focus efforts on the field, whether to move to another field of service, and whether it is time to hand the work off to the nationals and return home.

KNOWING GOD'S WILL

Entire books address knowing God's will with great wisdom and counsel that are beyond the scope of this chapter, but we do need to consider the ways God guides us on our journey to understand the missionary call. How can you know God's will?

Know God

When people ask me how they can know God's will, I tell them that the best first step is to know God. Some believers are so concerned with knowing the will that they miss the Source. Knowing God is the first step in any wise journey. Proverbs 1:7 teaches us, "The fear of the LORD is the beginning of knowledge; fools despise wisdom and discipline." Wisdom from God guides us to the answers for all the essential questions in life. James 1:5 says, "Now if any of you lacks wisdom, he should ask God, who gives to all generously and without criticizing, and it will be given to him."

Know God's Word

A crucial aspect of truly knowing God is to know his Word. He has revealed himself to us in the written Word. Without the Bible we would have limited knowledge of him. Psalm 19 and Romans 1 teach us that we would know that there is a Creator, but we would be without any specific knowledge of what he is like, what pleases him, and how we may enter into a right relationship with him through his Son Jesus Christ, among many other precious truths. Some people will go around the world to find God's will for their lives but will not go to the next room to read their Bible. Yet the desire to do what God has already revealed is crucial for receiving specific knowledge for your life. As you study the Bible, you will come to understand how he dealt with his people to guide them, to correct them when they strayed, and to enable them to do what they recognized was impossible for them by their own power. As you recognize the repeated biblical patterns throughout the history of his people, you will better understand why he deals with you as he does. In your study you will see that he compares his people to a flock of sheep who are dependent on their Shepherd to guide, protect, provide for, and love them.

God teaches us in his Word that we should be wise in our choices and how we invest our lives. However, we should rest in the sure knowledge that he is sovereign over every detail. Proverbs 16:9 teaches, "A man's heart plans his way, but the LORD determines his steps." When we need guidance, the path of wisdom is to trust him, not our own devices. Proverbs 3:5–6 states, "Trust in the LORD with all your heart, and do not rely on your own understanding; think about Him in all your ways, and He will guide you on the right paths." The wisdom in God's Word gives great guidance and great peace in the process of seeking his will.

Prayer

Prayer brings our heartbeat in tune with God's own. In prayer we come to God in worship. During times of praise and adoration, we are keenly aware of who he is, what he has done, and what his Word teaches us. This love for God leads us to contemplate his perfection and holiness. Like Isaiah, when we see the Lord high and lifted up, we are humbled and profoundly convicted of our sinfulness. How could such a holy God allow us to come into his presence? Mindful of his complete knowledge of all things, including our failures, we agree with him that we are sinners. We confess and renounce our sins. When we pour out our thanks to God for his forgiveness and many blessings, he is pleased. Someone has said that when a child says thank you for the first time without being prompted, he is well on his way to spiritual maturity. Parents are always pleased to see this development in their young children. God the Father is also pleased when we count our many blessings. Recounting our blessings and offering thanks to God make us mindful of the people around the world who do not have the blessings we have. We begin to pray for them and ask him to bless them.

The requests that are a natural part of praying to our God include the need to know what he would have us to do. This was Paul's experience when Christ came into his life.

> As I was traveling and near Damascus, about noon an intense light from heaven suddenly flashed around me. I fell to the ground and heard a voice saying to me, "Saul, Saul, why are you persecuting me?"
>
> I answered, "Who are you, Lord?"
>
> He said to me, "I am Jesus the Nazarene, the One you are persecuting!" Now those who were with me saw the light, but they did not hear the voice of the One who was speaking to me.
>
> Then I said, "What shall I do, Lord?"
>
> And the Lord told me, "Get up and go into Damascus, and there you will be told about everything that is assigned for you to do." (Acts 22:6–10)

Seek Counsel

The Bible teaches us that there is great safety and wisdom in seeking godly counsel. Two verses in the book of Proverbs make this clear.

1. Proverbs 11:14: "Without guidance, people fall, but with many counselors there is deliverance."
2. Proverbs 24:6: "For you should wage war with sound guidance—victory comes with many counselors."

God has placed people in our lives who have watched us grow as believers. They have been able to observe the gifts and abilities that we have shown in our Christian service. These people provide a balance and objectivity that we sometimes lack when we are on an emotional high about a new idea. Perhaps the new idea is indeed God's plan for our lives, and perhaps it is not. Great wisdom is in laying your situation before such a counselor, asking for insight and wisdom.

As you consider people from whom you could seek wise counsel, think about those who know you well and who have shown wisdom in the choices of their own lives. The combination of these two attributes can provide sound guidance in times of major life decisions. Beware of the tendency most of us have to seek out counselors who will tell us what we want to hear. Ultimately, what we want to hear is the truth. Godly friends with a proven track record of discerning God's will and making wise decisions in their own lives, who have watched you grow and exercise your spiritual gifts, and who love you are God's blessing in your life. Seek out their counsel and listen carefully to what they tell you.

Life Experiences

Your life experiences are important considerations for discerning God's will. Because God is sovereign, he has sent or allowed everything that has come into your life. He has done so for a reason, and he works everything together for your good and his glory. He has allowed you these life experiences to make you the person you are. As you look over your shoulder and consider the gifts, talents, abilities, personality, preferences, education, travels, friends, work experiences, and family that make up the composite picture of your life, you can ask yourself a question. Why has God allowed this mix of experiences? Is there a pattern that may help me see how he is preparing me for the future? God knows what you need in order to do what he has made you to do. He knows the skills or gifts that will enable the ministry and guarantee fruit in a future you cannot yet imagine.

Circumstances

The next step in seeking guidance should be circumstances. Many believers who are seeking God's will mistakenly believe that an open door or a closed door must be clear guidance from God. Of course, sometimes it is. Our sovereign God can certainly open and close doors—and does so daily. However, this is a fallen world, and circumstances are not always accurate indicators of God's will.

God warned us in his Word when he referred to Satan as "the god of this age" (2 Cor 4:4) and "the spirit now working in the disobedient" (Eph 2:2). Paul said that we should not be ignorant of Satan's schemes (2 Cor 2:11), forget that he masquerades as "an angel of light" (2 Cor 11:14), or forget that his activity may be marked by "false miracles, signs, and wonders" (2 Thess 2:9). Revelation 12:9 calls him "the one who deceives the whole world." With these passages clearly teaching you about the tactics of the one who loves to sidetrack you from finding and fulfilling the best use of your life, it is obvious that circumstances may not necessarily be a road map from the Lord.

Of course, circumstances are important components of God's guidance. Sometimes the doors that are open to us make no sense as we consider our plans, dreams, or understanding of God's will, but years later we may be able to see how God was clearly guiding us to a point of greater understanding. God has a plan in the many paths that we walk throughout our lives. The path you walk right now may not be of your choosing or desire, but there is a reason for it.

Timing

Many Christians know God, study his Word, spend time in prayer, seek the counsel of godly friends, factor in their life experiences, consider their circumstances, and believe they know what God is leading them to do. And, even though every- thing seems to point to a particular path, they have no peace in following it. God's Word suggests that open doors do not always mean we are to walk through them. Listen to the wisest king Israel ever had to understand the role of timing and God's direction.

> For everything there is a season, and a time for every matter under heaven: a time to be born, and a time to die; a time to plant, and a time to pluck up what is planted; a time to kill, and a time to heal; a time to break down, and a time to build up; a time to weep, and a time to laugh; a time to mourn, and a time to dance; a time to cast away stones, and a time to gather stones together; a time to embrace, and a time to refrain from embracing; a time to seek, and a time to lose; a time to keep, and a time to cast away; a time to tear, and a time to sew; a time to keep silence, and a time to speak; a time to love, and a time to hate; a time for war, and a time for peace. What gain has the worker from his toil? I have seen the business that God has given to the children of man to be busy with. He has made everything beautiful in its time. Also, he has put eternity into man's heart, yet so that he cannot find out what God has done from the beginning to the end. (Eccl 3:1–11)

We would be wise to remember that the opportunities with which we are faced should be evaluated in light of God's plan for us in that specific time.

The Desires of Your Heart

One more crucial element—a question, really—remains in the process of finding the will of God, and it sounds strange to many: "What do you *want* to do?" It strikes some as strange because they think God's will cannot be fun—or the more dis- tasteful the task, the more God is pleased with us.

God gives us desires in the direction he wants us to go, and then he fulfills those desires by allowing them to find expression and fulfillment in our lives. Psalm 139:16 says, "All my days were written in Your book and planned before a single one of them began." Before your first breath, God began to form in you a personality with preferences. He has given you life experiences, education, skills, gifts, and talents to make you exactly who you are so that you can be, do, and say all he desires for you. And he is giving you desires for the same. Our heavenly Father gives us our heart's desire when we delight ourselves in him (Ps 37:4). This biblical principle is so clear that some teachers simply stress that God guides us through our affections. In other words, what do you want to do?

However, a necessary warning must accompany this teaching: be careful to guard your heart. Proverbs 4:23 teaches, "Guard your heart above all else, for it is the source of life." If you delight in the world, you should not seek guidance by following your affections. I do not teach people to find God's will merely by following their heart because of the truth of Jeremiah 17:9: "The heart is more deceitful than anything else, and incurable—who can understand it?" And the worst thing about being deceived is that you do not know that you are. To delight yourself in God, you must know him, know his Word, spend time in prayer, and enjoy godly counsel. Finding God's will and the way to delight in him are not discovered by following one or two of these components; all of these steps are important to consider.

The way to find God's will is to become so close to him that your heartbeat resonates with his own. Study his Word. Spend time in prayer communing with him. Ask godly men and women to counsel you and listen carefully to what they say. Consider the life experiences God has given you to make you who you are. Examine your circumstances and factor them into your decision. Unfortunately, God does not always hang traffic lights at the crossroads of your life decisions to tell you when to go, stop, or slow down. Yet God's timing is a crucial element to consider in finding and following his will for your life. Finally, remember that God loves you. Jesus said that the Son of Man came that we might have life and have it more abundantly (John 10:10).

To enjoy the abundant life he has for you, consider carefully the desires God has placed in your heart.

CONCLUSION

A precise definition of the missionary call is elusive, and the options are as diverse as the people whom God has called. History shows that some define their call in terms of the need, others use God's Word, and others describe a sense of God's leadership that they cannot articulate. Carefully considering all that missionaries, theologians, and Bible commentators have written, we can distill the following definition for the *missionary call*: "The missionary call includes an awareness of the needs of a lost world, the commands of Christ, a concern for the lost, a radical commitment to God, your church's affirmation, blessing and commissioning, a passionate desire, the Spirit's gifting, and an indescribable yearning that motivates beyond all understanding."[5]

As we continue through our exploration of various facets of missions, we encourage you to pray each day for the Lord to reveal your role in missions. Are you a sender or a goer? It has been said that God cannot lead you based on information you do not have, so we hope the information in this text will be at least a part of what he uses to lead you into a deepening love for him and his kingdom as well as commitment to his service.

RESOURCES FOR FURTHER STUDY

Elliot, Elisabeth. *Shadow of the Almighty: The Life and Testament of Jim Elliot.* New York: Harper, 1958.

Kane, J. Herbert. *The Making of a Missionary.* Grand Rapids: Baker, 1975.

Sills, M. David. *The Missionary Call: Find Your Place in God's Plan for the World.* Chicago: Moody, 2008.

---

[5] Sills, *The Missionary Call*, 30.

SECTION 1

BIBLICAL AND THEOLOGICAL FOUNDATIONS FOR GLOBAL MISSIONS

CHAPTER 2

PANTA TA ETHNE: "ALL THE NATIONS"

Jesus did not merely send us out to make disciples and plant churches in all of the geopolitical countries of the world. If that were our task, the Great Commission would have been completed years ago. Because there are only about 200 countries in the world, it would be a comparatively easy task to look at a world map and then assure that a church is in each country. Any countries found to be lacking a church could be targeted and "reached" in a matter of months. Game over. That is not the task Jesus gave us in the Great Commission; rather, he has sent us to reach, make disciples, baptize, and teach *panta ta ethne*—all the ethnolinguistic groups of the world.

It is easy to get confused when reading books and perusing websites about missions. Some authors seem to use several terms synonymously, while others make distinctions between them. Some missions books include world maps with legends specifying the locations of world religions with different colors. Some tint entire continents and all the countries within them with the Christian color, while other regions are tinted with colors representing other religions, such as Buddhism, Islam, and Hinduism. Many readers seeking God's will for their place of service are not aware that these maps are simply intended to show the origin or concentration of the various world religions. Not every single individual living there is an adherent. However, the impression remains with some readers that certain continents are already reached for Christ and need no missionaries.

Other maps feature red dots, which represent the "unreached" peoples, to indicate the areas of the world in greatest need of missionaries. Unfortunately, world maps would be covered with red ink if they showed the locations where the world's undiscipled peoples live. The greater tragedy of the world today is not that it is "unreached" but rather that it is undiscipled, unless one understands that peoples are actually unreached until they are taught to understand all that Jesus commanded, as the Great Commission directs. Depending on definitions, it may be possible to be "reached" without being discipled, but it is impossible to be discipled without also being reached with the gospel. Many peoples who are designated as reached still lack sound churches; discipled members; biblically qualified, trained leaders; and Bibles in their language. This exploration of the challenges to understand and apply the basic terms of "reached" and "unreached" underscore the role that definitions play in missiological strategy. Understandably, individuals are often confused by diverse definitions and usages of many terms in missions today. This chapter will help us make sense of modern terms that populate missions books and conferences.

TAXONOMIES AND CHANGING WORLD

Every field of study has a taxonomy, a classification system or means of ordering data that includes the vocabulary specific to that discipline. The aviation industry has terms that enable efficient and precise communication, such as yaw, pitch, stall, airspeed, and aileron. Musicians also require terms pertinent to their art, such as baroque, modulation, key signature, and forte. The legal and medical fields each have their own specific terminologies as well. Such unique vocabularies facilitate clear communication. However, where fields and disciplines are changing, evolving, and developing rapidly, the terms must change just as quickly.

The discipline of missiology is changing and developing constantly in an effort to keep up with a world that changes so quickly that its every spin seems to present us with new challenges we did not have the day before. Just consider all that has been ushered in during this new millennium. In addition to 9/11 and the sea change this tragedy brought to international air travel, awareness of a burgeoning Islam, worldwide terrorism, and warfare, the world has also seen an unprecedented shift of global influence concerning economics, Christian population, political power, and technology from the North to the global South. Added to these dynamics are the relief efforts following the past century's devastating tsunamis, massive earthquakes, and wars, which increasingly are the best, easiest, or only platforms for gaining entrance to creative access countries.

Complicating the matter in the rapidly changing field of international missions is the challenge of sorting out how scholars and practitioners use the same terms but in different ways. Some of this will become clearer as we proceed through this chapter, especially for the missions scholars in our field who have been writing for years and began their prolific writing careers when terms were simpler. They often must continue using an older definition for a term to maintain continuity with their previous works, even while writing in the midst of the still-changing terms.

Another reason to understand the terms, rhetoric, and "sound bites" we hear in missions conferences is that they can easily sway our thinking—without actually thinking through their logical conclusions or how they fit together with others we have accepted. Consider this collection of challenges to mission conference attendees that Robertson McQuilkin found and how they contradict one another.

> Everyone should head toward missionary service until God stops him.
>
> No one should become a missionary if he can be happy doing anything else.
>
> If you haven't had a call, you must not be listening because Christ gave the call two thousand years ago. You are already called!
>
> The Great Commission is all the call you need.
>
> Don't move until God gives you a call.
>
> The need constitutes the call.

No one has a right to hear the gospel twice
until every one has heard it once.
Grow where you were planted.[1]

Sorting out which line to embrace can be confusing.

Beyond the sound bites we must be precise about even the
terms we use. Words have power to influence judgment and
instill prejudice. Referring to oral cultures as illiterate uses the
pejorative prefix "ill," which labels them as somewhat negative
or lesser than. Some missiologists prefer to use the terms *preliterate* or *nonliterate* to be less offensive, but even these terms
force us to describe entire peoples in terms of something they
cannot do. At a recent Urbana missions conference, the thousands of participants were affixed with a wristband to show
they had registered and should be allowed entrance to the daily
conference sessions and exhibition hall. Some began jokingly
to refer to themselves as "the people of the wristband" and the
others walking to work or school outside on the busy streets as
"nonwristband people." In a world where the wristband grants
an advantage, such as entrance to the venue, nonwristbanders
are seen as different, without access, and may eventually be seen
as inferior or "lesser than."

In the world of politics, some use the "hot words" and vola-
tile terms to sway opinion, stir up strife, or gain a hearing with
a certain crowd in ways that are often simply pedantic antics
with semantics. The media is able to shape public opinion in the
ways a news item is presented. However, mission agencies, missionaries, and missiologists usually do not use diverse terms for
any misleading or divisive purposes. Terms used correctly facilitate clear and precise communication. Confusion often leads
to unintended conclusions when readers are left to assume the
meanings of key terms.

A textbook such as this does not allow room for a thorough
etymological, missiological, and historical development of each
term, yet a general explanation of each will be helpful. Basic
missiological terms fall into general categories, and it is helpful
for understanding and remembering them if they are learned
this way. The basic categories of terms presented in this chapter

---

[1] Robertson McQuilkin, *The Great Omission: A Biblical Basis for World Evangelism* (Grand Rapids:
Baker, 1984), 72.

are culture, strategy, and orality. This short list is not exhaustive of the terms missionaries use, but many are relatively new to the field or are increasingly being used in more precise ways in the literature. Their definition will assist with clarity of meaning in the pages to follow.

CULTURE

Ralph Winter championed the cause of people-group thinking in missions during a presentation at the 1974 Lausanne Conference for World Evangelization. Prior to that time most mission agencies organized their efforts and deployed their personnel according to countries. Winter pointed out that Jesus had sent us to make disciples of *panta ta ethne* (all the people groups) and not merely the geopolitical entities of the world. Since that time mission agencies and missiologists began to focus on reaching the ethnolinguistic people groups of the world no matter where they were found. Specific cultures became the focus of missions strategy.

Since that day the need for more precise terms has resulted in a growing missiological vocabulary of precise definitions. In addition to referring to an ethnolinguistic people group, the word *culture* also refers to the rules of the game of life for a people. Just notice the common denominators in the following succinct definitions of the word *culture*.

- The total way of life of a people, composed of their learned and shared behavior patterns, values, norms, and material objects.[2]
- The partially integrated system of ideas, feelings, and values encoded in learned patterns of behavior, signs, products, rituals, beliefs, and worldviews shared by a community of people.[3]
- The anthropologist's label for the sum of the distinctive characteristics of a people's way of life.[4]

---

[2] Everett M. Rogers and Thomas M. Steinfatt, *Intercultural Communication* (Prospect Heights, IL: Waveland Press, 1999), 266.

[3] Paul G. Hiebert, *The Gospel in Human Contexts: Anthropological Explorations for Contemporary Missions* (Grand Rapids, MI: Baker Academic, 2009), 18.

[4] Sherwood G. Lingenfelter and Marvin Keene Mayers, *Ministering Cross-Culturally: An Incarnational Model for Personal Relationships* (Grand Rapids, MI: Baker Academic, 2003), 17.

- The conceptual designs, the definitions by which people order their lives, interpret their experiences, and evaluate the behavior of others.[5]

The list of the many definitions of *culture* could continue, but the fact that they are repetitive variations on the same theme is obvious. The discussions, literature, research, and ministry dealing with cultures have increased in volume and complexity over the past few decades. In the earlier days of missions, missiologists referred to any cultural interaction or involvement across cultures as *cross-cultural*. Books on cross-cultural communication, church planting, and ministry were extremely helpful to missionaries who needed the experience and wisdom of equipped men and women. The problem was that this term served for all things cultural. More precise terms were needed as the discipline of missiology developed. For instance, missiologists sometimes refer to cultural dynamics that are true to one degree or another in many cultures and at other times to specific interactions between cultures.

The term *cross-cultural* came to refer to realities present in many cultures at once. It was used to refer to dynamics that are more or less true across cultural lines, such as the fact that mothers love their children in all cultures, peoples of all cultures have favorite comfort foods, and women's rights exist in some measure in all cultures. Therefore, a cross-cultural study could be conducted on any of these components of reality, examining them among distinct people groups.

Another term for referring more precisely to the interaction of diverse cultures is *intercultural*. A medical team from North America ministering and treating disease in sub-Saharan Africa is an illustration of an intercultural medical experience. Finally, when referring to complex dynamics in a context where numerous cultures are present at once, such as a classroom, a megacity, or a church, the preferred term is *multicultural*. The successful teacher, urban church planter, or pastor must understand the multicultural dynamics, incorporating the necessary understanding of the cultures present in order to minister in culturally appropriate ways.

---

[5] Ibid., 18.

The term *cultural relativism* is yet another that causes some confusion among readers of modern missiological literature. Two different meanings of the term are in contemporary usage. One holds that cultural relativism "is the degree to which an individual judges another culture by its context (as opposed to ethnocentrism which judges others by the standards of one's own culture)."[6] This view of the term holds that no culture should be able to judge another by imposing its own standards upon others. For instance, let's suppose that Culture A always murders the second baby when twins are born, believing twins to be an evil omen. Culture B always kills the third baby born in a family, knowing that when attacked the family can escape with the father and mother running with one child each, but the third would slow down and endanger the whole group. Culture C kills all girl babies because their government has imposed a one-child policy in a culture where a male son is essential for religious rituals. Culture D kills any baby it wants to, as long as it is not actually born yet. Proponents of the first kind of cultural relativism would maintain that each of these cultures has found what works for it and should be allowed to make its own rules, mores, norms, and laws. They would maintain that imposing what one culture considers to be sin upon other cultures is theological, ethical, or cultural imperialism. Obviously, Christians would not hold to such an extreme view of cultural relativism. However, there is another usage of the term.

A second understanding of *cultural relativism* refers to the mutual respect that flows from understanding that unless God's Word speaks to an issue, a particular culture's expression of it may not be wrong, just different. Extrabiblical matters are matters of preference. For instance, people in Culture A live in mud huts, people in Culture B live in log houses, people in Culture C live in grass-walled houses with thatched roofs, and people in Culture D live in brick homes. Which is the most godly culture? We do not know; there is not enough information here. God did not say which kinds of houses he prefers his people to live in. One culture wears red shirts, another blue, and another white. These are extrabiblical matters. One culture wears leather shoes, another wears running shoes, and another does not wear

---

[6] Rogers and Steinfatt, *Intercultural Communication*, 266.

shoes at all. These matters are not spoken of in the Bible, so we must allow for differing opinions and show mutual respect; this is cultural relativism in a positive light. In the final analysis the missionary should study to know the culture and why it lives, believes, acts, reacts, and interacts as it does. Then study the Scriptures to see what God has said about the various aspects investigated and understood. Although an aspect of the host culture may seem strange to the outsider missionary, it is not necessarily wrong or unintelligent; it may simply be different.

Another term related to the culture family in our growing missions vocabulary is *ethnolinguistic group.* This term refers to a people group with its own language or dialect. Patrick Johnstone describes an ethnolinguistic group as

> a significantly large sociological grouping of individuals who perceive themselves to have a common affinity for one another because of their shared language, religion, ethnicity, residence, occupation, class or caste, situation, etc. or combinations of these. From the viewpoint of evangelization this is the largest possible group within which the gospel can spread as a viable, indigenous church planting movement without encountering barriers of understanding or acceptance.[7]

The first part of the word, *ethno*, comes from *ethne* in New Testament Greek and is translated "nations" in our Bible. From this word we also get our word *ethnic. Ethno* as a prefix is seen in an increasing number of terms in missiology, e.g., *ethnomusicology* is the study of music within a culture context; *ethnodoxology* is the study of praise within a specific culture context; *ethnocognition* refers to the distinct ways different cultures process information and think; *ethnohermeneutics* studies the ways a people group interprets texts in their own culturally specific ways; *ethnocentrism* is viewing and judging other cultures by one's own, believing one's own culture to be the center of the

---

[7] Patrick Johnstone, "People Groups: How Many Unreached?," *International Journal of Frontier Missions*, 7:2 (1990): 36–37.

ethnic universe; and *ethnography* is the science of researching other cultures and writing to describe them.

Every culture, or ethnic group, holds a unique *worldview,* which refers to the way they view all of reality, understand it, and develop culturally specific rules for living in harmony within it. Paul Hiebert described *worldview* as

> the logic used to form a coherent understanding of reality, and the fundamental cognitive, affective, and evaluative assumptions we make about the ultimate nature of things. A worldview is the most encompassing view of reality we share with other people in a common culture. *It is what we think with, not what we think about. It is the mental picture of reality we use to make sense of the world around us.*[8] (emphasis added)

Notice that worldview is not what we think about the world but rather the lens through which we see it. A worldview is much like your eyes; you don't see them, you see through them. And you naturally assume that everyone sees what you do. Tom Steffan describes worldview as "the linguistic-cultural assumptions and presuppositions founded and maintained by myths and stories that distinguish one people group or subculture from another."[9] A culture's worldview answers some of the big questions of life: Where did we come from? Where do we go when we die? Where does disease come from? A person answers such questions with a set of assumptions received from those around him and, in turn, passes them on more or less unchanged to the ones who come after him. In this way worldview shares a symbiotic relationship with culture. They each inform and spring from the other in endless cyclical fashion.

STRATEGY

The next family of words in missiological literature and practice relates to strategy. Much confusion has arisen from misunderstanding these terms. To illustrate, consider the term

---

[8] Hiebert, *The Gospel in Human Contexts*, 158.

[9] Tom A. Steffen, *Reconnecting God's Story to Ministry: Cross-Cultural Storytelling at Home and Abroad* (Waynesboro, GA: Authentic Media, 2005), 223.

unreached. Where did this term come from, and how can we measure a people group to know whether they are unreached? Does this mean no one has ever preached Christ among them? If the popular understanding of the term is revealed to be that or something similar, would they be considered reached if a mission team preaches among them during a two-week mission trip?

Because ideas do indeed have consequences, and what you think will drive what you do, let's start with the big picture and then focus in toward the middle. What is the mission Christ has given the church? Are we to preach Christ where he has never been named and evangelize the lost who have never heard? Or are we to bring in the harvest and concentrate workers in the responsive fields? When we allow others to dichotomize the Christian mission in this way, we list our tasks in a numbered fashion: (1) search out and evangelize all unreached peoples, and (2) bring in the harvest, disciple, and teach the reached. Once the list begins, there is a basis for prioritizing when money and times get tight. Missions administrators may say that we are strapped financially so we will concentrate on doing the first priority and later do the second when human and financial resources are more abundant. The main problem with such an approach is that the Great Commission is a both/and, not an either/or. Jesus said we are to go into all the world, make disciples, baptize them, and teach them all he commanded. We are to reach *and* teach them, not one or the other. Reaching and teaching are the two sides of the Great Commission coin. When we do one to the exclusion of the other, we are only doing half of the Great Commission. The sound-bite missiology that characterizes some missions appeals often uses terms that some readers misunderstand. A quick overview of related terms will help sort out some of the confusion.

Many use the term *unreached people group* today when challenging the church in developed lands to go to the unreached. Patrick Johnstone defines this term as a "people or people group among which there is no indigenous community of believing Christians with adequate numbers and resources to evangelize the rest of its members without outside (cross-cultural) assistance." Johnstone goes on to assert, "Yet we can be too simplistic. An unreached people group does not suddenly become reached by some magic statistic being attained! We are dealing with shades of grey rather than black or white."[10] The International Mission Board (IMB) defines an unreached group as "a homogeneous population group identified by a common language, heritage and religion with no church movement having sufficient strength, resources and commitment to sustain and ensure the continuous multiplication of churches,"[11] and "an Unreached People Group is a people group in which less than 2% of the population is Evangelical Christians."[12] The origin of the use of these terms was out of an agreement among research missiologists in need of a measurable descriptor they could commonly use to refer to the least reached.[13] Let it suffice here to say that the term is grossly misunderstood and misused by some well-meaning missions speakers.

As has been seen in many of our missions terms, more precise terms were needed in the growth and development of missiology. Just as it was necessary to have a commonly agreed upon metric for determining the unreached, so has it become necessary to refine that term as well. In addition to *unreached people groups* (UPG), we now refer to the *unengaged* (UUPG) and *uncontacted* people groups (UUUPG).

Unreached people groups are those groups with populations with less than 2 percent evangelicals, and unreached unengaged people groups are those with a population that is less than 2 percent evangelical *and* where no church planting has taken place among them for the past two years. It is possible that a church planting effort once existed, or that there may be a few Christians among them, but they are less than 2 percent evangelical and no active church planting efforts are underway in their midst. The IMB's Global Research office states:

---

[10] Johnstone, "People Groups: How Many Unreached?," 37.

[11] International Mission Board, glossary, accessed January 23, 2013, http://going.imb.org/details.asp?StoryID=7489&LanguageID=1709. The International Mission Board is the international missions agency of the Southern Baptist Convention.

[12] International Mission Board, definitions, accessed January 23, 2013, http://public.imb.org/globalresearch/Pages/FAQs.aspx#sixteen.

[13] M. David Sills, *Reaching and Teaching: A Call to Great Commission Obedience* (Chicago: Moody, 2010), 108–15.

A people group is unreached when the number of Evangelical Christians is less than 2% of its population. It is further called unengaged when there is no church planting methodology consistent with Evangelical faith and practice under way. A people group is not engaged when it has been merely adopted, is the object of focused prayer, or is part of an advocacy strategy.[14]

The Joshua Project further defines the term *unengaged*, with the following conditions:

At least four essential elements constitute effective engagement:

1. apostolic effort in residence;
2. commitment to work in the local language and culture;
3. commitment to long-term ministry;
4. sowing in a manner consistent with the goal of seeing a Church Planting Movement emerge.[15]

UPGs and UUPGs are joined by another term, *UUUPGs*, which refers to the *unreached, unengaged, and uncontacted people groups.* Uncontacted peoples are those hidden, hostile, or isolated people groups with whom no contact has ever been made for gospel advance. In some cases, because many are nomadic jungle people groups, researchers are not even sure *where* they are; they just know *that* they are. Missiologists and field missionaries are always seeking ways to introduce the saving gospel message to the unreached peoples of the world, considering for these groups the often-quoted words of Carl F. H. Henry, that for them the gospel is only good news if it gets there in time.

The Last Frontier is another term often heard in missions strategy. The IMB defines it as an "unreached people for which the majority of its members have little or no access to the gospel of Jesus Christ. This represents approximately 1.65 billion

---

[14] International Mission Board, "What Is a People Group," accessed January 23, 2013. http://public. imb.org/globalresearch/Pages/default.aspx.

[15] The Joshua Project, accessed January 23, 2013, http://www.joshuaproject.net/definitions.php. The Joshua Project, a ministry of the U.S. Center for World Mission, is a research initiative seeking to highlight the ethnic people groups with the fewest followers of Jesus Christ.

people in the world."[16] Where do these people live? They live in virtually every country of the world, but they are found in greatest concentration in the 10/40 Window.

The 10/40 Window is an imaginary box that encloses an area of the globe from 10 degrees north of the equator to 40 degrees north of the equator, and from Northwest Africa to East Asia. Not only does this rectangle contain the majority of the world's unreached lost; it is also home to three major religious blocs: Hinduism, Islam, and Buddhism, as well as the areas of greatest poverty.[17]

During the Cold War the U.S. and her democratic-industrial allies were referred to as the first world, the communist bloc countries were the second world, and all the rest were the third world. In recent decades some have used the fourth world to refer to the world's indigenous peoples who often live marginalized lives within the dominant cultures of others. The term many used to refer to the developing nations was *third world*, then the term *two-thirds world* was popular when it became obvious that there were many more of them than the developed Western nations. The term *two-thirds world* eventually became *majority world* for similar reasons.

Some have addressed the phenomenon referred to by the terms related to the majority world as

> that part of the world's population living outside Europe and North America. Terms such as non-Western, third world, two-thirds world, developing nations, and undeveloped nations have been used to designate such areas and peoples. No single term has been accepted by all, and all such terms have a negative political, economic, or social connotation. By using the term majority world, we simply recognize that people living outside Europe and North America

---

[16] International Mission Board, glossary, accessed January 23, 2013, http://going.imb.org/details.asp?StoryID=7489&LanguageID=1709.

[17] Joshua Project, "10/40 Window," accessed January 23, 2013, http://www.joshuaproject.net/10-40-window.php.

constitute the largest demographic block in the world.[18]

The church that exists in this vast area of the global south is called the *southern church.* Most recently, the term *global south* refers to the regions of the world encompassing Latin America, Africa, and Asia. These terms refer to the work of God going on in Africa, Asia, and the nations south of the Rio Grande in the Americas. The church is growing at breakneck speed in these countries. More Christians live there than in the United States, and they send out more missionaries than the United States and Western Europe. Yet the theological challenges and missiological needs therein are particular, so the distinction in terms to identify precisely is of importance and value.

ORALITY

Missionaries seeking to reach all the people groups of the world must give serious attention to the challenges of the world's unique peoples. Missionaries have traditionally sought to reach peoples the same way they themselves were reached, or they imagine would work among their own people. For years missionaries have served as colporteur missionaries (distributing Bibles, hymns, New Testaments, and tracts) or have given out tracts as a part of their witnessing effort. Unfortunately, we are now learning that about 70 percent of the unreached world does not read. Thousands of languages have not even been reduced to writing yet. It is no wonder we have found little success when working in literate ways among preliterate peoples.[19]

For years little attention was given to the ways cultures around the world engaged with written content. Our assumption was that they were like us. Without an understanding of the culture, we expected them to value the written word and understand how to engage it. We evangelized with gospel tracts, translated

---

[18] Michael Pocock, Gailyn Van Rheenen, and Douglas McConnell, *The Changing Face of World Missions* (Grand Rapids: Baker Academic, 2005), 16.

[19] The material contained within this section pulls heavily from the research of the International Orality Network and the work of the Orality Issues Group of the Lausanne Committee for World Evangelization, of which David Sills was a member. Additional information on this topic can be found in the Orality Issues Group paper "Making Disciples of Oral Learners" (presented at the Lausanne Committee for World Evangelization, Pattaya, Thailand, October 5, 2004).

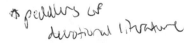
↑ peddlers of
   devotional literature

discipleship workbooks for training, and developed sermons that assumed their ability to follow along in the written text.

However, as missiologists rediscovered our call to people groups and began to learn about worldviews, they began to understand that the format in which information was communicated had broader challenges and implications due to the role the written word played in cultures. From this research and understanding, the designation of *oral learners* emerged. This is the designation that emerged for those people who cannot read or write the languages they speak. They learn, engage, and share information using only the spoken word. Once this designation was identified and research commenced, it became clear that this was the vast majority of the world. The study of the trends, challenges, and needs of those who are oral learners is the study of *orality.* One additional note should be made about this designation, however. While oral learners and orality are the widely accepted and used terms, *aurality* or *aural learners* actually are more accurate given that these are terms that refer back to hearing, rather than speaking, as does orality. Those in oral cultures learn by hearing, not speaking, so aural learners is a more accurate way to think about the process that is occurring.

In the highly literate West, we tend to think of literacy as simply whether or not someone can read. However, the reality is not so simple as merely having two options. In order to understand the world outside of the highly literate one in which those of you reading this text live, we need to understand a broader group of missiological designations for the peoples of the world and the ways they engage the written word—and really how they receive and process information in general. First in the levels of literacy are those who are *highly literate.* These are cultures where information tends to be written-word based, there is access to libraries, information is presented in sequential linear logic with abstract ideas, and individuals are expected to gain a significant portion of their learning on their own through written material. Second are those who would be considered *literate.* These are cultures or individuals where there is an understanding of the written word; they can interact with it and can rise to the occasion of accomplishing a task by engaging with a written task. The third level, *semiliterate*, refers to those who have probably received some high school level of reading but struggle to read well, and therefore do not do so as a pattern of life. The fourth level is *functionally illiterate,* which refers to those who can read basic instructions or headlines but live their lives as illiterates. They may be able to read basic written information but struggle to follow the author's argument or understand the ideas presented.

The final designation of the levels of literacy refers to those individuals or cultures that are *illiterate, preliterate,* or *nonliterate.* They have never learned how to make sense of the written words printed on a page. This is a designation that is manifest on the individual level. However, around the world we see cultures that are *preliterate.* In these cultures the written word is not valued, learning is not linear, and even when literacy is achieved, it is typically not highly valued within the culture. Thousands of ethnolinguistic cultures are in this category because their language has not been reduced to writing, and no concept of written communication exists. Given the centrality of God's Word in the life of a Christian, it is easy to see how the realities behind these designations inform everything from how the gospel is presented to how someone is discipled and how the church functions.

Thus far we have talked about the levels of literacy primarily around ability and values. *Primary oral learners* are those whom we've discussed as illiterate, preliterate, or nonliterate, which reveals that the delivery system of new information for them is primarily restricted to oral means. However, another segment of orality refers to individuals or cultures that choose to learn by oral means but who have the ability to read and learn through the written word. These are *secondary oral learners,* who are increasingly found in developed Western cultures where a high value on literacy is waning. Many university students read what is absolutely necessary or not at all. At a conference on orality, an attendee claimed that he had a master's degree and had never read a book in his life. He had read highlighted portions others had marked but never an entire book. According to the Lausanne Committee on World Evangelization, the challenges, needs, and strategies we would use to reach and teach primary oral learners are many of the same characteristics and strategies we should use with secondary oral learners.[20] We can draw application from this principle in the United States as the shift toward electronic media consumption grows and the dependency on books and written resources declines.

It is important to note that our understanding of the world around us not only leads us to new terms to describe those phenomena, but it also leads us to new methodologies, which then lead to even more new terms. This is probably seen most clearly in the field of orality given the challenges it has brought to our traditional understanding of missiological methodology. It is important to understand some of the terms and their contemporary uses for the key methodologies being used to reach oral learners.

The most prominent methodology that has emerged to reach oral learners is typically referred to as *Chronological Bible Storying.* This is the practice of crafting stories from key biblical passages from Genesis to Revelation and then telling them in sequence to impart the biblical metanarrative of God's plan of redemption and help reshape the hearers' worldview into a Christian one. Another key phrase for ministry in oral cultures is *watch and do.* Oral cultures learn through modeling in a mentoring or master-apprentice model of instruction. For many oral cultures this is the way they teach others, and the wise missionary will incorporate the model into his evangelism, discipleship, and leadership training.

The term *catechism* is one that is certainly established in our minds, but it finds distinct expression in ministry to oral learners and must be understood a little differently. Catechisms are used in some traditions as a teaching model, but with oral culture instruction the teacher uses it as a hook to hang other truths upon in the teaching session. For instance, "Who made you?" would be answered by "God made me" in the children's catechism. In oral contexts the teacher would drill them on the question and answer and then spend an hour or so talking about what it means that God made them and what the implications and application of that truth would be in daily life. The next session would review the previously learned questions and answers and then move to the next for the lesson of the current week.

---

[20] Orality Issues Group, "Making Disciples of Oral Learners."

Catechisms yield great fruit in oral cultures as a primary form of discipleship. The doctrinal positions that are succinctly captured in a catechism allow for *repetition,* which is one of the most helpful forms of instruction in oral contexts. It is true in every culture, but most especially in oral ones, that spaced repetition is the best teacher. Less literate and more contextual teaching tools are highly effective in oral cultures. These include *drama, songs, proverbs,* and *riddles.*

CONCLUSION

This chapter has been a whirlwind exploration of the key terms used in the study and practice of missions. Although for your purpose at this time it may amount to little more than definitions you need to know for a test, for missionaries around the world these terms represent the substance of their prayers and the fruits of their labor. We must always remember that definitions in the context of ministry never represent ideas that do not have implications in the lives of people created in the image of God. May we all take that which was shared in this chapter and use it to help us more faithfully serve Him.

RESOURCES FOR FURTHER STUDY

Hiebert, Paul G. *Anthropological Reflections on Missiological Issues.* Grand Rapids: Baker, 1994.

———. *The Gospel in Human Contexts: Anthropological Explorations for Contemporary Missions.* Grand Rapids: Baker Academic, 2009.

Lingenfelter, Sherwood G. and Marvin Keene Mayers. *Ministering Cross-Culturally: An Incarnational Model for Personal Relationships.* Grand Rapids: Baker Academic, 2003.

Piper, John. *Let the Nations Be Glad!* Grand Rapids: Baker Academic, 1993.

CHAPTER 3

THE MISSIOLOGICAL
BASIS OF THE BIBLE

E vangelical Christians believe the Bible is the final authority in everything they believe and do. Nothing can be significant in the life of the church unless it is taught in the Bible. For this reason it is customary to include a chapter on the biblical basis of missions in any book on missiology. It is possible to proof-text the issue of missions, point out that the Great Commission was a command of Jesus, and feel that the job is done. However, this is not the correct way to handle the Bible, and it is possible to make a far more comprehensive case for the centrality of missions in Scripture. To do so, it is necessary first to consider the nature of the Bible itself.

The Bible is one, coherent story. Indeed, it is *the* story that makes sense of everything else. All too often Christians treat the Bible as a random collection of sayings and commands, with some unconnected stories thrown into the mix. Different parts of the mix are then drawn out, interpreted, and applied without any real reference to the whole. Instead, the Bible should be regarded as a connected narrative, and each part should be interpreted in light of how it fits into the entire story. This story is absolutely true and absolutely definitive for our understanding of reality. It is, first and foremost, about God. He is the author, the main character, and the only real hero of the book. Who he is, what he has done, and what he plans to do are the main points of the Bible. He is before the story, above it, all through it, in control of it, and beyond it. All of it is to the praise of his glory. The Bible is fundamentally the Book of God.

The Bible is also the definitive book about humanity. It was written by humans in human languages, although those humans were guided by the Holy Spirit in such a way that they perfectly expressed what God wanted to say. It defines what it means to be human, as the image bearers of God. It describes what went wrong in the fall of the human race into sin, and it graphically describes the consequences of that rebellion against God, both in the pervasive depravity of human nature and in the tragic depravity of human history. It proclaims God's glorious plan to redeem sinful humans through the life, death, and resurrection of Jesus Christ, God himself become man. It shows the destiny of humanity, either in the glory of the new heavens and the new earth or in the judgment of hell. Humanity is not central to the message of the Bible. God is central. However, under God the Bible alone explains the human condition.

The setting of the narrative of the Bible is the universe that God has created. There are four main plot movements to the narrative of Scripture: creation, fall, redemption, and restoration. In creation, God (who alone is absolute, infinite, eternal, and uncreated) makes everything else that exists simply by the word of his power, out of the overflow of his greatness and goodness. All he makes is good. Angels are among his creatures, but the pinnacle of creation is humanity, male and female, created in his image and given the task of being fruitful, multiplying, filling the earth, and subduing it. Tragically, in the fall of the human race, our first parents rebel against God and introduce sin into God's good world. As a result of this treason, every person born in the line of Adam and Eve is guilty before God and deserves condemnation and hell. We are now alienated from God and from one another. We are all also corrupted in every aspect of our humanity—minds, bodies, affections, and wills—so that we are rendered totally incapable of accomplishing or even contributing to our own deliverance. The created order itself is subject to decay as a result of our disobedience, so that all creation groans under the weight of our rebellion.

The story could have stopped there. God could have destroyed humanity on the spot for its rebellion, or he could have left humans to the consequences of their sin as history rolled on. However, in his mercy and grace, God chose to inter- vene in human history in a glorious rescue mission of redemption. He did it all to the praise of his glory. Most of the Bible, following Genesis 3, is the story of God's redemptive work. That story reaches its climax in the life, death, and resurrection of Jesus Christ. After the risen Jesus returns to heaven, the Father and the Son send the Holy Spirit to God's people to witness to God's redeeming work in Jesus to the ends of the earth and to the ends of the age. The story comes to an end in restoration, when Jesus comes back, the dead are raised to life, all of humanity is judged, the old heavens and earth pass away, and all things are made new.

Mission ties the entire narrative together. It isn't simply one agenda item among many in biblical Christianity. It is, rather, one of the great, controlling themes of the narrative of Scripture. This can be seen in each of the plot movements of the Bible. In *creation* God makes everything that exists out of nothing, creating the stage on which the plot will unfold. Everything God makes is good. There is no absoluteness to evil—evil itself can never be more than perverted good. The material world is not bad or even neutral. The material universe declares the glory of God as it reflects his knowledge, wisdom, power, and beauty. When God created the first man and woman, he gave them a job to do. God was on a mission from the start—the display of his glory in the goodness of all he had made—and he set his people on a mission from the start—to reflect his glory by being fruitful, multiplying, naming his creatures, and tending his world.[1] The human race is intrinsically missional.

The *fall* changed things radically. Man and woman still had abilities that reflected the image of God, but now sin corrupted all of their abilities and every aspect of their characters. They no longer had the ability to fulfill the mission God had given them in creation, and they were no longer inclined to glorify God as

---

[1] The word *glory* does not appear in the first three chapters of Genesis, the texts that chronicle the creation and fall, but as will be demonstrated, later biblical texts highlight the centrality of God's pursuit of his glory in the creation and restoration of the cosmos and of man.

they were meant to do. They were spiritually blind and dead. They were running away from God, not toward him. Scripture says, "The LORD saw that the wickedness of man was great in the earth, and that every intention of the thoughts of his heart was only evil continually" (Gen 6:5). Humans were now guilty and worthy of condemnation. This changed both the nature of the mission and the context for the mission. The heart of the mission was the same—the praise of God's glory. However, the nature of the mission now involved the glory of God in judgment and the glory of God in redemption. The context of the mission was no longer a perfect world but rather a setting in which people were committed to sin and nature was subject to decay. A fallen world characterized by sin and death was now the stage on which God's mission would run.

Judgment and *redemption* began immediately at the fall. God is holy and just, and he cannot leave evil unpunished. Our first parents were judged immediately with the curses of the fall and with their expulsion from the garden. They died spiritually on the day they rebelled against God, and they were promised physical death in the future, a process that began even as they were expelled from the garden. However, God gave them the promise of redemption on that same day. God told the serpent, the embodiment of Satan, that there would be enmity between him and the Seed of the woman. Satan would strike the heel of the Seed, but the Seed of the woman would strike his head. This first, faint hint of hope would find its fulfillment when Jesus, the promised Seed, died on the cross and then rose again from the dead.

The following chapters of Genesis are a dismal tale of the downward spiral of human depravity as people grew further and further away from God, coupled with the relentless and bitter fruit of the death that God had promised. God exercised judgment against sin in the universal flood but showed redemptive mercy by rescuing Noah, his family, and the animals in the ark. Humanity demonstrated its rebellious pride at Babel, and God again displayed judgment by diversifying their languages. In doing so, however, he created the people group setting through which he would spread his work of redemption and the varied linguistic instruments through which he would be praised.

From this point on, the peoples, nations, tribes, and tongues of the earth would be a hugely important theme in Scripture.

Immediately after the peoples were separated at Babel, God narrowed his focus to one man: Abraham. However, he made plain that he was choosing Abraham for the purpose of blessing all the families on earth through him. He narrowed things further by choosing only one child of Abraham—Isaac—and only one child of Isaac—Jacob. But with each man God repeated his intention of blessing all the peoples of earth through them. In the Exodus, God chose, formed, and delivered a nation for himself. He did so in a manner that foreshadowed the redemptive work of Jesus through the substitutionary sacrifice of the Passover lamb. He also gave them his law, which perfectly reflected his character. He set up the tabernacle (and later the temple), which graphically proclaimed both the presence of God in the midst of his people and also the holiness of God in the arrangement of the courts and the separation of the holy of holies. Through the priesthood given to the Levite Aaron and his children and the sacrificial system, God stressed the seriousness of sin and the necessity of sacrifice to atone for it. In the separation ordinances God made clear to his people that he wanted them to be different from the wickedness of the nations around them. Through it all, however, he indicated that he intended to display his glory to the nations through them, and the invitation was always extended for Gentiles to come and see the greatness of the God of Israel. Even in this period of focus on one nation, the peoples of the earth were still in view.

The invasion and conquest of Canaan completed the rescue of Israel from Egypt and demonstrated the judgment of God against the nations. Through David, the greatest king of Israel, God demonstrated his rightful rule over both his people and the nations. Through the prophets God proclaimed hope for the nations. In the exile that followed the fall of Jerusalem to the Babylonians, God scattered his people among the nations. The focus was on Israel, but the nations were not forgotten. All of God's redemptive activity in the Old Testament was pointing to something—Someone—better. All of it was foreshadowing and preparation for the true Passover lamb, the true priest and sacrifice, the true prophet who was to come. This one to come would be a son of David; he would be the true King of Israel, one who would be greater even than his father David. The prophets promised that the Day of the Lord would come. It would be the day of the Messiah. It would be the day of the outpouring of the Spirit. It would also be the day of the ingathering of the nations. The prophetic vision of the Old Testament is inescapably redemptive, and it is just as inescapably global.

With the dawn of the New Testament, the vision of the Old Testament was perfectly fulfilled. Jesus was born, an heir of David, God in the flesh who is the Lord of the Old Testament Day of the Lord. As the Word of God made flesh, he is the ultimate prophet. As the Lamb of God who takes away the sin of the world (not just Israel!) by laying down his life on the cross, he is the ultimate priest and sacrifice, to whom the Aaronic priesthood was only a signpost. As the conqueror of hunger, disease, nature, sin, death, and hell, and as the perfect shepherd and ruler of his people, he is the ultimate king, of whom David was only a foreshadowing. When he died, the curtain of the temple was torn in two—not only for Jews but for the nations. The way into the holy of holies was open, perfectly but exclusively through the death and resurrection of Jesus. Salvation had now burst the bounds of Israel. When Jesus gave his Great Commission to his followers, he gave it more than once, indicating its importance. He laid out the mission of his people in explicitly global terms. This was no afterthought, nor was it a new twist on God's agenda. God had made clear throughout the Old Testament that he intended to bring the blessings of his salvation to all the nations and peoples of earth and that the Day of the Lord would be the day of the ingathering of the nations. The global mission of gospel proclamation that the risen Jesus gave his disciples was an intrinsic part of the redemptive mission of God from the beginning, made clear throughout the pages of the Old Testament.

With the outpouring of the Holy Spirit at Pentecost, the curse of Babel began to be reversed. The power of the Holy Spirit was explicitly for proclamation to the nations. The book of Acts is the story of the people of God sent to the nations. The Letters of the New Testament are missionary documents, written in the context of missionary advance. Everything about the New Testament is missionary in character. In the book of Revelation, the redemptive work of God culminates in *restoration*. Even here the nations are in view, as all the nations are represented in giving God the glory due his name.

In summary, the theme of the nations ties the Bible together. At Babel the different tongues and nations were created as an act of judgment from God on human arrogance. In Abraham, God chose one nation to bless all nations. In the exodus God rescued his nation in a manner that foreshadows the salvation that will come to all nations. Through Moses, God delivered his people, the children of Israel, and constituted them as a nation, making a covenant with them (the law) that is to govern their ethics, worship, and government. In the conquest of Canaan under Joshua (*Yeshua*, YHWH Saves), God brought his nation into the land of rest and judged the nations of the Canaanites for their wickedness. Under David, God ruled, protected, and provided for his nation and ruled over the nations around them. In the prophets God announced hope for the nations. In the exile God scattered his people among the nations where they spread the knowledge of the God of Israel and prepared the way for the advance of the gospel. In Jesus, God redeemed a people for himself from every tribe, tongue, people, and nation, and he sent them to all nations on earth. At Pentecost the reversal of Babel began with the proclamation of the gospel in languages spoken from southern Europe and North Africa to Central Asia, and the Holy Spirit was poured out to empower God's people to take the gospel to all nations. In Acts and the Epistles, the church burst through one barrier after another as it witnessed to all nations. In Revelation we see the fulfillment of God's focus on the nations as redeemed people from all people groups on earth worship him and enjoy him forever.

This is the big picture of the role of the nations and God's heart for the nations in the narrative of Scripture. We will now look more closely at the individual sections of the Bible to see how it is spelled out.

THE LAW

The Hebrew Bible is divided into three sections: the Law, the Prophets, and the Writings. The Law consists of the books of Genesis, Exodus, Leviticus, Numbers, and Deuteronomy, written by Moses. The book of Genesis is the absolutely essential foundation for understanding the rest of biblical revelation.[2] Genesis lays out the worldview that makes the rest of the Bible intelligible. In Genesis the reader is introduced to God as supremely powerful, as the Creator of all things, as distinct from his creation and infinitely above it while present everywhere in it, as wise and all knowing, as the Owner and Ruler of all things, as the righteous Judge who holds all people accountable for their deeds, as personal and relational, as holy, and as good. Genesis explains the material world as purposefully created by God, as owned by him, as subordinate to him, and as good. Genesis presents a view of time as having a beginning and as going somewhere. Genesis describes humanity as reflecting the image of God, as having amazing dignity and worth, as being created to work, as having a mission from the beginning, as having dominion under God over the earth, and as being intrinsically male and female in complementary gender distinctiveness. It also describes humanity as fallen into sin, and it graphically depicts the consequences of human rebellion in all its ugliness. It shows the impact of human sin on the entire created order, as corruption, disease, and death enter the picture with the fall of humanity. It guarantees the continuity of nature and of the seasons, despite human sinfulness. It shows what God requires of humanity—a righteous life in relationship with him—and it shows the consequences of failing to please God—judgment and death. It shows God reaching out in mercy to undeserving men and women and his requirement of sacrifice for their sin. It describes the origins of ethnic and linguistic diversity among people while maintaining the essential unity of the human race. It also lays the foundation for all that God would do in redemption through his sovereign choice of one man and his family and his sovereign dealings with that family to prepare the way for all he would subsequently do through them. That is an amazingly comprehensive worldview, and the entire rest of the Bible will presuppose it and build on it.

---

[2] Genesis is so essential for understanding the gospel that many times pioneer workers in a new unreached people group will begin Bible translation with a Gospel (such as Luke) and the book of Genesis at the same time.

The concept of nations and peoples actually began before the Tower of Babel. Genesis 10 describes the descendants of Noah and his sons. In the process it also describes the origins of the different nations of the earth, and it devotes significant energy to the subject. This is a matter of concern to the Bible. At the end of the chapter, we read, "These are the clans of the sons of Noah, according to their genealogies, in their nations, and from these the nations spread abroad on the earth after the flood" (Gen 10:32). The story of the Tower of Babel, and the curse of the division of the languages and the scattering of the peoples, follows immediately in chapter 11. The stage is now set for the story of redemption, and it is no mistake that the story of Abraham begins in that same chapter.

Genesis 12:1–3 is one of the most pivotal passages in the Bible. It is the call of Abraham.

> Now the LORD said to Abram, "Go from your country and your kindred and your father's house to the land that I will show you. And I will make of you a great nation, and I will bless you and make your name great, so that you will be a blessing. I will bless those who bless you, and him who dishonors you I will curse, and in you all the families of the earth shall be blessed."

God here called one single man out of all of humanity. That call involved separation (he was to leave his country, his kindred, and his father's house, and the idolatry that went with them), trust (he was going to a place he did not know), and blessing (promised over and over again). Yet the blessing did not terminate with Abraham. God focused particularly on one man in order to bless all the families of the earth through him. This will be the pattern of the rest of the Old Testament. God's focus was particular, on the descendants of Abraham who constitute the nation of Israel. Yet his final objective is universal, encompassing all the peoples of the earth in his saving purposes.

God repeated the promise to Abraham when he showed himself willing to give up his son Isaac at God's command. The passage in Genesis 22 is pregnant with gospel meaning, as Abraham prepared to sacrifice his only son and as God provided a substitute for that sacrifice. In the blessing God gave him after his act of faithful obedience, God said to Abraham, "In your offspring shall all the nations of the earth be blessed, because you have obeyed my voice" (Gen 22:18). God gave the same promise to Isaac (Gen 26:1–5) and then to Jacob (Gen 28:10–17). God started with one man—Abraham. He narrowed things further to only one son of Abraham—Isaac—and then only one son of Isaac—Jacob. At each stage of ever-increasing particularity, however, he restated his global intention to bless all the families and nations of the earth through them.

At the end of Genesis, Jacob called his twelve sons together and gave a combination of prophecy and blessing. As he turned to Judah, his prophecy became messianic: "The scepter shall not depart from Judah, nor the ruler's staff from between his feet, until tribute comes to him; and to him shall be the obedience of the peoples" (Gen 49:10). From Judah would come the royal line of David, and from the line of David would come the Messiah. Even here in Genesis that royal seed of Judah was to have universal rule, as all the peoples would obey him.

The book of Exodus furthers the theme of particularity, as God delivered the nation of Israel from bondage in Egypt and made a covenant with them to be his people. Even here, however, God's wider purposes can be glimpsed. In Exodus 12:38, we are told that a mixed multitude of people from other nations went out of Egypt with the Israelites, and they seem to have been absorbed into the nation of Israel. These were people who were not physical descendants of Abraham; yet they experienced deliverance along with the Israelites as they aligned themselves with Israel, the community of God. In the law that God gave to his people, he commanded them to separate themselves from the detestable practices of the nations. They were forbidden from intermarrying with the Canaanites or from making alliances with them, lest they be drawn into their idolatry. At the same time, however, God made provision for aliens and strangers from other lands who might come to live among them. "You shall not wrong a sojourner or oppress him, for you were sojourners in the land of Egypt" (Exod 22:21; see also 23:9). Most of the rest of the books of the Law focus on the details of the requirements God gave to Israel and on the story of their troubled journey from Sinai to the borders of the Promised Land. Even in giving his law, however, God had his eye on his fame among the nations. In Deuteronomy, Moses told the Israelites:

> See, I have taught you statutes and rules, as the LORD my God commanded me, that you should do them in the land that you are entering to take possession of it. Keep them and do them, for that will be your wisdom and your understanding in the sight of the peoples, who, when they hear all these statutes, will say, "Surely this great nation is a wise and understanding people." For what great nation is there that has a god so near to it as the LORD our God is to us, whenever we call upon him? And what great nation is there, that has statutes and rules so righteous as all this law that I set before you today? (Deut 4:5–8)

THE PROPHETS

Early in the history of Israel, God raised up prophets to call his people back to the covenant relationship he had established with them. Much of the focus of the ministry of the prophets, therefore, was on the sinfulness and waywardness of Israel. In the midst of this focus, however, God also directed the gaze of the prophets to the nations around them, and even more he directed their attention forward to the direction he was taking. Unlike the pagan conception of the gods of the nations, who were local in power and jurisdiction, the God of Israel is the God of the whole earth and the only true God. This is a major and revolutionary worldview issue that the prophets stressed again and again. They also saw history as linear, with a beginning and a destination. That destination was the Day of the Lord, and its consequences would be radical and global. The prophets saw a coming day in which the redemptive work of God would burst the bounds of national Israel and encompass the nations of the earth.

The book of Amos provides an example of these prophetic themes. The book begins by pronouncing God's judgment on Damascus, Gaza, Tyre, Ammon, and Moab, demonstrating God's power and authority beyond the boundaries of Israel.

Furthermore, his judgment on Moab was not because Moab had injured Israel but because it had injured Edom, indicating that his interest and authority extended completely beyond his own people. Amos ends with a vision of the restoration of Israel. This restoration includes "all the nations that are called by my name," showing that the people of God will extend further than ethnic Israel (Amos 9:12).

The book of Micah also gives a vision of an eschatological time to come in which the nations will come to the God of Israel.

> It shall come to pass in the latter days that the mountain of the house of the LORD shall be established as the highest of the mountains; and it shall be lifted up above the hills; and peoples shall flow to it, and many nations shall come, and say: "Come, let us go up to the mountain of the LORD, to the house of the God of Jacob, that he may teach us his ways and that we may walk in his paths." (Mic 4:1–2)

The latter days are seen as a time of peace and prosperity for the people of God, but they are also seen as a time of ingathering for the nations, who will be added to the number of God's people.

Habakkuk wrestles with the announcement that God planned to use the wicked, arrogant nation of the Chaldeans to punish his people for their sins. God answered by pointing his prophet to the future. In the near future other nations would plunder the Chaldeans themselves. For just a moment, however, God lifted the gaze of his servant beyond the short-term perspective to the ultimate destiny of human history: "For the earth will be filled with the knowledge of the glory of the LORD as the waters cover the sea" (Hab 2:14). God's aim was the display of his glory. The scope of that aim was nothing less than the entire earth. God's focus at this point in salvation history was on Israel. His goal, however, was nothing less than global.

Similar eschatological visions are in the other Minor Prophets. Zephaniah wrote, "For at that time I will change the speech of the peoples to a pure speech, that all of them may call upon the name of the LORD, and serve him with one accord" (Zeph 3:9). God said through Haggai, "And I will shake all nations, so that the treasures of all nations shall come in, and I will fill this house with glory, says the LORD of hosts" (Hag 2:7). Zechariah is even more explicit:

> Thus says the LORD of hosts: Peoples shall yet come, even the inhabitants of many cities. The inhabitants of one city shall go to another, saying, "Let us go at once and entreat the favor of the LORD and to seek the LORD of hosts; I myself am going." Many peoples and strong nations shall come to seek the LORD of hosts in Jerusalem and to entreat the favor of the LORD. Thus says the LORD of hosts: In those days ten men from the nations of every tongue shall take hold of the robe of a Jew, saying, "Let us go with you, for we have heard that God is with you." (Zech 8:20–23)

Even the messianic vision of Zechariah 9:9–10, which predicts Jesus' triumphal entry into Jerusalem on Palm Sunday, ends with the words, "And he shall speak peace to the nations; his rule shall be from sea to sea, and from the River to the ends of the earth." The last days, which will be the time of the Messiah, will also be the time when God gathers the nations to himself in redemption.

The most dramatic picture of God's heart for the nations in the Minor Prophets is the book of Jonah. Jonah's prophetic mission had nothing to do with Israel at all. Instead, he was called by God to go to the most cruel, destructive people of the ancient world: the Assyrians of Nineveh. The people of Nineveh would one day destroy the northern kingdom of Israel. Everyone in the ancient Near East feared and hated them. Jonah detested the idea of preaching to them, not because he was afraid for himself but because he was afraid that his mission might succeed (Jonah 4:1–3). He didn't want the Ninevites to be spared judgment, so he didn't want to give them an opportunity to repent. Rather than obey the call of God, Jonah sought to flee the presence of the Lord, reflecting the common idea of his day that gods were restricted to a given location. The idea was shown to be utter folly. God is clearly demonstrated in the book of Jonah to be sovereign over everything everywhere. He is sovereign over the sea. He is sovereign over Nineveh. It was God who hurled the storm at the ship carrying Jonah (1:4). It was God who appointed the fish who swallowed him (1:17), the plant that gave him shade (4:6), the worm that killed the plant (4:7), and the scorching wind that made him miserable (4:8). From the destinies of nations and the powers of nature to the activities of worms, God is completely in control. What bothered an ethnocentric nationalist like Jonah was that this sovereign God cared about a wicked people like the Assyrians and sent a Hebrew prophet to preach repentance to them. The real point of the book of Jonah is not his deliverance through the fish but God's grace and mercy to a hostile Gentile nation and Jonah's resentment over God's deliverance of Nineveh. Walt Kaiser believes the book of Jonah indicates that Israel had a mandate to take the knowledge of God proactively to the nations.[3] Others note that there is no specific command anywhere else in the Old Testament for such a missionary outreach and that even Jonah nowhere states that his mission is part of a larger missionary mandate.[4] However, whatever else this book may be, it is a clear demonstration of God's care and pity for the nations and a clear rebuke for Israel's failure to share that care and pity. The book of Jonah is a huge display of God's global agenda.

The book of Isaiah contains a series of eschatological visions and messianic prophecies that speak of God's redemptive plan for the nations. The second chapter begins with a verbatim repetition of the vision of the nations God gave Micah (2:1–4; cf. Mic 4:1–4). In the messianic prophesy that begins chapter 9, the day of the Messiah will be a day for the nations to come to God:

> They shall not hurt or destroy in all my holy mountain; for the earth shall be full of the knowledge of the LORD as the waters cover the sea. In that day the root of Jesse, who shall stand as a signal for the peoples—of him shall the nations inquire, and his resting place shall be glorious. (Isa 11:9–10)

[3] Walt Kaiser, *Mission of God in the Old Testament* (Grand Rapids: Baker, 2000), 65–71.
[4] Andreas Köstenberger and Peter O'Brien, *Salvation to the Ends of the Earth* (Downers Grove: IVP, 2001), 44–45.

The song of praise that follows in chapter 12 commands the people of God: "Make known his deeds among the peoples" (12:4). In the eschatological vision of Isaiah 19:19–25, Israel's ancient enemies, Egypt and Assyria, will know and worship the true God and will be counted as the people of God alongside Israel. The vision of Isaiah 24:14–16 foresees songs of praise to God from the ends of the earth. In Isaiah 25:6–8, the prophet says,

> On this mountain the LORD of hosts will make for all peoples a feast of rich food, a feast of well-aged wine, of rich food full of marrow, of aged wine well refined. And he will swallow up on this mountain the covering that is cast over all peoples, the veil that is spread over all nations. He will swallow up death forever; and the Lord GOD will wipe away tears from all faces.

This theme is seen with equal clarity in the songs about the Servant of the Lord in the second half of Isaiah's prophesy. The Servant of the Lord is a light for the nations. The first Servant song, Isaiah 42:1–9, says the Servant will bring forth justice to the nations (42:1) and calls him a light for the nations (42:6). Isaiah 42:10–12 is a summons to all the earth to praise God, including specifically non-Israelite nations. In 45:22, God issues a global invitation: "Turn to me and be saved, all the ends of the earth! For I am God, and there is no other." The second Servant Song, in Isaiah 49, lays out the mission of the Messiah in explicitly global terms: "It is too light a thing that you should be my servant to raise up the tribes of Jacob and to bring back the preserved of Israel; I will make you as a light for the nations, that my salvation may reach to the ends of the earth" (49:6). Similarly, Isaiah 52:10 promises, "All the ends of the earth shall see the salvation of our God." The song of the Suffering Servant, Isaiah 52:13–53:12, is a detailed description of the substitutionary nature of the sacrifice of the Messiah. It is also a declaration of the global scope of that sacrifice: "He will sprinkle many nations" (52:15). In a passage Jesus would quote when he cleansed the temple, God declared, "My house shall be called a house of prayer for all peoples" (56:7), in the middle of an extended promise that non-Israelites would enjoy salvation along with the people of

Israel. Finally, the eschatological vision of Isaiah 60:1–3 ends with the words, "And nations shall come to your light, and kings to the brightness of your rising." The book of Isaiah is permeated with a vision of the Day of the Lord and of the mission of the Messiah that is global in its scope.

The book of Daniel presents a glorious picture of the sovereignty of God over history and over all human power and authority. In that context it depicts the coming of the Messiah as the Son of Man.

> I saw in the night visions,
> and behold, with the clouds of heaven there
> came one like a son of man,
> and he came to the Ancient of Days and was
> presented before him.
> and to him was given dominion and glory
> and a kingdom,
> that all peoples, nations, and languages
> should serve him;
> his dominion is an everlasting dominion,
> which shall not pass away,
> and his kingdom one that shall not be
> destroyed. (Dan 7:13–14)

This is no local savior. The Son of Man will have a dominion that encompasses all peoples, languages, and nations. The Messiah will be a global Messiah.

In summary, the prophets present a vision of the end of history that includes salvation among all nations. They also look forward to a Messiah who is a Savior for all nations. History is moving toward a day when God's redemptive activity goes global.

THE WRITINGS

The third section of the Hebrew Bible contains those books that are not in the Law or the Prophets. By far the longest book in the Writings (and in the Bible as a whole) is the book of Psalms. Psalms is a book of prayer and praise. Not surprisingly, in light of what we have already seen in the rest of the Old Testament, God's intention that he should be glorified among the nations and by the nations is a frequent theme of the Psalms. It begins in Psalm 2, which celebrates both the universal sovereignty of

God and the global inheritance of the Son. Psalm 22 predicts the suffering of the Messiah, and it ends with these words:

> All the ends of the earth shall remember and
> turn to the LORD,
>   and all the families of the nations shall wor-
> ship before you,
>   for kingship belongs to the LORD,
>   and he rules over the nations. (vv. 27–28)

Psalm 46 contains the oft-quoted words, "Be still, and know that I am God." The context is less frequently mentioned; however, immediately after those famous words, the psalmist writes, "I will be exalted among the nations, I will be exalted in the earth!" Psalm 47 begins with a universal summons to praise: "Clap your hands, all peoples! Shout to God with loud songs of joy!" It ends with an astonishing declaration of the global scope of the people of God: "The princes of the peoples gather as the people of the God of Abraham." Psalm 57 speaks of the worship of God in the presence of the nations:

> I will give thanks to you, O Lord, among
> the peoples;
>   I will sing praises to you among the nations.
>   For your steadfast love is great to the heavens,
>   And your faithfulness to the clouds.
>   Be exalted, O God, above the heavens!
>   Let your glory be over all the earth! (vv. 9–11)

Psalm 67 is one of the most blatantly missionary passages in the Old Testament. It begins with a clear reference to the Aaronic blessing laid out in Numbers 6:24–26. It goes on, however, to make clear that the blessing of God is not intended to terminate on the people of God, but that they are blessed to be a blessing. That blessing, explicitly, is the knowledge of God and the experience of his salvation among all nations. The ultimate goal is that God would be praised by all the peoples of the earth.

The vision of universal worship continues in Psalm 86. "All the nations you have made shall come and worship before you, O Lord, and shall glorify your name. For you are great and do wondrous things; you alone are God" (Ps 86:9–10). In Psalm 87, foreigners are counted as natives of Jerusalem. "Among those who know me I mention Rahab and Babylon; behold, Philistia and Tyre, with Cush—'This one was born there,' they say" (Ps 87:4). All of Psalm 96 speaks of the global obligation to worship God and the global scope of the witness of God's people. "Sing to the LORD, all the earth!" (96:1). "Declare his glory among the nations, his marvelous deeds among all the peoples!" (96:3). "Ascribe to the LORD, O families of the peoples, ascribe to the LORD glory and strength! Ascribe to the LORD the glory due his name; bring an offering, and come into his courts!" (96:7–8). "Tremble before him, all the earth!" (96:9). "Say among the nations, 'The LORD reigns!'" (96:10). Psalm 96 presents a picture of missionary proclamation as an act of worship, as God's people praise him by declaring who he is and what he has done for all the nations to hear. Psalm 100 repeats the global summons to worship: "Shout for joy to the LORD, all the earth" (NIV). So, likewise, does the shortest psalm in the Bible:

> Praise the LORD, all nations!
> Extol him, all peoples!
> For great is his steadfast love toward us,
> And the faithfulness of the LORD
> endures forever.
> Praise the LORD! (Psalm 117)

In summary, the theme of the book of Psalms is that worship must be global. God deserves nothing less. For that to happen, the knowledge of God must also be global. Psalms establishes a close connection between worship and missions.[5]

SUMMARY OF THE OLD TESTAMENT ON THE NATIONS

God created the diversified speech of the nations as an act of judgment at the Tower of Babel. That linguistic diversity would prove to be the setting and scope of God's redemptive plan. God narrowed his focus by choosing Abraham, Isaac, Jacob, and the nation of Israel, but he did so for the sake of the nations. Israel was created to display the glory of God to the nations. The theme of God's dealings with Israel was, "Come and see the works of the Lord." The Old Testament looks ahead in an eschatological vision of all nations knowing and worshipping the one true

---

[5] John Piper, *Let the Nations Be Glad* (Grand Rapids: Baker Academic, 2003), 17, 231.

God. The messianic vision of the Old Testament is that Israel's Messiah would be the Savior of all nations. The ultimate goal of everything is worship from the ends of the earth, as the languages that were diversified as an act of God's judgment became instruments of God's praise.

THE INTERTESTAMENTAL PERIOD

For 400 years, from the death of the last of the Old Testament prophets to the birth of John the Baptist, there was no fresh word from God. That does not mean, however, that nothing was happening. God had providentially scattered his people among the nations. He providentially preserved them during these centuries through times of relative peace and times of intense persecution. This was the period of Second Temple Judaism, centered around the temple rebuilt in Jerusalem after some of the exiles returned from Babylon. Was this a period of Jewish missionary outreach? Was the missionary enterprise of the early church simply an extension of what Second Temple Judaism was already doing? At first glance the answer would seem to be yes. Jesus, after all, said to the religious leaders of his day, "Woe to you, scribes and Pharisees, hypocrites! For you travel across sea and land to make a single proselyte, and when he becomes a proselyte, you make him twice as much a child of hell as yourselves" (Matt 23:15). Without question the Jews of this period did proselytize Gentiles, and Gentiles converted to Judaism. However, Judaism was no monolith, and there was no tight organizational system. The work of proselytism seems to have been sporadic and regional, and there was no centralized or sustained missionary outreach.[6]

All the same, the period of the Babylonian exile and the subsequent Diaspora of Jews around the ancient world was hugely significant for the advance of the gospel. In the providence of God, during the centuries leading up to the birth of Jesus and the missionary expansion of the early church, Jewish synagogues were established from the western Mediterranean to China. Through those synagogues the knowledge of the God of Israel spread widely among the Gentiles. Some Gentiles converted,

---

[6] For an excellent discussion of this issue, see Michael F. Bird, *Crossing over Land and Sea* (Peabody, MA: Hendrickson, 2010).

but more became Godfearers who were attracted to God and his law but were reluctant to undertake the arduous process of full conversion to Judaism. In the sovereignty of God, those synagogues and pockets of God-fearing Gentiles were the fertile soil through which the gospel would explode once the fullness of time had come. Once again God used even an act of judgment (the scattering of the Jews following the fall of Jerusalem to the Babylonians) to advance his redemptive purposes in the world.

NEW TESTAMENT

With the arrival of Jesus, the hopes of the Old Testament began to be fulfilled. The Gospels demonstrate that Jesus is the promised Messiah who inaugurated the kingly rule of God on earth. With Jesus the Day of the Lord had arrived, and once he had completed the work the Father had given him to do, the Spirit was poured out and the ingathering of the nations began. The New Testament was written in the context of the rapid missionary expansion of the church, and it cannot be properly understood otherwise.

Gospels

The Gospel according to Matthew has a decidedly Jewish feel to it, with its extensive quotation from the Old Testament. It even begins with a Jewish genealogy. Even here, however, Matthew makes a point of mentioning three Gentile women—Tamar, Rahab, and Ruth—where a conventional genealogy only needed to mention the men (Matt 1:3, 5). This awareness of God's purposes beyond the bounds of Israel is even more dramatically displayed by the coming of the magi (Matt 2:1–12). Among the first worshippers of Jesus were Gentile Iranians who were probably astrologers. One of the few people in the Gospel whom Jesus commended unreservedly is a Roman centurion, and Jesus responded to his faith by saying, "Truly, I tell you, with no one in Israel have I found such faith. I tell you, many will come from east and west and recline at table with Abraham, Isaac, and Jacob in the kingdom of heaven, while the sons of the kingdom will be thrown into the outer darkness" (Matt 8:10–12). When Jesus condemned the Pharisees for their lack of faith, he used two Gentile examples of faith, the men of Nineveh and the Queen of the South, to shame them (Matt 12:38–42). Matthew 24:14 unambiguously links the return of Christ with the global spread of the gospel to all people groups: "And this gospel of the kingdom will be proclaimed throughout the whole world as a testimony to all nations, and then the end will come." The Great Commission in Matthew 28:18–20 therefore comes as no surprise. Jesus had concentrated his focus on the house of Israel during his ministry prior to his death and resurrection (Matt 10:5–6). With his resurrection and the sending of the Holy Spirit, God's redemptive focus rests on nothing less than all peoples and nations on earth.

The Great Commission in Matthew merits closer examination, for it makes many aspects of a biblical missiology explicit. Jesus began by asserting that all authority in heaven and on earth had been given to him. He is the King of the kingdom of heaven, which has now invaded the earth. His universal *authority* is the foundation of Christian mission. He has the authority to command his followers to go to every people group, whatever the cost. He also has authority over every government, every culture, and every spiritual power, including those that oppose his gospel. His authority gives his followers both the right to take the gospel to every nation, whether they welcome it or not, and the obligation to take it to every nation, whether it is safe and convenient or not. The *basic task* of Christian mission is found in the imperative verb in the Great Commission: make disciples. It is never enough for Christians simply to do works of mercy. It is also never enough simply to seek decisions for Christ. The goal of Christian mission is not decisions but disciples who abide in an intimate relationship with him, who grow progressively in his likeness, and who learn and obey everything he commanded. This discipleship is marked in its beginning by baptism in the name of the triune God, which signifies dying to everything you were before Christ and rising to walk in newness of life and radical identification with Christ (Rom 6:3–4). The *scope* of Christian mission is all peoples. The word *ethne* means far more than geopolitical countries. It refers to people groups identified by language, culture, common history, or anything else that gives a group of people a sense of "us" as opposed to "them." The Great Commission is thus rooted firmly in the Old

Testament vision of the peoples and nations of the earth. God's *provision* for Christian mission is the promise of his presence to the end of the age—a promise that is only given in the context of fulfilling his mission.

The Gospel of Mark begins with quotations from Malachi 3:1 and Isaiah 40:3, which link the coming of Jesus with the eschatological promise of the Old Testament. Jesus made that link explicit with his first recorded words in Mark: "The time is fulfilled, and the kingdom of God is at hand; repent, and believe in the gospel" (Mark 1:15). His next recorded words were a summons to evangelistic outreach: "Follow me, and I will make you become fishers of men" (Mark 1:17). Jesus' first recorded contact with Gentiles in Mark is the curious story of his conversation with the Syrophoenician woman, in which he rebuffs her at first and then grants her request in light of her persistent faith (Mark 7:24–30). When he entered Jerusalem for the last week before his crucifixion, however, all ambiguity was gone. He cleansed the temple of buyers and sellers and money changers. The part of the temple that was defiled by their activity was the court of the Gentiles, and he quoted from Isaiah to justify his action: "My house shall be called a house of prayer for all nations" (Mark 11:17, cf. Isa 56:7). Their crass commercial activity was preventing Gentiles from approaching the God of Israel, and that provoked his anger.

Luke also connects the coming of Jesus with the ingathering of the nations. When Mary and Joseph brought the baby Jesus to the temple, Simeon prayed, "Lord, now you are letting your servant depart in peace, according to your word; for my eyes have seen your salvation that you have prepared in the presence of all peoples, a light for revelation for the Gentiles and for glory to your people Israel" (Luke 2:29–32). When Jesus preached in the synagogue in Nazareth, he identified himself as the Servant of the Lord from Isaiah, and he infuriated the congregation by speaking of God's mercy to Gentiles like the widow at Zarephath and Naaman the Syrian in the Old Testament. At the end of Luke, Jesus claimed that his life, death, and resurrection have fulfilled the Law, the Prophets, and the Psalms. His immediate conclusion was that repentance and forgiveness of sins should now be proclaimed in Jesus' name to all nations (Luke 24:44–49). Here as elsewhere, Jesus also connected the fulfillment of the Old Testament and the proclamation of salvation to all nations with the coming of the Holy Spirit, linking together all the elements of the promised Day of the Lord in the Old Testament. The task Jesus gave his followers (who were almost certainly more than the Eleven) was to proclaim the gospel to all peoples on earth in the power of the Holy Spirit.

As with the other three Gospels, the Gospel of John has a global perspective from the beginning. In his prologue John speaks of the Word of God made flesh, and he speaks of him coming into the world, not just to his own people. In fact, he observes that Jesus' own people did not receive him, and he goes on to assert that the right to become children belongs not to those with the right ethnic pedigree but to those who receive him (John 1:1–13). When John the Baptist saw Jesus, he called him the Lamb of God who takes away the sin of the world, not just the sin of Israel (John 1:29). In Jesus' famous conversation with Nicodemus, he said that God loves the world, not just the Jews, and he offered salvation to anyone who believed in him (John 3:16). Jesus had another famous encounter, with the woman at the well in Samaria, in which he acknowledged that salvation and legitimate worship had belonged to the Jews up to that point in history, but he clearly stated that a great transition was about to take place in which ethnicity and location will no longer matter, and he linked that transition to the ministry of the Holy Spirit (John 4:19–26). Throughout the Gospel of John, Jesus repeatedly announced that his hour had not yet come, but when some Gentiles sought him in Jerusalem at Passover, Jesus declared that the hour of his glorification had come and predicted his imminent death (12:20–33). Finally, at the end of John, Jesus sent his followers into the world as he had been sent, and he connected that sending with the gift of the Spirit (John 20:21–23).

The message of the Gospels is consistent. In the life, death, and resurrection of Jesus, the turning point of the ages has happened. The Day of the Lord, promised in the Old Testament, has now come. God has stepped into human history in the person of the Messiah, and his kingly rule has broken into human history. The repeated promise of God to bless and save the nations through Israel is now being fulfilled. The day of the outpouring of the Spirit has arrived, and he is given to the followers of the Messiah to empower the proclamation of the gospel to all the peoples of the world. The Gospels end with the people of God sent on a mission of gospel witness to the ends of the earth, in fulfillment of all God had done in the Old Testament.

Acts

The book of Acts is the story of the expansion of the church as its members carry out their mission of proclaiming the gospel to the nations. It begins with yet one more presentation of the Great Commission in Acts 1:1–11. The stated task is to be witnesses to Jesus. This is linked with the Holy Spirit, who is given for the purpose of empowering that witness. This is also set in the context of eschatology, as the words of Jesus are bracketed by questions from the disciples and declarations by the angels about the end of history. The scope of the task is given as a series of ever-expanding circles that reach to the ends of the earth. The beginning of Acts recapitulates the commission given at the end of the Gospels, in all the same theological frameworks.

Acts then tells its story through a series of turning points that propel the gospel forward into the world. The first is the day of Pentecost (Acts 2:1–41). Peter's sermon, with its quotation from the book of Joel, explained the outpouring of the Holy Spirit as the fulfillment of Old Testament promises, and he made explicit the linkage between the giving of the Spirit, the last days, and missions. In Pentecost we see the beginning of the reversal of the curse of Babel. We also see the role of the Jewish Diaspora, as Diaspora Jews were the audience who heard the gospel in their heart languages,[7] and as many of them will have returned home after the feast, taking the gospel with them. The next turning point is the gospel harvest in Samaria, which is the first time a significant number of non-Jews come to faith in Jesus (Acts 8:4–25). This is almost immediately followed by the conversion of the Ethiopian eunuch, a Godfearer who was doubly banned from the Jewish congregation as a Gentile and a eunuch (Acts 8:26–39). Saul of Tarsus was then converted

---

[7] The Jews of the Diaspora used Hebrew in their synagogue worship, but for most it was not their heart language, i.e., the language they knew best and used in daily life.

and given a commission to take the gospel to the Gentiles (Acts
9:15). The next major step forward comes with the conversion
of Cornelius, a Roman army officer, and his household (Acts 10).
This step was so fraught with controversy that God endorsed
it ahead of time with a dramatic vision, and Peter explained it
carefully to the church in Jerusalem afterward. After this there
could no longer be any doubt that the gospel was intended for
the Gentiles. In Acts 11, we read that the church in Antioch,
established by anonymous refugees from the persecution that
followed the death of Stephen, reached out both to Jews and
Gentiles, with significant fruit for the gospel among the Gentiles. Once again this was sufficiently controversial for the
church in Jerusalem to send Barnabas to Antioch to make sure it
was legitimate. The missionary journeys of Paul begin in Acts 13
when the church in Antioch sent him and Barnabas, and those
journeys occupy much of the rest of the book. Paul went first to
the Jews in each city, but he always then turned to the Gentiles
and shared the gospel with them. The most significant break in
Paul's journeys is the meeting in Jerusalem, recorded in Acts
15, to discuss whether or not Gentiles needed to become Jews
in order to become Christians. This was a theological question,
but it had profound missiological implications. The conclusion
of those gathered at the meeting—that Gentiles did not have
to become Jews in order to be saved—set the stage for the contextualization of the gospel in the Gentile world. The end of the
book details Paul's arrest, his arraignments in Palestine, and his
journey to Rome to stand trial before Caesar. At the conclusion
of Acts, the gospel has gone from a small group of people who
could fit in one building in Jerusalem to a growing movement
that had spread from Palestine to the capital of the Roman world.
It is entirely a missionary story.

The Epistles

Paul was a missionary, and the letters of Paul were part of
his missionary strategy.[8] Paul was seldom able to stay long in

---

[8] Eckhard Schnabel questions whether Paul can legitimately be called a missionary, as he never left
the country of his birth (the Roman Empire) and was able to minister in Greek everywhere he went.
However, Schnabel fails to take into account that Rome was a huge conglomeration of nations and
peoples under one imperial government, not a country in the modern sense of the word, and Paul
certainly encountered multiple cultures in the course of his travels. He went where the gospel had

any city because of opposition and persecution. When he could, as in Ephesus, he stayed longer. Wherever people came to faith, he established churches and appointed elders. When he left, he did not abandon those churches but stayed in touch as best as he could. When possible, he revisited the churches he had planted. At times he sent others he trusted—Timothy, Titus, Priscilla, and Aquila—to check up on them. He stayed in touch and stayed abreast of the issues. His letters were thus part of his church-planting strategy, demonstrating the need for ongoing input, theological instruction, and pastoral care for new churches made up of new converts.

Paul wrote most of his letters in response to specific issues in the churches. Two of them, however, are less "occasional" than the others: Ephesians and Romans. Part of the second chapter of Ephesians teaches that an intrinsic piece of the work of the cross was the breaking down of the dividing wall between Jew and Gentile. It also indicates that the body of Christ, the church, is now the holy temple where God dwells, so that the New Testament antitype has replaced the Old Testament type. In chapter 3, Paul said that the mystery of the gospel was that the Gentiles—the nations—were fellow heirs with Israel and members of the same body. His mission was to preach to the Gentiles the unsearchable riches of Christ. The letter to the Romans is an extended exposition of the gospel. In the opening of the book, Paul made clear that Jews and Gentiles were both alike under condemnation and that Jews and Gentiles both were saved only by grace through faith in Christ as proclaimed in the gospel. In Romans 10:5–17, Paul based the necessity of missionary effort and gospel witness in the logic of the gospel itself. Salvation comes only to those who call upon the Lord to be saved, which requires faith in the Lord Jesus Christ. Faith is not possible unless the gospel is heard. Hearing the gospel is not possible without someone proclaiming it. No one will proclaim the gospel unless they are sent. The conclusion is clear. No one will be saved without intentional, proactive missionary sending, and without intentional, proactive evangelistic proclamation. Paul explained his own ministry in terms of the imperative of the gospel. In Romans

---

never been heard. He certainly was a cross-cultural, pioneer missionary. See Eckhard Schnabel, *Paul the Missionary* (Downers Grove: IVP, 2008), 317–34.

15:14–23 he described his own ministry as bringing the Gentiles to the obedience of faith. In doing so, he adopted the language of the temple priesthood and saw his missionary work as the fulfillment of the temple ministry. His accomplishment was that he had fulfilled the ministry of the gospel from Jerusalem as far as Illyricum (modern-day Croatia). He could say this not because everyone in that territory had heard the gospel but because he had planted churches across the area, and those churches continued the work of evangelism in their locations. His ambition was to preach the gospel where Christ was not yet known, and he saw this as a fulfillment of the Old Testament vision of the Day of the Lord and of the purpose of the Atonement.[9] Paul's letter to the Romans firmly connects the content of the gospel with the imperative of missions.

In 1 Corinthians, in the course of dealing with issues in the Corinthian church, Paul gave significant insights into his understanding of the missionary task. In 1 Corinthians 3:5–17, he explained the complementary roles that he and Apollos played in establishing the church. Paul was the pioneer church planter who laid the necessary foundation of the church in the gospel. Apollos was the church development missionary who continued the work Paul had begun, investing in the growth and health of the baby church. Both were valid and essential ministries, and those who tried to value one over the other missed the point of what God was doing. God alone got the credit, as he alone gave the growth. The church lies at the heart of God's missionary strategy.[10] It belongs to God, and he takes it seriously. This passage is not about the individual life of a Christian, as it is so often taken, but rather about the church, and it gives a sober warning about the importance of treating the church carefully and building on the foundation of the gospel wisely.

First Corinthians 9 is a famous passage on Paul's missionary method. The primary focus in the passage is on his decision to lay down his rights for the sake of the gospel. In this context he

---

[9] In support of his explanation of his ministry and his ambition, Paul quotes Isa 52:15, from an eschatological passage that includes the most profound description of the atoning work of the Messiah in the Old Testament.

[10] Consequently, any missionary strategy that neglects church planting and church development is subbiblical. Given what Paul says in 1 Corinthians 12 about the essential role of spiritual gifts and the body of Christ in the health of any believer, and what he says in Eph 4:1–16 about the necessary role of the church in growing to maturity as a disciple of Jesus, this makes sense.

said, "I have become all things to all people, that by all means I might save some" (1 Cor 9:22). Paul was not talking about compromising his own integrity or the content of the message in any way. His parenthetical statement in verse 21 ("Not being outside the law of God but under the law of Christ") makes that plain, as does the consistent message of all of his letters. Paul never tolerated immorality in the churches, he never tolerated theological diversity, and he never tolerated compromise of the message in order to make it more acceptable to those who heard it. Rather, this context speaks to his willingness to give up things he had a legitimate right to enjoy, like taking along a believing wife or eating certain kinds of foods, if doing so would give him a better hearing for the gospel. Within the bounds of Scripture (an all-important caveat), he was willing to adapt to the culture, and even the scruples, of the people he was trying to reach. This is the foundation for a biblical approach to contextualization.

The other letters of Paul contain numerous references to his understanding of the missionary task. He was committed to maintaining integrity in both his message and his methods (2 Cor 2:14–17; 4:1–2). He saw the gospel message as urgent, and he believed it was valid to use persuasion and to express that urgency when he proclaimed the gospel (2 Cor 5:11–21). He regarded it as natural and expected that churches would engage in evangelistic outreach where they lived (Phil 1:12–18; 1 Thess 1:8). He spoke plainly, worked hard, maintained holiness of life, and opened up his life and his heart in affection and love (1 Thess 2:1–12). His pastoral epistles, to Timothy and Titus, are extended instructions to church development missionaries. Paul's letters have been rightly applied to established churches and to the lives of individual Christians through the ages. In their original context, however, they are missionary documents, and they are rich sources for missionary passion, the missionary message, and missionary method.[11]

Paul was not alone in writing letters as part of his missionary method. Peter wrote his first letter to new Christians in central and northern Anatolia (modern-day Turkey), and he

---

[11] See Roland Allen's classical book, *Missionary Methods: St Paul's, or Ours?* (Grand Rapids: Eerdmans, 1962). For more recent explorations of the missiology of Paul, see Köstenberger and O'Brien, *Salvation to the Ends of the Earth*, and Robert Plummer and J. Mark Terry, *Paul's Missionary Methods* (Downers Grove: IVP Academic, 2012).

addressed them as "elect exiles of the Dispersion" (1 Pet 1:1), connecting these largely Gentile believers to the Jewish Diaspora after the Babylonian exile and indicating his sense of the basic continuity of New Testament missionary expansion with Old Testament promises.[12] His letter is set in the context of suffering and persecution. Yet even here he expected his readers to use their suffering as an opportunity for witness: "In your hearts honor Christ the Lord as holy, always being prepared to make a defense to anyone who asks you for a reason for the hope that is in you" (1 Pet 3:15). The apostolic pattern is clear and consistent. They shared the gospel and planted churches where Christ was not yet known. They nurtured those churches and followed up with them regularly, building carefully on the foundation of the gospel and responding quickly to false teaching, unethical leadership, or immoral behavior. They expected those churches to continue the work of evangelism where they lived so that the apostles could continue to press into new areas that had not yet heard the gospel. As they went, they looked for people whom God had gifted for either pioneer or church development missionary service (people like Timothy, Titus, Luke, John Mark, Silvanus, Priscilla, Aquila, and others), and they mentored them. They did not regard the task as complete as long as there were people who had not heard the gospel.

Revelation

The Bible closes with a dramatic picture of how the history of the world will end. This is consistent with the worldview of the entire biblical revelation. History is not aimless. It had a beginning in creation. It has a purpose—the display of God's glory in redemption and judgment—and it has a destination—the restoration of all things in the new heavens and the new earth. The point and plotline of this present time between the first and second comings of Jesus is the advancement of the gospel to every people group and nation on earth, even as the world grows more wicked. The theme of God's heart and plan for the nations comes to a climax in the book of Revelation. Revelation 5 connects the atoning work of Christ directly to the global scope and

---

[12] James does the same thing at the start of his letter, addressing it "to the twelve tribes of the Dispersion."

the people group focus of God's redemptive purposes: "Worthy are you to take the scroll and to open its seals, for you were slain, and by your blood you ransomed people for God from every tribe and language and people and nation" (5:9). The fulfillment of those purposes, and the complete undoing of the curse of Babel, is seen in Revelation 7:9–10:

> After this I looked, and behold, a great multitude that no one could number, from every nation, from all tribes and peoples and languages, standing before the throne and before the Lamb, clothed in white robes, with palm branches in their hands, and crying out with a loud voice, "Salvation belongs to our God who sits on the throne, and to the Lamb!"

The nations will bring their glory and honor into the New Jerusalem (Rev 21:22–26), and the leaves of the tree of life are for the healing of the nations (Rev 22:1–2). The point of history will not be complete until the gospel has reached every people group on earth and until every language spoken on the planet worships Jesus.

RESOURCES FOR FURTHER STUDY

Bird, Michael F. *Crossing over Land and Sea: Jewish Missionary Activity in the Second Temple Period*. Peabody, MA: Hendrickson Publishers, 2010.

Grudem, Wayne, C. John Collins, and Thomas R. Schreiner. *Understanding the Big Picture of the Bible*. Wheaton: Crossway, 2012.

Kaiser, Walter C., Jr. *Mission of God in the Old Testament*. Grand Rapids: Baker Academic, 2000.

Köstenberger, Andreas, and Peter O'Brien. *Salvation to the Ends of the Earth: A Biblical Theology of Mission*. Downers Grove: IVP, 2001.

Plummer, Robert L., and John Mark Terry, eds. *Paul's Missionary Methods*. Downers Grove: IVP Academic, 2012.

Schnabel, Eckhard J. *Paul the Missionary*. Downers Grove: IVP Academic, 2008.

Wright, Christopher J. H. *The Mission of God*. Downers Grove: IVP Academic, 2006.

CHAPTER 4

THEOLOGICAL FOUNDATIONS FOR GLOBAL MISSIONS

Missiology is applied theology. What we do flows from what we believe. Indeed, what we do reveals what we truly believe and value, whatever we may say. As evangelical Christians, theology is simply an account of what we believe God has revealed to us in his Word about the things he regards as essential for us to know regarding the ultimate questions of life. Missiology is a description of what we believe we have been called by God to do in the world and how we believe we ought to do it. As followers of Jesus, we regard ourselves as under the authority of God. Therefore, theology should control missiology, and our missiology should flow from our theology.[1]

This approach is deeply biblical. The apostle Paul followed a typical pattern in his letters. He began with theological truth in the first part of his letters and then transitioned with the word "therefore" to the application of that truth to the lives of believers.[2] Paul clearly thought that what Christians believe has profound and controlling consequences for how they live. In a pragmatic culture like contemporary North America, it is all too common to assume that Jesus gave the basic task when he gave the Great Commission but then left it up to his people

---

[1] Bruce Riley Ashford, "A Theologically Driven Missiology," in *Theology and Practice of Mission: God, the Church, and the Nations,* ed. Bruce Riley Ashford (Nashville: B&H Academic, 2011), 294–95.

[2] See, for example, Eph 4:1; Phil 2:12; Col 2:16; 1 Thess 4:1.

to figure out how to do it, leaving them free to explore whatever methods produced the greatest numerical results. In reality the theology of biblical Christianity gives a far more thorough understanding of the nature and goal of the task of missions, and has a far greater impact on how that task should be done, than evangelical pragmatism would seem to assume. The task of this chapter is to unpack this connection between theology and missiology.

What is theology? Properly speaking, evangelical theology is the summary of what the Bible teaches on the key subjects of Christian faith and life. Good theology addresses two types of subjects. First and foremost, whatever is central in Scripture should be central in theology. Certain things clearly lie at the heart of the biblical message: God, God's Word, God's creation, humanity, sin and its consequences, the person and work of Jesus Christ, the Holy Spirit, the church, and the progress and destiny of history. Because the Bible views these as central, they must be central in any presentation of Christian theology, wherever in the world one may be and whatever the cultural context. Second, however, different cultural contexts raise different particular issues that must be addressed from Scripture. These may vary from place to place and from time to time. For example, at the beginning of the twentieth century, the concept of marriage as a lifelong monogamous union between a man and a woman, and the idea that human life began at conception, and the nature of gender roles in the church were all part of the cultural consensus of the West. Consequently, most confessions of faith did not address them. In the early twenty-first century, all of those issues are matters of debate, and all of them now need to be considered carefully. Church history therefore plays a helpful role in the shaping of theology, not because tradition is authoritative but because the experience of our brothers and sisters across the ages helps us see the importance of certain issues, and it also helps us see the consequences of going down different paths of interpretation. To give one important example, the early church wrestled hard with the issue of the full divinity and full humanity of Christ, and they went down many blind alleys in the process. Under the sun little is new, and Christians in the twenty-first century would be fools not to learn from their experience.

Everyone is a theologian. Theology is not the preserve of academia. Anytime anyone speaks on any issue of Christian belief and life (and biblical Christianity encompasses all of life), they are engaging in the task of theology. Even if they are quoting Scripture, they have engaged in the theological task of connecting and applying certain texts to certain issues. Those who claim to have no interest in theology or denigrate theology as impractical simply show that they do not understand what they are talking about. Every Christian does the work of a theologian every day, and those who think otherwise guarantee that they will do it poorly.[3]

Properly done, theology should result in worship. It is not enough to know the truth. Even demons believe orthodox truths like "God is one" (Jas 2:19). Evangelical theology combines *knowing* the truth with *loving the truth*, something neither demons nor unbelieving academicians are capable of doing. For those who have been born again of the Spirit, it should not be possible to think about God and his ways without falling on our faces in worship. Certainly, no one in the Bible was able to do so.[4] Theology that does not flow into worship is blasphemous because worship is the only appropriate response to the glory of God revealed in his truth. On the other hand, worship that is not rooted in theology is idolatry because it is worship of a different god than the one true God as he has revealed himself exclusively in the teaching of Scripture. Scriptural theology must provide the content of worship, or it is not worship of the God of Scripture. Theology and worship are absolutely inextricably interconnected.

Both theology and worship then lead inevitably to mission. The debt owed by missiology to theology has already been stated. At the same time, theology must flow into mission or it degenerates into disobedience. What we believe doesn't only inform our action; it impels it. If God is who our theology says he is, and if we are who our theology says we are, and if Jesus Christ has done what our theology says he has done, and if salvation

---

[3] Wayne Grudem, *Systematic Theology* (Grand Rapids: Zondervan, 1994), 21–30.
[4] See, for example, Exod 3:1–6; 20:1–21; Isa 6:1–8; Matt 17:1–8; Acts 9:1–9; Rev 1:9–18.

comes about the way our theology says it does, then the truth
we believe compels us to action. Anyone who says they believe
orthodox evangelical theology yet feels no compulsion to take
the gospel into the world either has not understood that theology fully or has not believed it transformingly.

In the same way, worship flows directly into mission. John
Piper has done a convincing job of drawing the link between
worship and mission.[5] Worship is the fuel of mission as it stokes
the fire of our passion for the glory of God. It is also the goal of
mission as the entire missionary enterprise aims at recruiting
more worshippers for the choir of heaven. In addition to these
points made by Piper, is also the content of mission. Missionary
proclamation is declaring his glory among the nations, his marvelous deeds among all peoples (Ps 96:3); it is proclaiming the
excellencies of him who called us out of darkness into his marvelous light (1 Pet 2:9). The evangelistic message of the church
is not the bare recitation of a formula for escaping hell. It is an
act of worship, proclaiming the character and deeds of our saving God, and a summons to worship, calling sinners to give him
the glory due his name in repentance and faith.

What is the mission of God's people? A mission is a task
someone is sent to complete. The definition implies three elements: a sender, the person or persons sent, and the task to be
accomplished. Christian mission fits this definition perfectly.
The sender is God himself. The ones who are sent are his people.
The task is his assignment to them to make disciples out of every
tribe, tongue, people, and nation. The penultimate goal of this
mission is the redemption of a global people who will glorify him
and enjoy him forever; the final result will be the restoration of
the entire created order; and the ultimate end of this mission is
that the earth be filled with the glory of the Lord as the waters
cover the sea. Each of these elements is pervasively theological
in content and motivation, and each can only be properly understood in the context of worship.

The grand narrative of Scripture is creation–fall–redemption–restoration for the display of God's glory and out of the overflow of his grace. God created everything that exists and declared
it good. The crown of his creation was man (male and female),

---

[5] John Piper, *Let the Nations Be Glad* (Grand Rapids: Baker, 2003), 17–18.

who bore his image and served as his vicegerent on earth. The first man and woman, Adam and Eve, were historical persons who willfully chose to rebel against God. Adam stood as federal head of the human race, and in his fall all subsequent humanity descended into both actual guilt and a corrupted nature. Their fall also introduced corruption and disorder into the rest of creation. God, before the foundation of the world, purposed to redeem a global people for himself out of fallen humanity and to guide the history of this world from its beginning in creation to a climactic conclusion in which he restores all things and dwells with his redeemed people forever. God supremely accomplished his redemptive purpose through the life, death, and resurrection of Jesus, God the Son in human flesh, and through the sending of the Holy Spirit. The mission of the people of God nests within this grand narrative of Scripture. Based on the redeeming work of Jesus, and in the power of the Holy Spirit, God has sent his people on his mission as his ambassadors to make disciples of all peoples, to the praise of his glorious grace.[6]

Because Christian mission is God's mission, it is fundamentally a theological task. It is rooted in the nature, character, plan, and deeds of God; it is based on the authority and sufficiency of Scripture; it is set in the context of what Scripture teaches about the nature of fallen man; it flows from the person and work of Christ; it is carried out by the church in the power and gifts of the Holy Spirit; and it is inextricably tied to the eschatological destiny of history. Any understanding of mission that is not rooted in the theology of Scripture is not Christian mission, and any missionary approach or methodology that is not controlled by such theology is illegitimate.

GOD: THE AUTHOR, RULER, AND GOAL
OF CHRISTIAN MISSION

There is one and only one living and true God. He is an intelligent, spiritual, and personal Being, the Creator, Redeemer, Preserver, and Ruler of the universe. God is infinite in holiness

---

[6] See Bruce Riley Ashford, "The Story of Mission: The Grand Biblical Narrative," in *Theology and Practice of Mission*, 6–16; Zane Pratt, "The Heart of Mission: Redemption," in *Theology and Practice of Mission*, 48–59.

and all other perfections. God is all powerful and
all knowing; and His perfect knowledge extends
to all things, past, present, and future, including the future decisions of His free creatures.
To Him we owe the highest love, reverence, and
obedience. The eternal triune God reveals Himself to us as Father, Son, and Holy Spirit, with
distinct personal attributes, but without division of nature, essence, or being.[7]

The triune God of Scripture is the author of Christian mission. The world belongs to God, who created it (Genesis 1), who
rules over it and guides its history (Dan 4:34–35), and who will
bring that history to a close (Rev 20:11–22:5). God the Father
sent God the Son into that world to be the appointed Redeemer.
God the Father and God the Son together send God the Holy
Spirit to direct and empower God's people to do the task God
has given them. God the Son sends us, his people, on his mission (John 14:16–17, 26; 20:21). The Great Commission is based
on the universal authority the Father has given the Son (Matt
28:18–20). The mission of the people of God belongs to God
and is based on his authority. There are three implications to
this. First, it is under his rule. No one has the right to tamper
with the nature, the task, the scope, the appointed means, or the
obligation of his mission. Second, it is based on his authority;
his people have a *right* to carry it out, regardless of what fallen
human cultures or fallen human governments may say to the
contrary. Third, also because it is based on his authority, his people have an *obligation* to carry it out, whatever the cost.

Just as God is the author and the ruler of Christian mission, so also his glory is the ultimate goal of that mission.[8] The
redemption of sinners from all of the people groups on earth
is a penultimate goal of Christian mission, but it can never be
the ultimate goal because people are not ultimate. God is. The
glory of God is the ultimate goal of everything. God created the
world for his own glory. Everything he made reflects the glory
of his being and his character (Ps 19:1). The angels in Isaiah's

---

[7] Baptist Faith and Message 2000, http://www.sbc.net/bfm/bfm2000.asp.
[8] Piper, *Let the Nations Be Glad*, 20–36.

vision of God cried out, "Holy, holy, holy is the LORD of hosts; the whole earth is full of his glory!" (Isa 6:3). God designed the human race to glorify him (Ps 96:7–8). God created men and women in his own image, and sin is fundamentally a failure to live up to the glory of that image and to give him the glory that naturally belongs to him (Rom 3:22–23). Idolatry is the foolish exchange of the true glory of the living God for the shoddy false glory of man-made gods: "They . . . exchanged the glory of the immortal God for images resembling mortal man and birds and animals and creeping things" (Rom 1:22–23). The final objective of the work of the triune God in redeeming fallen people, Paul argued, is "the praise of his glory" (Eph 1:3–14). Those who are redeemed are commanded to live entirely for God's glory (1 Cor 10:31). The missionary message of the people of God is a declaration of the glory of God as revealed in his saving acts: "Declare his glory among the nations, his marvelous works among all the peoples!" (Ps 96:3) Ultimately the destiny of creation is universal knowledge of the glory of God: "For the earth will be filled with the knowledge of the glory of the LORD as the waters cover the sea" (Hab 2:14). The mission of God has the glory of God as its driving passion and its ultimate goal, as God reveals the amazing spectrum of his glory in creation, judgment, redemption, and restoration.[9]

God is also sovereign. He rules over everything. Whatever God decides to do occurs exactly as he planned it. He is in control of everything. This does not mean God is the author of evil (Jas 1:13–15). Nor does it mean he does violence to the wills of his creatures. It does mean he is so completely in charge that even evil things end up accomplishing his purposes (Gen 50:20). God is sovereign over human history, sovereign over nature, and sovereign over the events in our lives. He is sovereign over the salvation of sinners. Far from discouraging evangelism and missions, the sovereignty of God is the bedrock on which they stand. Believers can take the gospel boldly into a hostile world, knowing that our sovereign God will break down every barrier, open every necessary door, and accomplish his stated purpose of

---

[9] Pratt, "The Heart of Mission: Redemption," in Ashford, *Theology and Practice of Mission*, 49.

redeeming a people for himself from every tribe, tongue, people, and nation.[10]

It is absolutely critical that everyone who engages in Christian mission understand how fundamentally theocentric that mission must be. God himself issues the marching orders. He defines the task. He prescribes the means. He provides the resources and the power to accomplish it. He gets all the glory. A healthy obsession with the glory of God safeguards his people from the idolatry of thinking they are primary, and it also purifies their methodology because if the end is his glory, then the means must glorify him as well. Because he is sovereign, missionaries will not be tempted to engage in manipulative means, and they will not despair in the face of opposition. Furthermore, the mission of the people of God is not some minor addendum to the life of the church but God's assigned task to them that connects them to God's design for all of human history. Because it is fundamentally God's mission, it is not an option.[11]

SCRIPTURE: THE RULE OF CHRISTIAN MISSION

God exercises his lordship through his Word, illuminated and applied by his Spirit. The way to know the nature of the task God has given his people, the means he has prescribed, and the parameters he has set is through Scripture. The sixty-six books of the canonical Old and New Testaments were given by inspiration of the Holy Spirit in such a way that what Scripture says, God says (2 Tim 3:16; 2 Pet 1:20–21). Evangelical theology has historically affirmed a series of consequences that flow from this understanding of divine inspiration, and each of these consequences has serious implications for a genuinely biblical missiology. First, because the Bible was inspired by God, who is Truth, the Bible itself is truth without any mixture of error in everything it teaches on every subject on which it touches (John 17:17).[12] Scripture is fully reliable. It is the only completely trustworthy source of instruction on anything, including the task of missions. Second, because it is the word of the

---

[10] J. I. Packer, *Evangelism and the Sovereignty of God* (Downers Grove: IVP, 1961).

[11] For more information, see Timothy George, "The Nature of God," in Daniel Akin, ed., *A Theology for the Church* (Nashville: B&H Academic, 2007), 176–241.

[12] The best book on the inerrancy of the Bible remains J. I. Packer, *"Fundamentalism" and the Word of God* (Grand Rapids: Eerdmans, 1958).

sovereign Lord of the universe, it bears his authority. The Bible is absolutely authoritative over everything we think, believe, and do. What the Bible says, God says, and what God says goes. This makes Scripture the final word over every aspect of mission theory and practice. Both of these first two propositions are generally affirmed by the majority of evangelical missiologists.

Under the influence of contemporary culture, however, many professing evangelicals can affirm the inerrancy and authority of Scripture and yet fail to make any connection between what Scripture actually says and how they go about the missions enterprise. This is because two more consequences of divine inspiration receive far too little attention in this current, postmodern, cultural environment.

First, because it is inspired by God and because God has the power and ability to accomplish what he sets out to do, his Word is clear in everything we need to know, believe, and do. God is not a failure at communication. The fact that unregenerate men and women are capable of reading contradictory messages into the text of Scripture is no reason to despair of the ability of believers, with the illumination of the Holy Spirit, to discern the meaning of Scripture clearly. Many methods of popular Bible study do indeed lead to wildly divergent interpretations of the text, but such methods often have little to do with what the text actually says in its context, and responsible exegesis leads to remarkably consistent results.

Second, Scripture is sufficient. God has given us everything we need for life and godliness. Much of what passes for evangelical missiology nods to biblical inspiration and inerrancy but then looks to secular sources for its methodology as though the Bible were inadequate. However, because the Bible is inerrant, authoritative, clear, and sufficient, it not only has the final word in all legitimate evangelical missiology; it also has the formative word.[13] All truth that is genuinely true belongs to God and is consistent with his Word. Under the judgment of Scripture, we can make use of knowledge from secular sources. However, because we have a solid, clear epistemological foundation on which to stand, we need not resort to a secularly defined pragmatism; and

---

[13] See Wayne Grudem's discussion of the attributes of Scripture in section 1 of his *Systematic Theology*.

because we have a reliable, sufficient guide in Scripture, we need not let secular marketing techniques or the latest social science fads dictate our method. Scripture rules, shapes, directs, and judges all of our mission theory and practice.

HUMAN REBELLION: THE CONTEXT
OF CHRISTIAN MISSION

God created man and woman in his image (Gen 1:26–27).[14] This image provided a basic compatibility between God and humanity that allowed Adam and Eve to have an intimate relationship with God that was not possible for lesser creatures to have. Adam and Eve were created altogether good. They were without sin, and they were able not to sin, but they were not confirmed in their righteousness in such a way as to be unable to sin. Sadly our first parents chose to rebel against God. Because Adam stood as federal head of the human race, his rebellion bequeathed to all his posterity both real moral guilt and all-pervasive corruption (Rom 5:12–21).[15]

According to Scripture, sin has affected every aspect of the human person. Every man and woman born into this world since Adam, other than Christ, is a fallen sinner (Rom 3:23). Fallen people are blind to the gospel (2 Cor 4:4). Fallen people are unable to understand spiritual truth (1 Cor 2:14). Fallen people are not free at all but are slaves to sin (Rom 6:17). Fallen people do not seek God: "No one understands; no one seeks for God" (Rom 3:11). Fallen people cannot obey God or please God (Rom 8:7–8). Fallen people justly fall under the wrath of God (Eph 2:3). Fallen men and women are not spiritually healthy or even spiritually sick; they are spiritually dead. "You were dead in the trespasses and sins in which you once walked" (Eph 2:1–2). A sick person can cooperate in his or her healing, but a dead person contributes nothing to his or her resurrection. This is the biblical picture of fallen humanity. By nature fallen people are spiritually dead, enslaved to sin, unable to understand the things of God, unable to obey God, unable to please God, and unable to do anything about it. They are justly under the wrath of God and

---

[14] For a helpful discussion of the biblical understanding of humanity, see Anthony Hoekema, *Created in God's Image* (Grand Rapids: Eerdmans, 1986).

[15] John Murray, *The Imputation of Adam's Sin* (Phillipsburg, NJ: P&R, 1959).

headed for an eternity in hell. They are not looking for God; they are looking to escape God.

This biblical reality about the human race is the context in which Christian mission must be carried out.[16] It has several implications.

First, human guilt is real. It is not a psychological state or a result of cultural conditioning but an objective reflection of our standing before a holy God.

Second, there is such a place as hell (Matt 25:46; Rev 20:11–15). It is eternal, terrifying, and just. We all deserve to go there. Unregenerate people face eternity there. Because of the guilt and corruption of the human race, fairness is exhausted by hell. Anything else is pure grace.

Third, no one goes to hell because they haven't heard the gospel. They go to hell because their sins deserve judgment and condemnation. It is an inescapable conclusion from Scripture that those who haven't heard the gospel are lost and headed toward condemnation.

Fourth, human religion is not an attempt to seek God. No one seeks God. Human religion is an attempt to evade the true and living God in favor of substitute gods we can manipulate on our own terms.

Fifth, despite the protests of postmodernism, there is such a thing as human nature; and in addition to this common inescapable nature, God has uniquely but definitively crafted the individual abilities and limitations of each human being. People are not free to invent or reinvent themselves. Fallen sinners need redemption, not reinvention.

Sixth, every aspect of human nature is corrupted by the fall, and this includes human reason. Unaided fallen reason cannot ever gain an accurate understanding of reality.

Seventh, human culture is not neutral. The Holy Spirit restrains the full effects of sin, and common grace manifests itself in every culture. However, human culture is corrupted by sin and must come under the judgment and correction of Scripture.

---

[16] Doug Coleman, "The Agents of Mission: Humanity," in Ashford, *Theology and Practice of Mission*, 39–41. See also Grudem, *Systematic Theology*, 490–514.

Finally, fallen people by nature are incapable of responding to the gospel. They cannot understand it, and they are not looking for it. They aren't sick—they are dead, and they are incapable of contributing anything at all to their own salvation. Therefore, no marketing technique, rhetorical device, or psychological method will ever accomplish anyone's salvation. It may produce a crowd, and it may even produce some sort of "decision"; but it will never produce disciples. Only the power of God can make a dead person alive. God has ordained that his power works through the unvarnished truth of his word, through the testimony of the changed lives of his people, and in response to prayer. A proper understanding of the biblical picture of fallen humanity should compel missionaries to focus on the proclamation of the whole message of the gospel (including the parts that are offensive to proud sinners), on their own reflection of the winsome holiness of Christ, and on the hard work of prayer, in the conviction that God alone can save sinners. It should compel missionaries to maintain the priority of evangelistic proclamation as the solution to the deepest and most desperate need of every human being, even while meeting other human needs. Finally, it should compel missionaries, churches, and mission agencies to prioritize getting the gospel to those who have never heard because, in their sin, such people have no other hope.

JESUS CHRIST: THE HEART OF CHRISTIAN MISSION

God the Son was begotten by his Father before time began.[17] He was, is, and always will be fully God. In the fullness of time, he took on humanity and became fully one of us as a human being while remaining fully divine (Phil 2:6–11). Our Lord Jesus Christ was conceived by the Holy Spirit and born of the virgin Mary (Luke 1:35). He lived a perfect, sinless, holy life—the life we should have lived and owed to God (2 Cor 5:21).[18] He spoke the word of God. He performed incredible miracles, demonstrating his power over sickness, hunger, demons, nature, and even death. He then died the death we deserve to die. He died as our substitute, paying the just penalty for our sins and bearing on

---

[17] Daniel Akin, "The Person of Christ," in *A Theology for the Church*, 480–544.
[18] For a rigorous defense of the importance of the active righteousness of Christ, see John Piper, *Counted Righteous in Christ* (Wheaton: Crossway, 2002).

himself the wrath of God against our rebellion (Rom 3:25; 2 Cor 5:14–15). He rose again from the dead on the third day, victorious forever over sin, death, and hell (Luke 24:33; 1 Cor 15:1–4). By his resurrection from the dead, his sacrifice was vindicated, and he was declared triumphantly by the Father to be the Son of God (Rom 1:4).[19] He ascended into heaven, where he sits at the right hand of God the Father and intercedes for his saints (Acts 2:33; Heb 8:1). He will come again visibly, with power and great glory, to judge the living and the dead, and there will be no end to his reign (Luke 1:33; Acts 1:11; 10:42).

As Messiah, Jesus is the perfect prophet, priest, and king,[20] and he perfectly meets all the needs of fallen humanity. As the ultimate Prophet (Heb 1:1–2), he not only spoke the word of God; he *is* the Word made flesh. He not only told us what God is like; he showed us what God is like in his own person. As the ultimate Priest (Heb 2:17), he had no sins of his own requiring atonement; and he has perfect, unhindered access to the Father. Because he is fully one of us as a man, and fully pure and holy, he perfectly represents us as our sacrifice; and because he is fully God, his sacrifice was of infinite worth. Unlike the provisional sacrifices of the Old Testament, his sacrifice of himself totally and permanently atones for all the sins of everyone who believes in him. Because he is eternal, he lives forever to intercede for his people. As the ultimate King (1 Tim 6:15–16; Rev 17:14), he has defeated our worst foes—sin, death, and hell—and he has infinite power and wisdom to lead us, guide us, and guard us until we are safely home with him. Jesus is the perfect Redeemer.

Jesus Christ is the center of Christian theology, and redemption in Jesus is the center of Christian missiology.[21] Scripture presents Jesus as the only way to know God and as the only Savior from sin (e.g., John 14:6; Acts 4:12; Rom 10:9–17; 1 John 5:11–12). Christian mission must be based on those same convictions. The message of the mission of the church is redemption in Christ alone. It is carried out under the authority of King

---

[19] There are many excellent books on the death and resurrection of Jesus. Among the best are Leon Morris, *The Apostolic Preaching of the Cross* (Grand Rapids: Eerdmans, 1965), and John Stott, *The Cross of Christ* (Downers Grove: Intervarsity, 1986). An outstanding recent contribution is Steve Jeffery, Michael Ovey, and Andrew Sach, *Pierced for Our Transgressions* (Wheaton: Crossway, 2007).

[20] John Calvin, *Institutes of the Christian Religion*, Book II, chapter XV.

[21] Pratt, "The Heart of Mission: Redemption," in Ashford, *Theology and Practice of Mission*, 55–57.

Jesus, who has been given all authority in heaven and on earth. The aim of that mission is to make disciples of Jesus, who cultivate intimacy with him in the Holy Spirit, who learn and obey everything he taught, and who are his body to one another and to the world. The standard toward which they are growing as disciples is conformity to his image. Jesus, the second Adam, is the true picture of authentic human life precisely because he is God in the flesh and humans were created to bear the image of God. Everything about authentic Christian mission must revolve around the Jesus of the Bible and his gospel. Anything else is just religiously tinted humanitarianism.

THE HOLY SPIRIT: THE AGENT OF CHRISTIAN MISSION

The work of redemption was and is the work of all three Persons of the Trinity.[22] God the Father chose to save us and gave us to his Son to redeem us; God the Son accomplished our redemption through his perfect life, his atoning death, and his victorious resurrection; God the Holy Spirit now applies the redeeming work of Christ to our lives. We believe the Holy Spirit is a Person of the Trinity and not some vague impersonal force. He is the Spirit of God (Rom 8:9) and the Spirit of Jesus Christ (Phil 1:19). He inspired the writers of the Old and New Testaments in such a way that they perfectly wrote God's words, and he illuminates believers now to understand the Word of God. He convicts the world of sin, righteousness, and judgment (John 16:8–11). He makes dead sinners alive in Christ (born again = born of the Spirit, John 3:1–8), sealing us for the day of redemption (Eph 1:13–14), baptizing us into the body of Christ (1 Cor 12:13), putting sin to death in us (Rom 8:13), creating the character of Christ in us (Gal 5:22–23), and gifting and empowering us for service (1 Cor 12:4–11). His work in our lives is both a promise and a foretaste of the restoration that will come to the adopted children of God.[23]

The power of the Holy Spirit promised to believers is power for proclamation (Acts 1:8). There can be neither fruitful Christian living nor fruitful service to God apart from that power. It is therefore essential that those who engage in the mission God

---

[22] Grudem, *Systematic Theology*, 249.
[23] Ibid., 634–53.

has given his people walk in step with the Spirit (Gal 5:16–26). According to Scripture, it is possible to quench or grieve the Holy Spirit by the way we live, but to do so cuts the believer off from the only power available for effective ministry. Therefore, it is not possible to separate ministry from the life of discipleship. Personal holiness is essential to effective mission work.[24] Intimacy with Christ through the Holy Spirit is necessary for fruitful service. The crucial role of the Holy Spirit in every form of ministry also highlights the importance of the gifts of the Spirit. The Holy Spirit has chosen how he will gift each believer. He has done so in such a way as to make no one self-sufficient and to make everyone dependent on others in the body of Christ. Every gift matters. Mission work is not a lone-ranger enterprise. Christian workers should work in such a way that most of their time and energy is invested in the areas where the Holy Spirit has gifted them, and they should seek to work together with others who have gifts they don't possess rather than proudly attempt to achieve omnicompetence. Finally, a biblical understanding of the essential role of the Holy Spirit in the conversion of others should drive us to prayer. Prayerlessness is a sign of self-reliance. If only the Holy Spirit can convict sinners, bring the dead to life, and conform sinners into the image of Jesus, it makes sense for Christian workers to spend much time on their knees asking him to do what only he can do.

SALVATION: THE MESSAGE OF CHRISTIAN MISSION

God is holy and just. He hates sin and must punish it. He is also loving and gracious, and he has mercifully chosen to redeem people who do not deserve anything from him but condemnation. Every member of the human race is a sinner. All people are sinful, spiritually dead, under God's wrath, and unable to do anything at all to rescue themselves (Eph 2:1–4). In astonishing grace God became a man in the person of Jesus Christ, lived the life of perfect obedience we owe to God, and then died the death we deserve to die, bearing in himself the wrath of God against our sin. He rose again from the dead, vindicated by his Father as the sin-bearing Son of God. He has gone to the right hand of the Father, where he intercedes for his people, and he will

---

[24] J. I. Packer, *A Passion for Holiness* (Wheaton: Crossway, 1992), 34–37, 219.

come again at the end of history to judge the world and make all things new. Jesus accomplished a perfect salvation. How do sinners come to share in that salvation?

God has ordained that salvation comes to sinners by grace alone through faith alone in Christ alone.[25] Grace is God's unmerited favor. No one deserves salvation, and no one ever earns it. It is a free gift from God. Faith is the instrument through which guilty sinners are declared righteous before God. No one is justified through their own works. Even justifying faith is a gift from God (Eph 2:8–9). Faith itself is only as valuable as its object. Saving faith is faith in Christ as he is presented to us in Scripture. Just as an electrical plug has no value in itself, and only works when plugged into a legitimate electrical socket, so also faith per se only leads to salvation when it connects the believer to the saving work of Christ on the cross. When a believer trusts in Christ, God reckons the righteousness of Jesus to that person because Jesus has had the sin of that believer reckoned to him (Romans 4; 2 Cor 5:21). Saving faith is more than mental assent. It involves radical trust and reliance on Christ alone for salvation, and it involves entrusting all that one is and has to Jesus for time and eternity. God has ordained that faith comes by hearing the word of Christ (Rom 10:17). Saving faith is always accompanied by repentance, as the other side of the same coin. Salvation is to discipleship; that is, believers are saved to become disciples, not merely converts. Jesus commanded his followers to make disciples, not to count decisions, and a reported decision for Christ that is not followed by a life of discipleship is almost certainly not real. True believers grow in holiness of life, in conformity to the image of Jesus, as they walk with him, become like him, and learn to obey everything he commanded. Real believers never finally fall away from faith, but they are kept by the power of God for salvation.

This is the essence of the gospel message, and it is the essence of Christian mission. God has sent his people into the world to proclaim who he is, what we have become in our sin, what he has done for us in Jesus Christ, and how we are to respond. If the full gospel message is not proclaimed, what results is not Christian

---

[25] For a concise, helpful summary of the message of the gospel, see Greg Gilbert, *What Is the Gospel?* (Wheaton: Crossway, 2010).

mission. Believers who encounter human suffering will respond with compassion. They cannot help but meet human need, if they have the heart of Christ. However, they are never content to relieve human suffering but leave lostness untouched. Community development and moral improvement are good things, but they are never enough. A biblical understanding of salvation should impel believers to preach the gospel.[26] It should encourage them to leave in the offensive edges of the gospel that rub against sinful human pride, because redemption is the goal of our mission and inflated self-esteem is actually the enemy of one's soul. Knowing the response God requires from sinners should lead Christian workers to press for repentance and faith. It should be done without deceit or manipulation; the apostles pleaded with people to believe the gospel and be saved, and if we understand the stakes, we should as well. Finally, a biblical understanding of salvation clearly indicates that a lifelong process of discipleship is the goal. It is not enough to ask for a decision and then move on. The cost of discipleship should be clearly told up front, and evangelism should flow smoothly into follow-up, discipleship, and leadership training.

DOES EVERYONE HAVE TO HEAR AND BELIEVE THE GOSPEL TO BE SAVED?

This biblical understanding of human sin, the person and work of Christ, and the way of salvation also speaks directly to the issue of those who have never heard or never believed the gospel. Throughout the history of the church, many positions have been held on the destiny of such people. These positions may (at the risk of oversimplification) be considered under four categories: pluralism, universalism, inclusivism, and exclusivism.

Pluralism holds that all religions are potentially equally valid. On a popular level, this is sometimes expressed as the conviction that most religions teach essentially the same thing. The most charitable thing that can be said for this form of pluralism is that its adherents don't actually know what different religions teach. At a far more sophisticated level, pluralists like John

---

[26] For a thoughtful discussion on the centrality of the proclamation of the gospel and the Great Commission task of making disciples in the mission of the church, see Kevin DeYoung and Greg Gilbert, *What Is the Mission of the Church?* (Wheaton: Crossway, 2011).

Hick[27] acknowledge that the incredible diversity of beliefs and worldviews represented by the world's great religions cannot simply be amalgamated into any coherent synthesis. The differences are too profound and too blatantly contradictory. Instead, Hick and others like him see a transcendent reality behind all religions that is legitimately experienced in each of them. This understanding of religion is only possible by redefining the truth claims of all of the existing religions in a way that leaves them unrecognizable to the ordinary adherent of each faith. The problem with this approach, of course, is that it ends up creating a new conception of religion that falsifies all other religions to some degree or other. This defeats the purpose of pluralism and leaves it as an unsatisfactory position.

Universalism holds that everyone will be saved in the end. There is considerable diversity within this position. In its most popular and unreflective form, some hold that everyone will be saved simply because that seems most fair or most loving. It is also possible to be a universalist based on an unlimited view of the atonement. If the atoning work of Christ is unlimited both in its scope (intended for the salvation of every individual) and in its efficacy (actually accomplishing the salvation of all those for whom it was intended), universalism is the inevitable conclusion because God would be unjust to condemn anyone whose sin had been entirely atoned by the blood of Jesus. Universalism can flow from a high view of the love of God divorced from a high view of his holiness and justice or from a high view of humanity combined with a low view of the offensiveness of sin. Whatever the foundation, universalism is profoundly unbiblical. Jesus talked about hell a lot (Matt 5:29–30; 10:28; 13:41–42; 18:9; 25:41–46, just to give a few examples). So did his apostles (2 Thess 1:9; 2 Pet 2:4–10; Jude 5–7; Rev 20:15). Scripture repeatedly talks about two destinies for humanity—eternal life and eternal condemnation—with faith in Jesus as the deciding factor (John 3:18; 1 John 5:11–12). Universalism may be a popular position, but it is not a biblical one.

Inclusivist positions hold that Christianity is uniquely true, and Jesus is the only grounds of salvation, but that it is possible for someone to be saved outside of conscious faith in Jesus

---

[27] John Hick, *An Interpretation of Religion* (New Haven: Yale University Press, 1989).

in this lifetime. Roman Catholic theology since Vatican II has considered the possibility of "anonymous Christians," individuals who are recipients of the redemptive work of Christ without knowing it. C. S. Lewis gave popular expression to inclusivism in his children's fantasy novel *The Last Battle*.[28] Even though he had served the demonic god Tash his whole life, Emeth the Calormene ends up in heaven because he had offered good service to a bad god, and Aslan (the representation of Christ in the novel) accepted that good service as offered to him. On a more sophisticated level, Clark Pinnock makes a case for inclusivism in *A Wideness in God's Mercy*.[29] He presents several arguments to provide support for this idea and to explain how it could happen. He separates the ontological basis of salvation from the epistemological basis, arguing that it is possible to be saved by Christ (the ontological basis) without knowing about Christ or the gospel (the epistemological basis). He contends that the presence of faith is more important than the content or object of that faith. He separates the work of the Holy Spirit from Christ so that the Holy Spirit can regenerate people without explicit reference to Jesus. As a final measure he suggests the possibility that God offers the gospel to people after they have died but before they go to their final destiny so that even those who lived and died without any witness to Christ have an opportunity to trust him. In one form or another, inclusivism is popular among Christians who live in Western societies as it fits well with the tolerant and inclusive climate of their culture.

In contrast to pluralism, universalism, and inclusivism, the position the Bible advocates is exclusivism. Simply stated, exclusivism is the belief that salvation is only possible based on the work of Christ, his life, death, and resurrection, and it is only appropriated through conscious faith in Christ. Therefore, in order to be saved, one must hear and believe the gospel, the good news of salvation in Jesus Christ. How does the Bible develop and defend exclusivism?

The place to begin is the Old Testament. The Old Testament world was awash in religious diversity. There were more gods than there were nations, and most people operated under the

---

[28] C. S. Lewis, *The Last Battle* (New York: Harper Collins, 1956), 205.
[29] Clark Pinnock, *A Wideness in God's Mercy* (Grand Rapids: Zondervan, 1992).

assumption that all gods had some sort of ontological reality. Most people also assumed that gods were territorial, each with his or her particular national jurisdiction. The Old Testament never adopts a pluralist, universalist, or inclusivist position toward the religions of the nations around Israel. It never ascribes reality to pagan idols, views other religions as possible ways to God, or sees the gods of the nations as the true God under another name. Indeed, the Old Testament makes a big deal about the name and the identity of the true God. It bluntly asserts that the God of Israel is the only God. It expresses a holy jealousy on the part of that one true God, who refuses to share his glory with another and refuses to accept divided loyalties. It pours scorn on all religion other than that which the God of Israel revealed, and it even forbids worshipping that God in the wrong way.[30] The Old Testament is explicitly and even loudly exclusivist.

The New Testament assumes everything the Old Testament teaches and expands on it in the same direction. Jesus said that those who believe in him have eternal life but those who do not believe in him are condemned. This is not generic faith but faith with a specific content: the person and work of Jesus (John 3:16–18). Right before he was crucified, he linked that work of the Holy Spirit so tightly with his own person and teaching that it is impossible to separate the convicting, regenerating, and teaching role of the Spirit from the person and teaching of Jesus (John 14–16). He also said, "I am the way, and the truth, and the life. No one comes to the Father except through me" (John 14:6). It would be difficult to imagine a more specific statement of exclusivity. In the book of Acts, Peter reflected the same exclusive understanding when he said, "There is salvation in no one else, for there is no other name under heaven given among men by which we must be saved" (Acts 4:12). Not only did Peter assert that there is salvation in no one other than Jesus, but he also made the specific identity of the Savior essential by referring to his name. Consistently in the book of Acts, the apostles made clear in their preaching that they regard knowing and trusting the gospel of Jesus Christ essential to salvation (Acts 2:14–47;

---

[30] The second commandment is not simply a repetition of the first but a prohibition of worshipping the true God by means of images.

3:11–26; 4:5–12; 10:34–48; 13:16–41, 44–48; 16:25–34). It was the motivation behind the urgency of their mission.

The apostle Paul gives an extended explanation of the gospel in his letter to the Romans and in the process lays the foundation for gospel exclusivism. He begins by stating, in categorical terms, that salvation comes to those who believe in the gospel. He then sets the background for understanding the gospel in the depravity of the human race and the righteous wrath of God against sin. In the process he states that knowledge about God is evident in what God has created, but his only application of the reality of that knowledge is that all people are without excuse because they suppress that knowledge in unrighteousness (Rom 1:19–22). He never states, or even hints, that such knowledge is sufficient to save sinful people.

In Romans 2:6–11 Paul makes a case for the impartial justice of God, including the statement that those who persevere in well-doing will gain eternal life. However, he proceeds to state in Romans 3 that no one is righteous and no one does good, so the theoretical category of those who gain eternal life by doing good proves to be an empty set. Similarly, in Romans 2:12–16 Paul states that even the Gentiles can know what is right through nature and conscience, but both the immediate context and subsequent statements in chapter 3 make clear that no one is saved through this knowledge.

The heart of the matter is found in Romans 3:9–23. No one is righteous. No one seeks for God. No one does good. By the works of the law, no one is justified before God. All have sinned; all have fallen short of the glory of God. This is the ultimate context for understanding biblical exclusivism. Everyone in the world who has ever lived deserves condemnation because of sinful rebellion against God. Fairness is exhausted by hell.

When Paul went on to explain the glorious good news of justification based on the sacrifice of Jesus, who bore the wrath we deserved because of our sin, he was explicit that this justification is received by faith alone (Rom 3:21–28). There simply is no other way in the economy of God. This background then makes sense of the logic of the gospel expressed in Romans 10:5–17. In this passage Paul was talking about his own people, the Jews, and he went to some lengths to assert that there is only one way of salvation for Jew and Gentile alike. Salvation comes to those who call on the name of the Lord, making the specific identity of Jesus essential to salvation. He then worked out the logical implications of this reality. Calling on the Lord for salvation requires faith. Saving faith has a content that must be heard and known to be believed. In order for the gospel to be heard, someone must preach it. In order for someone to preach it, they must be sent. A powerful motivation for missions lies precisely in the fact that people must hear the gospel and believe it or they will not be saved. This gracious salvation of sinners, in turn, redounds to the glory of God, which is the ultimate motivation for missions.

The apostle John made the same point, although in simpler and starker terms: "And this is the testimony, that God gave us eternal life, and this life is in his Son. Whoever has the Son has life; whoever does not have the Son of God does not have life" (1 John 5:11–12). The witness of Scripture is consistent. Everyone deserves condemnation because of sins. God, in sheer mercy, has chosen to save people who only deserve his wrath. His appointed means of saving sinners is the gospel of Jesus Christ. God requires sinners to repent of their sins and believe in the gospel in order to receive his gracious gift of salvation. There is no other way. Therefore, those who have not believed are lost, and that includes those who have never heard the gospel. This should provide a powerful motivation for Christians to obey Christ's command to take the gospel to every person and every people.[31]

ALL PEOPLES: THE SCOPE OF CHRISTIAN MISSION

From the beginning God made clear that the scope of his redemptive mission was global. In his promises to Abraham (Gen 12:3), Isaac (Gen 26:4), and Jacob (Gen 28:14), God told each of the patriarchs that his purpose in blessing them was to bless all peoples on earth through them. This global scope was repeated in the Prophets (Isa 49:10 and Hab 2:14, among many other references) and in the Psalms (Psalms 67 and 96, among others). The Great Commission specifically states that

---

[31] For an excellent analysis of each of these positions, and a solid presentation of the case for exclusivism, see Todd Miles, *A God of Many Understandings?* (Nashville: B&H Academic, 2010).

the people of God are to make disciples of every people group on earth. Revelation 5:9 tells us that the redeeming work of Christ was intentionally both global and people-group oriented: "You were slain, and by your blood you ransomed people for God from every tribe and language and people and nation." Revelation 7:9 assures us that God accomplished exactly what he set out to do in the atoning work of Christ, as there will be people worshipping God around his throne from every nation, tribe, people, and language. Accordingly, Christian mission must be global in scope and have an intentional people-group focus.

CHURCH: THE INSTRUMENT OF CHRISTIAN MISSION

Sin not only shattered the relationship between people and God; it also shattered the relationship among people. Correspondingly, redemption not only reconciles men and women to God. It also reconciles men and women to one another in the fellowship of the church. In Christ, the second Adam, God is creating a new humanity in which old dividing walls of hostility are broken down (1 Cor 15:45; Gal 3:28; Eph 2:11–22). The church is therefore one of the fruits of God's redemptive mission. At the same time it is an instrument of that mission. The core task of mission is making disciples, and disciples only mature in Christ in the fellowship of the body of Christ (Eph 4:1–16). Therefore, it is impossible to carry out the Great Commission fully without establishing churches wherever there are new believers. Furthermore, the work of Christian believers is carried out through the empowering and gifting of the Holy Spirit. His gifts are designed to function in the context of the body of Christ, and he has deliberately gifted his people in such a way as to make them interdependent on one another (1 Cor 12:1–30). Therefore, those who do the work of disciple-making need the body of Christ themselves in order to be effective. The church is the means, the context, and the measure of the mission God has given his people.[32]

This crucial role of the church has three implications in the work of Christian mission. First, if discipleship can only occur in the context of the church, the advance of the gospel must

---

[32] For a concise description of the biblical doctrine of the church, see Mark Dever, *The Church: The Gospel Made Visible* (Nashville: B&H Academic, 2012).

be accompanied by intentional church planting where there are no churches. Evangelism and individual training do not fulfill the biblical mandate to make disciples apart from the church. Second, Christian workers themselves need the church as the context for their own life as disciples. This need is not fulfilled by technical membership in a church halfway around the world that they only see once every three or four years. Workers need the fellowship of the church where they live as much as new believers do. Third, new churches in a mission setting need to be fully biblical in every aspect of their life and ministry. If the church matters this much, Christian workers must be rigorously biblical in how they build the church on the foundation of Jesus Christ (1 Cor 3:3–17).

ESCHATOLOGY: THE HISTORICAL
FRAMEWORK OF MISSION

The Bible presents a clear understanding of history. Time is linear, with a beginning and an end. Furthermore, it is not aimless, but it is a story with a destination. History has been going somewhere since the moment of creation. God is the author, ruler, and goal of history's story. The major plot movements of that story are creation, the fall, God's redemptive work climaxing in Jesus, and the final restoration of all things in the new heavens and the new earth. Jesus is coming back. The dead will be raised. Evil will be destroyed forever. All people who have ever lived will be judged, and all who have not received God's undeserved mercy through the gospel will be justly condemned because of their sin. God will be worshipped forever by a multitude no one can count from every tribe, tongue, people, and nation. We cannot yet even begin to imagine the glory and joy of our final state, face-to-face with him for all eternity.[33]

This is eschatology, the study of the "last days." Properly speaking, it is broader than that—it is the study of the progress and destination of history under the sovereign hand of God. There is both a cosmic dimension and a personal dimension to eschatology. At the cosmic level the Bible tells us that history is proceeding toward the day when Jesus comes back, judges the world, and makes all things new. At the personal level the Bible

---

[33] Grudem, *Systematic Theology*, 1091–67.

teaches us that every person who has ever lived will live forever. Those who are in Christ will be raised to eternal life in resurrection bodies like that of the risen Jesus and will live with him forever in indescribable glory and joy. Those who die in their sin will be raised to eternal condemnation in hell. Eschatology is fundamentally a missionary subject. Global history is the story of the mission of God to display his glory through creation, judgment, redemption, and restoration. It will end when Jesus comes back, and he himself linked his return to completion of the global spread of the gospel (Matt 24:14). The mission of the church nests within that mission of God. So does the mission of individual Christians. God is not up to one thing in history and something totally different in the lives of his children. God's purpose for each of his followers fits within what he is up to in history and in the mission of the church.

The biblical account of the last days has given rise to an incredible amount of speculation about the details of how it will all happen. In the Bible itself, references to the return of Christ are always given for one of two reasons: to comfort and encourage the afflicted or to warn the complacent. The twin realities that our earthly lives will end and that the earth itself will burn are intended to reset the values and priorities of Christians. The mission of God, and the mission that God has given his people, cannot fail. Everything else will inevitably fail and pass away. Those who engage in the hard work of the gospel can take strong encouragement to persevere, knowing that their labor in the Lord is not in vain (1 Cor 15:58). Those who live for the things of this world should take warning from the fact that everything in this world will go up in flames and that they themselves will pass from this life, taking nothing from this life. For those whose lives nest within the mission of God, the worst thing that can happen to them is that they die—and go straight into the presence of Jesus. A solid grasp of biblical eschatology gives believers in Jesus every reason to give up everything and persevere through anything for the sake of God's global glory through the gospel.

RESOURCES FOR FURTHER STUDY

Akin, Daniel, ed. *A Theology for the Church*. Nashville: B&H Academic, 2007.

Ashford, Bruce, ed. *Theology and Practice of Mission*. Nashville: B&H Academic, 2011.

DeYoung, Kevin, and Greg Gilbert. *What Is the Mission of the Church?* Wheaton: Crossway, 2011.

Grudem, Wayne. *Systematic Theology*. Grand Rapids: Zondervan, 1994.

Miles, Todd L. *A God of Many Understandings?* Nashville: B&H Academic, 2010.

HISTORICAL FOUNDATIONS FOR GLOBAL MISSIONS

CHAPTER 5

THE EXPANSION OF CHRISTIANITY, PART 1

EARLY CHURCH THROUGH THE REFORMATION

The history of Christian missions begins as quickly as Jesus delivered the Great Commission. In our first primary source Luke recorded Jesus' command, "You will be My witnesses in Jerusalem, in all Judea and Samaria, and to the ends of the earth" (Acts 1:8). From there he described how the gospel and, therefore, the church spread from a small group of disciples toward the farthest reaches of creation. This chapter and the next will describe that expansion with particular emphasis on application to contemporary missiology.

WHY STUDY MISSIONS HISTORY?

For some people the study of history is a tedious endeavor—memorizing dates and names and battles. If a reader does not connect past moments with present ministry, missions history can seem just as irrelevant. Why does it matter that Boniface cut down a sacred oak tree or that unnamed merchant believers carried the gospel into China in the seventh century? Understanding the past is an important facet of missiology and can help twenty-first-century Christians continue the work started by first-century disciples.

First, and perhaps most obviously, missions history helps us avoid the mistakes and grow from the successes of the past. Early Catholic missionaries in Europe and South America made contextualization errors that continue to bear fruit today. Centuries later others learned to avoid those problems by thinking more deeply about the relationship between old beliefs and new. History does not repeat itself, but history helps us not to repeat past problems.

Closely related to that point is the fact that historical study helps us think more humbly about ourselves and our ideas. Our nature is to think of our strategies and philosophies as original and faultless. We have good reasons for thinking as we do, and it's easy to pick out the faults of our forebears. The more we know about those upon whose shoulders we stand, however, the more we see the reality of our own situation. Ecclesiastes 1:9 reminds us that "there is nothing new under the sun." Our "original" ideas often turn out to be quite ancient. That's not a bad thing, but it's good to know that we stand in a long line of Christians seeking to make disciples to the ends of the earth. Second, we discover that mistakes occur even with the best of intentions. It's easy to find fault in the methodologies of early missionaries, but we should be reminded frequently that we, too, are subject to mistakes and errors in judgment. Humility makes good historians and good missionaries.

Another reason to study missions history is that it helps us to become more aware of our own cultural blindness and presuppositions. One of the basic tenets of missionary philosophy is that we must understand another culture in order to share the gospel among its people. In the process of discovering a new culture, the oddities and beauty of our own culture become clearer. In the same way, historical study illuminates our own assumptions about the world and about our own place in history. During our education many of us make assumptions about history (especially that of our hometowns and countries) that further study shows to be unfounded. In the process of making those discoveries, we can also see a multitude of fascinating and cultural reasons for those presuppositions. We come to know ourselves and our own heritage better as a result of that study.

Finally, and equally important, we can gain inspiration from the stories of missionaries across the ages. David Brainerd struggled with the difficulty of preaching the gospel to native peoples on the early American frontier and died young. But his story touched men like Jonathan Edwards and William Carey, who read his journals and took inspiration from his work. We are propelled by Brainerd's perseverance. When we read about Jim Elliot, Nate Saint, Ed McCully, Pete Fleming, and Roger Youderian, we cannot help but be touched by their passion. When we hear of Adoniram Judson working seven years before the first Burmese convert or Ann Judson's suffering, we can be heartened for our own slow progress. Knowing that thousands of missionary stories will never be told, we can work for God's glory among the nations without fear, seeing the big story that will end in eternal worship by the redeemed of every tribe, tongue, and nation.

Why study the history of missions? Because it's worth the effort in order to join the 2,000 year stream of men, women, and families in the Great Commission task. The history of missions displays God's glory at work through fallible people. When we see our place in that story, we are equipped and challenged to press on boldly and well.

MISSIONS IN THE EARLY CHURCH

Luke recounts that at the coming of the Holy Spirit on Pentecost, Jews from many nations were gathered in Jerusalem. The city was situated between two competing empires: Rome to the west and the Parthian Empire to the east. Cyrenes to Elamites, Romans to Arabians, Jews and proselytes had gathered for the Passover (Acts 2:5–11). The indwelling Holy Spirit gave the disciples the ability to speak in tongues previously unknown to them, and the crowd reacted in amazement. At that moment the curse of Babel was reversed, and the gospel began to spread forth from Jerusalem as many of the 3,000 converted presumably returned to their scattered homes.

In the earliest days of the church, believers faithfully proclaimed the good news of Jesus Christ to those around them.

Many were converted, and the growing church prayed for bold-
ness in witness (Acts 4:23–31). As the church grew, so did persecution of the believers. Stephen, who had been chosen with six
others to serve the needs of the growing and diverse congregation, was arrested and stoned to death following a bold and passionate witness (Acts 6–7). As a result, many of the believers left
Jerusalem and journeyed to other cities in the regions of Judea
and Samaria (Acts 8:1).

Philip, one of the seven along with Stephen, went first among
the despised Samaritans (Acts 8). God drew many to himself
through Philip's evangelistic ministry, to the point that Peter
and John went to Samaria to investigate. Later Philip met an
Ethiopian (from modern-day Sudan and Ethiopia), with whom
he shared the gospel. The African proselyte likely returned to his
home country to spread further the gospel.

Two critical moments in the history of missions took place
in the conversions of Saul and Cornelius. Saul persecuted Christians vehemently before he met Christ on the road to Damascus
and became the most important missionary figure in the early
church (Acts 9). Peter's vision in Acts 10 opened the way for the
gospel to go beyond the Jewish community to "all nations" and
led to the conversion of Cornelius, a Roman military officer, and
his family.

The Expansion of the Church. Eusebius, an early church
historian, described the spread of the gospel this way:

> Thus with the powerful cooperation of Heaven,
> the whole world was suddenly lit by the sun-
> shine of the saving word. At once, in accor-
> dance with the Holy Scriptures, the voice of
> its inspired evangelists and apostles went forth
> into all the earth, and their words to the ends of
> the world. In every town and village, like a well-
> filled threshing floor, churches shot up burst-
> ing with eager members. Men who through the
> error they had inherited from generations of
> ancestors were in the grip of the old spiritual
> sickness of idol-worship, by the power of Christ
> and through the teaching of His followers and
> the miracles they wrought were freed, as it were,

from cruel masters and found release from gall-
ing fetters. They turned their backs on devilish
polytheism in all its forms, and acknowledged
that there was one God only, the Fashioner of all
things. Him they honoured with the ordinances
of true religion through that divine, reasonable
worship of which our Saviour sowed the seed in
the life of men.[1]

One important example of the churches that "shot up"
during this period was the congregation at Antioch. Luke records
that the church formed when persecuted believers arrived in the
city—the third largest in the empire (Acts 11:19). It was a trade
crossroads with a multinational population. The church there
reveals several factors in the expansion of the early church.

First, laymen founded the church at Antioch. According to
Luke, the initial lay missionary preaching took place among
Jews, but at Antioch the believers crossed religious and ethnic
boundaries with the gospel (Acts 11:20). Without question much
early evangelism took place through witnesses going about their
daily lives. The Roman roads that crisscrossed the empire and
connected the major cities provided relatively easy travel. Merchants and soldiers were converted and carried their message of
salvation as they went.

These earliest missionaries displayed a noticeable passion
for proclaiming the gospel. Christianity remained illegal in the
empire for more than two centuries, but believers freely shared
the good news. At Antioch men from Cyprus and Cyrene spoke
both with Jews and with Gentiles, "proclaiming the good news
about the Lord Jesus" (Acts 11:20). When the church at Jerusalem heard of the events in Antioch, they sent Barnabas to
investigate. He, in turn, asked Saul to join him, and they spent a
year teaching the Scriptures to new believers. This zeal for God's
Word was a second reason for the rapid expansion of the church
beyond Jerusalem, Judea, and Samaria.

A third feature of the Antioch congregation, and broadly of
the early church, was the believers' engagement of human need

---

[1] Eusebius, *The History of the Church from Christ to Constantine*, trans. G. A. Williamson (Minneapolis, MN: Augsburg, 1975), 76.

and struggle. Antioch was a divided pagan city, and Christians crossed physical, ethnic, and social barriers to share the gospel and minister to those in need. In the fourth century the Roman emperor Julian fretted about the care shown to outsiders, declaring that Christianity

> has specially advanced through the loving ser-
> vice rendered to strangers, and through their
> care for the burial of the dead. It is a scandal
> that there is not a single Jew who is a beggar,
> and that the godless Galileans care not only for
> their own poor but.for ours as well; while those
> who belong to us look in vain for the help that
> we should render them.[2]

Christians were known for caring for the sick and needy, for gathering infants left exposed on the streets of Roman cities, and for feeding the hungry. The tie between these social ministries and the congregation's proclamation of Christ resulted in the believers first being called "Christians" at Antioch (Acts 11:26).

Finally, persecution had a significant impact on the expansion of the early church. For the church at Antioch, attacks by Jewish leaders drove them to new fields. For others, martyrdom provided the occasion to show the strength of their faith in the face of death. While persecution was not constant in the empire, waves of anti-Christian movements came for the first three centuries of Christian history.

Apostolic Missions. With the exception of Paul, the Bible gives little information on the missionary activity of the apostles. Church tradition records that many of the apostles spread across the region and the world to preach and start churches. While impossible to verify, Eusebius placed Thomas in Parthia, Andrew in Scythia, and Peter eventually in Rome. John went to Asia. Further, tradition places Thomas in India and other apostles as far as Spain and the British Isles.

A vital contribution of the church at Antioch was its role in the preparation of Paul for missionary evangelism. After he and Barnabus spent a year teaching in the city, both were sent

---

[2] Stephen Neill and Owen Chadwick, *A History of Christian Missions,* 2nd ed., rev. Owen Chadwick (Harmondsworth, Middlesex, England: Penguin Books, 1986), 38.

out by the congregation on the first of three major missionary journeys recorded in Acts. Paul and his teams planted numerous churches, taught the Scriptures, and raised up leaders for the congregations.[3]

By the end of the second century, Christianity had touched every major province of the Roman Empire. By the end of the third century, some Christian witness had been established in every major city. Persecutions continued until the Edict of Milan in 313, which made Christianity the religion of the empire.

Missions to the East. Luke generally recorded the movement of the gospel and the church westward toward Rome. During that expansion, however, a significant missionary movement to the east also took place. Outside of the empire, Edessa (in Syria) had a church established during the second century. Though closely identified with the various Christological controversies after the fourth century, churches in Persia, India, and China came into existence early in Christian history.

Missionary Bishops. While lay missionaries were the most significant force in the early expansion of the church, church leaders were an important factor as well. Men like Irenaeus, bishop of Lyons late in the second century, and Gregory Thaumaturgus, bishop of Pontus in the third century, led efforts to expand the church into rural areas surrounding key cities. Thaumaturgus substituted festivals celebrating Christian martyrs for the pagan feasts common in his region.

MISSIONS AFTER CONSTANTINE

The legalization (and encouragement) of Christianity following the Edict of Milan had a massive impact on the growth of the church. Inside the Roman Empire church membership grew rapidly thanks to the end of persecution. On the fringes of the empire, where tribal groups like the Visigoths, Burgundians, and Franks maintained a constant warfare, Christians continued to share their faith. The mercantile interchange between peoples, as well as the enslavement of Christians by "barbarians," provided a means by which the gospel spread.

Missionary bishops continued to play an important role as they led churches in the remote corners of the crumbling

---

[3] See chap. 10 on church planting for more on Paul's church planting work.

empire. Martin of Tours, a soldier turned monk, was bishop of that city in the late fourth century. Like Thaumaturgus, Martin sought to expand the church into rural areas surrounding his city. He introduced missionary monasticism and destroyed pagan shrines and temples, replacing them with churches. John Chrysostom, famous for his preaching as bishop of Constantinople, was a contemporary of Martin. He, too, commissioned missionaries to preach in the countryside.

Patrick of Ireland. Perhaps the best-known missionary of this period was Patrick of Ireland. Born in the late fourth century in Britain, Patrick came from a Celtic Christian family. When he was sixteen years of age, he was kidnapped and carried into slavery in rugged and pagan Ireland. He suffered greatly at the hands of his captors, spending long periods alone in harsh conditions tending sheep. He escaped captivity only to return to Ireland around 432 as the result of a vision reminiscent of Paul's Macedonian call in Acts 16:9. Patrick spent the remainder of his life among his former captors, proclaiming the gospel and seeing the conversion of thousands to the Christian faith.

The Role of Monasticism. The rise of monasticism after Constantine has been well noted in church history. As Christianity and culture became more intertwined in the fifth century, some began to separate themselves to a more ascetic life. While some who committed to the monastic movement remained completely separate, monks became an important part of the missionary movement of the Middle Ages.

One example of missionary monasticism was Columba. A spiritual descendant of Patrick, Columba was an Irish nobleman who joined the priesthood at a young age. In 563, he formed a monastic community on the island of Iona. He and a group of monks lived a typical monastic life, but one that was geared toward the expansion of the church into Northern and Eastern Europe. Columba led his followers to start small missionary villages with a school and church. As pairs of monks went out to scout new locations, others remained in the new villages to learn the local language, teach the Scriptures, and engage pagan religions. They did so by teaching biblical truth rather than confronting the pagan error, a strategy that contrasted with Roman Catholic monasticism. Columba himself started multiple monasteries and churches that, in turn, sent multitudes of monks into the British Isles and Europe.[4]

A second prominent example of missionary monasticism was Winfried or (Wynfrith), later called Boniface. Boniface was born in Britain, entered the monastic life at a young age, and developed an evangelistic passion early. After a failed mission into Frisia (modern-day northwest Europe), he sought out a papal commission to go to Germany, where he spent most of his ministry during the seventh century. Boniface is best known for his confrontation of pagan religions and the syncretistic faith of nominal Christians. Most famously, Boniface cut down the "sacred oak of Thor" at Geismar, demonstrating God's power over the demonic pagan gods. He also destroyed shrines devoted to other deities.

As with the early church, most missionary monks remain unnamed to history. As the Roman Empire collapsed and the so-called Dark Ages began, missionary monks carried the gospel and the church back into Europe. Their humble existence and service to communities, as well as their evangelistic passion, had an impact throughout the Middle Ages.

THE "THOUSAND YEARS OF UNCERTAINTY"

Kenneth Scott Latourette, the most influential historian of missions in modern history, called the years between 500 and 1500 the "thousand years of uncertainty." As the church grew in political influence and wealth, missions fervor waned. Islam began its march through North Africa, once the stronghold of the early church, and into Europe. The Crusades, beginning in 1095, had a detrimental impact on the church that continues to impact missions among Muslim peoples. The church continued to grow in Europe but quite little outside of the old Roman Empire. Not until the end of the period did a renewal of Roman Catholic missionary advance coincide with the Protestant Reformation.

One notable exception to the decline in missionary activity during this period was Raymond Lull. During the period of the Crusades, Francis of Assisi had attempted to evangelize Muslims with little success. Lull, a wealthy courtesan from the island of

---

[4] Ruth Tucker, *From Jerusalem to Irian Jaya: A Biographical History of Christian Missions* (Grand Rapids, MI: Zondervan, 1983), 41.

Majorca, took up that challenge, leaving his affluent life and family to become a Franciscan monk. His vision included not only preaching to Muslims but also the institution of monasteries devoted to the training of missionary monks. Lull learned Arabic himself and encouraged language learning in his schools.

Lull journeyed on several occasions into North Africa—first to Tunis and later in Algeria. He developed an apologetic method in which he challenged the Muslim rejection of Christ as God's Son and the Christian doctrine of the Trinity. When he arrived in the city, Lull approached the Muslim leaders and offered to debate their beliefs. He was persuasive, but most of his debates ended in his imprisonment. Lull saw several Saracens convert, and on his final visit to the town of Bugia in 1314 to teach and encourage the Christians there, Lull was killed by an angry mob.

Certainly Lull was not the only missionary during the period preceding the Reformation, but he was one of few. While he focused mainly on Muslims, Lull also worked among European Jewish populations who were under intense persecution. His emphasis on language, apologetics, education, and preaching served as an example to later missionaries.

ROMAN CATHOLIC MISSIONS ON THE EVE OF THE REFORMATION

The growth of Roman Catholic missions on the eve of the Reformation went hand in hand with the expansion of colonialism led by Spain and Portugal. In 1454, Pope Alexander V sought to alleviate the competition between the colonial powers by dividing the known world among them. The Spanish queen Isabella, who financed much of the early exploration, believed that the primary reason for such exploration was the conversion of native populations. Members of the missionary Franciscan and Dominican orders, and later the Jesuits, accompanied the explorers for the purpose of establishing the Roman Catholic Church in new lands.

Portugal was given patronage over Brazil in the New World, Africa, and the West Indies. As they developed trade settlements along the coastal areas, the Portuguese, hand in hand with the monks, overcame the indigenous religions, generally by force.

In Africa settlement was more difficult due to the climate and cooperation with the slave trade.

The Spanish developed the *encomienda* system by which indigenous peoples were brought into settlements for the supposed purpose of teaching and evangelism. In reality, however, the system was little more than slavery. In spite of efforts by missionaries like Bartholomew de las Casas, who fought against forced conversion and servitude, the tie between church and conqueror made missionary work difficult. The church was established, but it remained a foreign religion to most.

Several individuals stand out in the history of Roman Catholic missions during this period. Portuguese Jesuit Francis Xavier pioneered work in India and Japan. Ignatius Loyola had founded the Jesuits in opposition to the Protestant Reformation, and he found a vibrant and active follower in Xavier. After a sudden appointment to go to India, Xavier wholeheartedly engaged the Hindu populations and saw numerous conversions. He focused on baptizing children and teaching them the doctrines of the Catholic Church. After several years in India, Xavier moved on to Japan where social instability opened the door for the implantation of the church. While it was left to Xavier's followers to see large numbers of conversions in Japan, his initial work with the difficult language opened the country to the church. Xavier's influence, though he was only a missionary for ten years before his death, was tremendous.

In China, Matteo Ricci followed in the footsteps of the early Nestorian Christians and later efforts to reintroduce Christianity. In the late thirteenth century, John of Monte Corvino, a Franciscan monk, had worked in China to great success. Cultural insensitivities dictated by Rome stifled the movement, and Ricci started on generally new ground. Ricci's unique methodology included first taking on the image of a Buddhist monk then later a Confucian scholar. He was highly educated in fields like astronomy and mathematics, and this learning gave him opportunities to work among the upper classes of Chinese society. He was known to bring clocks into the country to give away. Unfortunately, Ricci and other Jesuits came under fire for allowing Confucian thought to mix with Christian doctrine. Several

Chinese intellectuals professed faith in Christ, and Ricci's influence was lasting.

Whether in the New World or in Asia, the lasting legacy of Roman Catholic missions was often a syncretistic mix of Catholic Christianity and animistic religions. Forced conversions, cultural differences, and poor methods of contextualization left many "converts" continuing to worship their old gods but with different names. Churches replaced shrines and saints replaced pagan gods, but only on the outside. Roman Catholic missions opened the world to Christianity, but later missionaries, both Catholic and Protestant, faced great difficulty in unraveling the mix left behind by the early conquering churches.

MISSIONS AND THE PROTESTANT REFORMATION

On October 31, 1517, Martin Luther launched the Protestant Reformation when he declared his conflict with the Roman Catholic Church by nailing ninety-five points of doctrine on a church door in Wittenberg, Germany. Luther was not alone in his growing understanding of the key Reformation values of biblical authority and salvation by faith alone through grace alone. A combination of factors, including political unrest, church corruption, and nationalism, made Europe ripe for Luther's movement. Printing press technologies made the Scriptures more readily available and facilitated the spread of ideas. In Geneva, John Calvin was also leading a significant movement against the Roman church based on the same principles.

While there is little question of the necessity and importance of the Reformation, missiologists and historians have questioned the Reformers' commitment to missions. Compared to the growth of missionary activity in the Roman Catholic Church over the century preceding the Reformation, Protestant missions appeared insignificant. To characterize the Reformers as indifferent, however, is an overstatement.

The Protestant churches faced several factors that made missions difficult. First, Luther and Calvin were heavily occupied with doctrinal issues and spreading the Reformation throughout Europe. Both faced significant, even violent, opposition; they were involved literally in a life or death struggle. The Reformation was both a religious and a political movement that required tremendous effort. While such preoccupation does not excuse a lack of missionary zeal, it does make it more understandable.

A second factor in Protestant missions was geography. Luther was German and Calvin worked in Switzerland. As we have seen, Spain and Portugal dominated global exploration and sea power, and both were strongly Catholic countries. Quite simply, the Protestant churches had neither a broad geographic knowledge nor access to mission fields.

Finally, and perhaps most importantly, both Luther and Calvin understood that the Great Commission passages applied to and were fulfilled by the apostles. For example, Calvin argued that the biblical "office" of apostle (Eph 4:11) was charged with the proclamation of the gospel and the expansion of the church. In his own time Calvin believed there was no longer any need for such an office, except in extraordinary circumstances, because the church was well established.

We cannot say, however, that missionary activity was completely absent from the Protestant Reformation. Calvin himself commissioned missionaries to work in France, and he sent a mission to Brazil that failed after facing established Catholicism. Another of Calvin's younger contemporaries, Adrian Saravia, argued against the Protestant hermeneutic, saying that "the command to preach the gospel to all nations, once received by the apostles who are now departed, continues to obligate the church."[5]

Another stream of the Reformation had a much more active missionary sentiment: the Anabaptists. The Anabaptists followed an ecclesiology that stood in stark contrast to the magisterial Reformers like Luther and Calvin. They rejected a church closely associated with the political state and viewed the local congregation as primary. Such a view, along with a strong emphasis on personal evangelism, fostered church planting. While the Anabaptist movement did not move broadly outside of Europe for some time, their motivation for missionary activity drove them to preach openly and call for repentance.

The missionary movement among the Protestant Reformers was mixed, but the Reformation itself had a significant impact

---

[5] Norman E. Thomas, *Classic Texts in Mission and World Christianity* (Maryknoll, NY: Orbis, 1995), 41.

on the future of Christian missions. A renewed focus on the authority of biblical revelation opened the way to later missions pioneers who viewed the Great Commission as applicable beyond the apostles. The Reformation emphasis on the importance of Bible translation into vernacular languages, as well as the relatively widespread availability of the printing press, put the Scriptures into the hands of common people. Most importantly, the Reformation laid a theological foundation of salvation by faith alone that fueled missionary preaching.

THE RISE OF PIETISM AND PROTESTANT MISSIONS

In the century following the Protestant Reformation, many of the Anabaptist fears of a stagnant state church came to pass. Decades of warfare and a cold orthodoxy settled on the churches such that they were in need of significant revival. Pietism was a movement that started among Lutherans in response to the decline in biblical spirituality in the churches. The movement began from a home Bible study led by Philipp Jakob Spener around 1675. Spener encouraged in-depth Bible study and Christlike living for both laypeople and clergy. He emphasized personal evangelism and prayer, along with education and missions. He influenced the founding of the University of Halle in 1691, which became a center for Pietist education.

One of the earliest professors at Halle, August Francke, had been heavily influenced toward Pietism by Spener. Francke exemplified both the spiritual and the practical aspects of Pietism, starting small Bible studies, an orphanage, and a school for children at Halle. As a theology professor and pastor, Francke had the opportunity to disseminate the ideals of Pietism widely, including its emphasis on missions and evangelism.

The Danish-Halle Mission. The first significant Protestant missions effort was the Danish-Halle mission, called for by Denmark's King Frederick IV in 1705. In the early seventeenth century, Denmark had developed a colonial trading post at Tranquebar in India. Frederick, burdened by the need for Christian missions in South Asia, asked for missionaries to be sent to the post. Two of Francke's students, Bartholomew Ziegenbalg and Heinrich Plutschau, answered the plea and departed for Tranquebar in 1706. Plutschau served for five years before returning home for health reasons, but Ziegenbalg worked in India for fifteen years.

The Danish-Halle missionaries developed a series of missionary principles that reflect early church and Celtic patterns and serve as a model for modern missions. Upon entering the city, they first set up a school and studied the local language. The men were concerned to translate the Scriptures into the vernacular tongue so that local clergy could receive training. They studied the culture extensively and focused heavily on personal evangelism with a goal toward individual conversion.

The Moravian Mission Movement. After several years on the field, Ziegenbalg returned to Europe to report on the mission and to raise support. While visiting Halle, one of Francke's students, Nickolaus von Zinzendorf, heard Ziegenbalg speak. Zinzendorf was a German nobleman with a large estate. A group of Christians from Moravia fled to Germany under persecution, and Zinzendorf allowed them to live on his land as part of a settlement called Herrnhut. As the community grew, Zinzendorf became the bishop of the Moravian church, leading them toward pietistic principles.

During a visit to Copenhagen for the coronation of Christian VI, Zinzendorf heard pleas for missionaries in the New World. He challenged the Herrnhut Christians to respond to the missionary call, and the Moravian missionary movement was born. Beginning in 1732, the Moravians sent more than 200 missionaries to ten different countries, including the Virgin Islands, Suriname, Ghana, and Jamaica. Many from among the community relocated to the British Colonies in New England to work with Native American populations. Despite financial, political, and some doctrinal problems, the Moravians continued to send missionaries well into the twentieth century, eventually numbering almost 3,000.

Zinzendorf's missionary force followed many of the principles developed by the Danish-Halle mission, including an emphasis on personal evangelism and Scripture translation. Notably all Moravian missionaries practiced a trade and were self-supporting. They were required to work alongside the people among whom they shared the gospel. As churches were formed, the Moravians insisted that the congregations be self-governed and self-supporting. Zinzendorf himself traveled extensively, including a brief stint as a missionary working in New England. Moravian missionary principles were much ahead of their time and continue to have value for modern missionaries.

BRITISH MISSIONS IN NORTH AMERICA

The Danish and Moravian missionaries were not the only Protestants working during the seventeenth and eighteenth centuries. Beginning around 1639, Anglicans formed several missionary societies to minister among Native Americans. The Society for Promoting Christian Knowledge launched in 1698, followed three years later by the Society for Propagating the Gospel in Foreign Parts. Like the Roman Catholic missionaries before them, British colonists believed the church and evangelization were integral parts of colonization. In fact, the most notable missionaries of the colonial period in North America were not directly associated with the missionary societies but were rather pastors of local churches.

John Eliot arrived in Massachusetts in 1631 to pastor a small frontier church. After more than a decade of ministry there, he recognized the spiritual needs of Algonquin Indians living nearby and began to preach among them. He struggled to learn the language but eventually saw some of the group converted. Eliot advocated for the Algonquins and arranged for a settlement of several thousand acres that became a "praying town" of Native Christians. He spent several years translating a catechism and the New Testament into the Algonquin language, and as more "praying towns" formed, he concentrated on training leaders for the churches. Eliot spent the remainder of his life working among the Native Americans, even in the face of opposition from other colonists and a devastating war. His work influenced the formation of the Society for Propagating the Gospel in Foreign Parts and inspired other colonists to proclaim the gospel among other tribal groups.

Thomas Mayhew Sr. was the colonial governor of Martha's Vineyard, an island off the coast of Massachusetts, at the same time that Eliot was working outside Boston. His son, Thomas Mayhew Jr., was a local minister with a desire to evangelize the Native American population. The younger Mayhew started a church and school and saw several hundred believers on the island. When he was lost at sea on the way to England to mobilize support, the elder Mayhew took up the work in spite of his advanced age. Two younger generations continued the ministry for decades.

Perhaps the best-known missionary of the period was David Brainerd, a Congregationalist pastor whose influence spread far beyond his missionary work among Native Americans on the New England frontier. As a young man Brainerd enrolled at Yale, only to be expelled for insulting a professor. He joined the work of the Society for the Propagation of Christian Knowledge in 1742 and began his preaching ministry among the native populations in the Massachusetts colony. Brainerd first preached without any interpretation, so he saw no results. His melancholy disposition, made worse by his expulsion from Yale and the meager results, came through in his journal. Brainerd worked hard, building his own homes and spending long hours on horseback as he traveled from one preaching opportunity to another.

Brainerd persevered, however, and eventually saw an awakening among a group of Indians in New Jersey. He gathered new believers into a village where he continued to preach and teach. Unfortunately, his health began to fail, and Brainerd went to stay with Jonathan Edwards, whose daughter Brainerd planned to marry. He died of tuberculosis in 1747 at the age of twenty-nine. Brainerd's lasting influence was not in the number of Christians resulting from his ministry. His journal, which Edwards published, became one of the most important pieces of missionary literature from the period of the Great Awakening. It influenced many of the missionary heroes of the nineteenth century, including William Carey.

LESSONS FROM THE FIRST 1,800
YEARS OF MISSIONS HISTORY

By the end of the eighteenth century, Christianity had become a truly global faith. Many fields remained unreached, but every continent had been touched. From a band of scattered believers in cities like Jerusalem and Antioch, thousands of unnamed missionaries had faithfully carried the gospel to the ends of the earth. And yet the "Great Century" of Christian missions was just on the horizon.

Twenty-first-century students of missions can gain considerable inspiration and education from the early history of the expansion of the church. Several factors stand out:

- First, the most fruitful efforts of early missions history displayed a focus on preaching and teaching the Word of God. Whether it was Barnabus and Paul teaching at Antioch, Celtic monks building schools to teach, or Pietist translation efforts, missions meant the proclamation and dissemination of the Scriptures. Paul wrote to the Roman church, "So faith comes from what is heard, and what is heard comes through the message about Christ" (Rom 10:17). Faithful missions have always meant the faithful teaching of the Bible.

- Hand in hand with the preaching of the Scriptures went a passion for evangelism. Early missionaries heard clearly the Great Commission and understood that "making disciples" meant evangelism. While most missionaries from the New Testament period on also met human needs and provided for education, their primary drive was to lead nonbelievers to Christ.

- Early missionaries also understood that discipleship best takes place in the context of local churches. Anywhere they saw conversions, missionaries planted churches.

- In the first eighteen centuries of Christian missions, we also see good and bad examples of contextualization. Positively, groups like the Celtic monks led by Columba and the Moravians led by Ziegenbalg and Zinzendorf studied cultures. They strove to understand how best to communicate eternal truth within worldviews different from their own. Sometimes, as in the case of sixteenth-century Roman Catholic missionaries, weak efforts led to syncretism. Others found ways to remain faithful to Scripture while communicating in local languages and with indigenous cultural forms. Modern missionaries can learn much from those efforts.

- Finally, early missionaries provide a model of sacrifice that is both instructive and inspirational. Whether they ministered in the face of persecution or of strange diseases, faithful men and women often gave their lives for the sake of getting the gospel to those who had never heard it.

The first 1,800 years of missions history laid the groundwork for a massive expansion of cross-cultural evangelism and missions over the past 200 years, Filled with the instruction and inspiration of history, Christians at the end of the eighteenth century launched the "Great Century" of missions.

RESOURCES FOR FURTHER STUDY

DuBose, Francis M. *Classics of Christian Missions*. Nashville: Broadman, 1979.

Moffat, Samuel Hugh. *A History of Christianity in Asia*. 2 vols. Maryknoll, NY: Orbis, 1999, 2003.

Neill, Stephen, and Owen Chadwick. *A History of Christian Missions*, 2nd ed., rev. Owen Chadwick. Harmondsworth, Middlesex, England: Penguin, 1986.

Terry, John Mark, Ebbie Smith, and Justice Anderson, eds. *Missiology: An Introduction to the Foundations, History, and Strategy of World Missions*. Nashville: B&H Academic, 1998.

Tucker, Ruth. *From Jerusalem to Irian Jaya: A Biographical History of Christian Missions*. Grand Rapids: Zondervan, 1983.

CHAPTER 6

THE EXPANSION OF CHRISTIANITY, PART 2

THE GREAT CENTURY AND BEYOND

Just before the turn of the nineteenth century, a series of factors came providentially together to create a perfect atmosphere for the launch of what came to be known as the modern missions movement. Global exploration had shifted from Spain and Portugal to the formation of the French and British Empires. Changing technologies had led to the Industrial Revolution that, in tandem with improvements in transportation, made travel relatively much easier. And the Great Awakening that had produced David Brainerd, John Wesley, and George Whitefield had brought renewed attention to the importance of evangelism and missions.

Just as God providentially brought together circumstances and opportunities that facilitated the spread of the gospel and the expansion of the church in the first century, he did so at the end of the eighteenth. The first-century context of the Roman Empire provided a road system for ease of travel, general peace throughout the Mediterranean region, and a generally common language. At the beginning of the nineteenth century, world trade and exploration opened new avenues to missionaries, as did growing British and American influence around the globe.

The "Great Century" was marked by numerous well-known missionaries and movements. William Carey, Adoniram and Ann Judson, David Livingstone, Lottie Moon, and Hudson Taylor made important contributions. Methodologies and philosophies developed by these, along with indigenous church strategies and organizations like the Student Volunteer Movement, changed missionary strategies and practice. The development of missionary societies outside of church structures was perhaps the most notable distinction of the period. These factors resulted in an unprecedented expansion of the global church.

WILLIAM CAREY

Justice Anderson ties the beginning of the Great Century to the formation of the Baptist Missionary Society (BMS) in 1792.[1] William Carey, who led the creation of the BMS with local church pastor Andrew Fuller, is often called the Father of the Modern Missions Movement. Carey was born in 1761 near Northampton, England, and was a shoemaker by trade and a local church pastor by calling. He was self-educated and had an affinity for languages and geography, even making for himself a world map out of scraps of shoe leather. Also a voracious reader, Carey studied the stories of David Brainerd, John Eliot, and Captain James Cook, who explored much of the South Pacific.

The combination of Carey's biblical studies and his missionary reading developed in the pastor a growing sense that British evangelicals had left a key component out of their ministries: Great Commission missions. In 1792, Carey wrote and published an eighty-seven-page pamphlet entitled *An Enquiry into the Obligations of Christians to Use Means for the Conversion of the Heathens*. The work was a response to the common understanding among Carey's Particular Baptist friends that the Great Commission had applied to the early church alone and that if God wanted to bring redemption to non-Christians, he would do so himself.

---

[1] John Mark Terry, Ebbie C. Smith, and Justice Anderson. *Missiology: An Introduction to the Foundations, History, and Strategies of World Missions* (Nashville, TN: B&H Academic, 1998), 200.

Carey's *Enquiry* reflected his own belief that the Great Commission was still binding on his own age. He confronted the prevailing ideas, writing:

> It seems as if many thought the commission was sufficiently put in execution by what the apostles and others have done; that we have enough to do to attend to the salvation of our own countrymen; and that, if God intends the salvation of the heathen, he will some way or other bring them to the gospel, or the gospel to them. It is thus that multitudes sit at ease, and give themselves no concern about the far greater part of their fellow-sinners, who, to this day, are lost in ignorance and idolatry.[2]

Hyper-Calvinist sentiments had caused some of Carey's fellow pastors to reject missionary activity. Not long after publication of the *Enquiry*, on May 31, 1792, Carey preached at a meeting of the Northampton Baptist Association (a cooperative body of local Baptist churches). As his text Carey chose Isaiah 54:2–3, declaring, "That we should expect great things, that we should attempt great things."[3] While he faced some opposition because of his "enthusiasm," Carey pressed on, and the gathering concluded with a resolution to form a new missionary society.

On October 2, 1792, the pastors gathered in Kettering for the formation of "The Particular Baptist Society for Propagating the Gospel amongst the Heathen," later called the Baptist Missionary Society. The society immediately began taking financial subscriptions from individuals and churches for the support of missionaries. In a later meeting they discussed missionary qualifications and fields of ministry, asking, "In what parts of the heathen world do there seem to be the most promising openings?" Carey suggested consideration of India, where Dr. John Thomas had already begun preparations.

---

[2] Francis M. DuBose, *Classics of Christian Missions* (Nashville: Broadman, 1979), 26.

[3] Baptist Missionary Society, *Periodical Accounts Relative to a Society Formed Among the Particular Baptist for Propagating the Gospel Among the Heathen* (London: J. W. Morris, 1800, no.1 p. 3); accessed May 2, 2013, http://www.wmcarey.edu/carey/per-acct-vol1/bms-founding.pdf.

After struggling to find a suitable missionary, the Society asked Carey to consider taking the first missionary appointment of the young association. At the January 9, 1793, meeting of the Society, Carey agreed to go, describing India as a deep and dark gold mine and declaring, "I will go down, but remember that you must hold the ropes."[4] In June, after significant opposition from the British East India Company and aborted attempts at departure, Carey, his wife and children, his sister-in-law, Kitty, and Thomas left England on board a Danish ship bound for Calcutta. They arrived five months later.

William Carey spent the next forty-one years in missionary labor. Those years were costly, including the loss of his wife Dorothy, who had never fully accepted Carey's missionary calling, and their son Peter. But Carey's ministry in India was also fruitful beyond his own work. The society model of local-church missions support provided for the expansion of the modern missionary movement throughout the Great Century. Carey's high view of Scripture, the church, and culture led to a focus on Bible translation and church planting. He was personally involved in at least thirty-five translations into local languages. With Thomas, Carey started the first Baptist church in India in 1795. After seven years of labor, he baptized the first Indian convert, Krishna Pal, in December 1800. Over his career Carey recruited numerous missionaries, trained national pastors, and launched Serampore College (started in 1819 and still operating today).

One of Carey's important contributions, along with his colleagues William Ward and Joshua Marshman, was the "Serampore Agreement." Carey had moved to Serampore in January 1800, where he joined Marshman and Ward. In October 1805, the three (often referred to as the "Serampore Trio"), along with six other missionaries, signed an agreement that laid out the principles, philosophies, and strategies of the Baptist Missionary Society working in India. It was a document influenced by history yet contemporary and forward thinking. It outlined ten principles that reflect missionary practice during the Great Century and are thus worthy of examination.

---

[4] Timothy George, *Faithful Witness: The Life and Mission of William Carey* (Birmingham, AL: New Hope, 1991), 73–74.

The missionaries (Ward most likely drafted the text of the agreement) began with an affirmation of the importance and priority of evangelism. They declared their Calvinistic theological heritage but added, "Nevertheless, we cannot but observe with admiration, that Paul, the great champion for the glorious doctrines of free and sovereign grace, was the most conspicuous for his personal zeal in the work of persuading men to be reconciled to God."[5] With great passion they declared, "It is absolutely necessary that we set an infinite value upon immortal souls." The trio believed that the first work of missions was the generous proclamation of the gospel to the unconverted.

Much of the agreement focused, then, on how best to communicate the gospel and make disciples. First, the missionaries argued, they must understand well the culture in which they work. The agreement advocated studying literature, observing customs and ceremonies, and conversing with the people. By such means, "we would gain their attention to our discourse, and would avoid being barbarians to them." Translation of the Scriptures into local languages was the natural result of such concern for culture.

An understanding of culture would lead to a lifestyle that would not unnecessarily offend nonbelievers. Carey and his colleagues agreed together that they should neither live a lifestyle that offended Indian sensibilities, like cruelty to animals, nor attack "with acrimony" Hindu practices. Rather, missionaries must demonstrate love and humble themselves before those who need to hear the gospel. Closely related to this point, the trio committed themselves to preach Christ alone, to always be accessible to those around them, and to "watch all opportunities of doing good."

A final category of resolutions revolved around leadership development and church planting. Carey believed strongly in the establishment of churches led by national believers. New believers should receive training, and then missionaries should submit to their leadership. While some of the language in the agreement continued to reveal the paternalism common to the time, the missionaries committed themselves to raising up churches that reflected the culture and community. "We can

[5] "The Serampore Form of Agreement," *Baptist Quarterly* Vol 12, no. 5 (Jan 1947): 125–38.

never make sacrifices too great," they wrote, "when the eternal salvation of souls is the object, except, indeed, we sacrifice the commands of Christ."

The Baptist missionaries agreed to pursue wholeheartedly their own prayer and spiritual growth. They recognized that the life of the missionary was one of the most powerful tools to their task. The final section of the agreement declared,

> A competent knowledge of the languages current where a missionary lives, a mild and winning temper, and a heart given up to God in closest religion, these, these are the attainments which, more than all knowledge or all other gifts will fit us to become the instruments of God in the great work of human redemption.

At a gathering to constitute the church at Serampore, the trio and six other missionaries signed their names to the agreement. They also included a provision that the document would be read aloud three times every year, on the first Sundays of January, May, and October. The resolve of the Serampore Agreement reminded the missionaries of their heritage (referring, for example, to David Brainerd's devotion) and pointed them toward healthy practices for the future. "Let us give ourselves up unreservedly to this glorious cause." The agreement concluded, "Oh, that He may sanctify us for His work!"

William Carey's influence spread far beyond his work in India. The society model of missions support spread with the formation of groups like the London Missionary Society in 1795 and the Church Missionary Society in 1799. Excitement about missions overseas led to the implantation of new churches and the growth of existing churches in England. In the young United States, local societies began to appear, as well. The American Board of Commissioners for Foreign Missions (ABCFM) was formed in 1810 by a group of Congregationalist churches. The General Missionary Convention of the Baptist Denomination in the United States of America for Foreign Missions (commonly called the Triennial Convention because it met every three years) followed soon after in 1814.

In August 1806, five students at Williams College in Massachusetts gathered to discuss missionary theology. When a sudden thunderstorm arose, they ran to a nearby haystack where they began to pray for the lost in Asia. Out of what came to be known as the "Haystack Prayer Meeting," a larger gathering of students began to meet. The group called themselves "the Brethren" and continued to pray, eventually calling on churches to form the ABCFM in 1810.

One young student impacted by the haystack meeting (though not part of the original group) was Adoniram Judson. Judson had been raised in a Congregationalist home but did not become a believer until he was a student at Andover Seminary. In 1810, he was one of four young men who so impressed the Congregationalist General Association meeting that they formed the ABCFM. The following year Judson was part of the first group of American missionaries commissioned to go to Asia.

On February 19, 1812, Judson, Ann Hasseltine Judson (his wife of two weeks), Samuel and Harriett Newell, and Luther Rice set sail for Calcutta. En route the two Judsons entered into an intense Bible study on the subject of baptism. They became convinced of the truth of believer's baptism and, upon arrival at Calcutta in June, were baptized by William Ward, one of the Serampore Trio. Naturally, this change in doctrine was a conflict with their Congregationalist-sending churches, so Luther Rice (whose health had declined) returned to America to seek the support of the Baptists. Rice's labor resulted in the formation of the Triennial Convention.

The Judsons did not remain long in Calcutta. Local authorities and the British East India Company opposed their presence, so the couple moved to Burma in 1813. Their first years in Burma were difficult. They were isolated from other Christians and faced a difficult culture and language in which conversions were punishable by death. After six years and several failed attempts to engage the Burmese (including wearing the robes of a Buddhist teacher), Judson noticed that Buddhist leaders commonly constructed a *zayat*, a roadside building where people gathered to hear religious teaching. Judson built a *zayat* close to his home and started waiting for people to gather, sometimes crying out to people passing on the road. After seven years in Burma, Judson saw his first Burmese convert to Christianity. By 1822, there were eighteen believers.

Judson's missionary life was characterized by hard work and suffering. He spent decades translating the Bible into the local language, completing the task in 1840. His translation is still in use today. The Burmese church grew exponentially over his career and remains strong. Such fruit came at great cost, however. The Judsons had already lost two children. Judson was imprisoned for almost two years during a war between Burma and the British. Ann worked tirelessly to care for him, even as she tried to care for a newborn daughter, Emily (their third child). In October 1826, soon after Judson was released, Ann died, followed soon by their daughter. Judson entered into a period of severe depression and retreated to the jungle to con- template death and suffering. He even dug a grave where he sat for hours every day.

Thanks to the ministry of other missionaries and Burmese Christians, Judson returned to his work. He married Sarah Boardman, widow of another missionary pioneer, George Boardman, in 1834. They had eight children together, three of whom died early in childhood. She died in 1845, and Judson married a third time. In April 1850, Judson died aboard a ship bound for America and was buried at sea.

Adoniram Judson's missionary legacy is immense. In addi- tion to his tireless translation work, he and his coworkers led the formation of a strong Burmese church that endures today, especially among the Karen people group. Judson's story, passed on through letters and reports, inspired a missionary awakening among American Christians. He became a missionary hero, and, on his one visit back to America, Judson mobilized many to mis- sionary service.

MISSIONARY PIONEERS OF THE GREAT CENTURY

While Carey and Judson were pioneers in the evangelical missions movements in the late eighteenth and early nineteenth centuries, they were not alone in their passion to take the gospel to the nations. Robert Morrison (1782–1834) was the first mod- ern Protestant missionary to China, arriving in 1807 with the London Missionary Society. He spent sixteen years translating the Bible into the local language. Like Carey and Judson, Morrison waited seven years before he saw fruit from his labor, and he only baptized twelve converts in almost thirty years on the field. Morrison considered his translation work to be his greatest legacy, supposedly saying, "By the Chinese Bible, when dead, I shall yet speak."

One of the earliest missionaries to Africa, Robert Moffatt (1795–1883) was appointed by the London Missionary Society in 1817 to work in South Africa. He, too, believed strongly in Bible translation, completing his Bechuana Bible in 1857. Moffatt and his wife, Mary, worked in South Africa for fifty-three years. They established the "mission station" approach, building a settlement around their home and church. From there Moffatt's ministry extended to multiple tribal groups, often as a result of tribal emissaries coming to ask for Moffatt to bring the gospel to their people. The Moffatts returned to England where he spent the remaining years of his life mobilizing missionaries and support for the African work. Their legacy included not only the Bible translation but also many indigenous pastors, numerous churches, and five children serving in missions.

David Livingstone (1813–73) married one of Robert and Mary Moffatt's daughters. A trained physician, Livingstone was appointed by the London Missionary Society in 1841 to serve alongside Moffatt at the mission station in Kuruman. Livingstone is often remembered as a pioneer who opened the African interior to exploration and fought against the slave trade, but he was first and foremost a missionary. He became a well-known hero in Britain and popularized missions there.

One of the most influential missionaries of the Great Century was Hudson Taylor (1832–1905), a Methodist physician who went to China in 1854 under the appointment of the China Evangelization Society. In 1854, Taylor resigned but remained in China. Most missionaries in China lived and worked in the large coastal cities where outsiders were allowed, but Taylor was burdened for the Chinese interior. In 1865, after a brief return to England, he founded the China Inland Mission with a goal to send missionaries into every Chinese province.

China Inland Mission (CIM) was unique in several ways thanks to Taylor's vision of a "faith mission." Missionaries with

CIM did not appeal for funds from churches or individuals but rather relied on their own work and on unsolicited support. Taylor based the administration of the mission in China rather than in England or the United States, and he accepted missionaries from any denomination regardless of educational level or gender. He advocated identification with the Chinese culture as much as possible.

Taylor was a strong leader with a focused vision, and CIM grew rapidly. By 1882, CIM had missionaries in every inland province. In 1895, Taylor led a missionary force of more than 600, comprising half of the entire Protestant presence in China. And by 1929, CIM had grown to be the largest Protestant missions organization in the world with 1,300 missionaries.

China Inland Mission was not the only organization sending women to the mission field. The Foreign Mission Board of the Southern Baptist Convention, formed in 1845, appointed Charlotte Diggs Moon and her sister, Edmonia, as missionaries to China in 1873. The Moons were from an affluent Virginia family and were well educated. Charlotte, or Lottie as she is better known, began ministry as a teacher but was also involved in evangelism and church planting. She died during a famine in 1912, leaving behind a legacy of thirty churches and of financial mobilization among her Southern Baptist denomination.

Amy Carmichael (1867–1951) was from Northern Ireland and served fifty-five years in India. She worked mainly among children, rescuing hundreds through the Dohnavur Fellowship she established in 1901. A prolific author, Carmichael inspired many of the twentieth century's most influential missionaries.

GREAT MOVEMENTS DURING THE GREAT CENTURY

While many great missionaries were at work during the Great Century, the period was also characterized by great movements within Christian missions. Some, like the growth of faith missions mentioned above, were tied to individuals like Hudson Taylor. Others were more general in nature. Regardless of their origin, however, these movements had a significant impact on missions that continues today.

While early missionaries like the Celtic monks and William Carey all recognized the importance of understanding local culture for the planting of healthy churches, leaders in the early nineteenth century grew concerned that missionaries were transferring Western forms and structures into other places. Working independently of one another, Henry Venn (1796–1873) and Rufus Anderson (1796–1880) called for an indigenous movement in missions. Venn and Anderson were leaders of the Church Missionary Society and the ABCFM, respectively.

The term *indigenous* comes from horticulture and indicates a plant that thrives in its native soils and environment. Venn, Anderson, and others understood that for the church to thrive in a new culture, it had to reflect that culture within biblical parameters. Venn and Anderson developed a "formula" to describe indigenous churches. First, they argued, churches must be self-supporting; they must not depend on outside sources (including missionaries) for financial or other means. Second, churches must be self-governing. Missionaries often served as pastors of new churches, but Venn and Anderson contended that missionaries should move quickly to raise up, train, and turn over authority to national believers. Finally, indigenous churches would be self-propagating; they would plant new churches that are indigenous. With these three characteristics in place, they argued, churches would best engage local cultures and would be healthier.

Another proponent of indigeneity in missions was John L. Nevius (1829–93). Nevius was a missionary first in China and later in Korea. He mourned the fact that many new believers were drawn out of their own cultures and networks to enter a mission compound and adopt Western culture. He was a proponent of Venn's and Anderson's "three self" formula (without calling it such) but added theological education and broader national leadership. In his influential book, *The Planting and Development of Missionary Churches* (1886), Nevius advocated providing means by which national pastors could receive theological training without leaving their homes and neighborhoods, suggesting short intensive courses. He argued that church buildings should reflect indigenous architectural styles and that music should reflect local styles (though he did suggest that hymns and liturgy should be translated).

Other missionary scholars and practitioners spoke into the developing indigenous movement well into the twentieth century. Roland Allen, an Anglican missionary in China, wrote two books that influenced modern missions: *Missionary Methods: St. Paul's or Ours?* (1912) and *The Spontaneous Expansion of the Church* (1927). Allen suggested that the biblical example of the apostle Paul should be the model for contemporary missions. He emphasized the role of the Holy Spirit, local leadership, and financial independence.

In the twentieth century, anthropologist Alan Tippett added to the understanding of indigenous churches by adding "self-theologizing" to the list. He argued that indigenous leaders and theologians should be free to develop theologies that reflect their own cultures. Such a move would allow Christianity to become more than a foreign religion, a problem keenly felt in many fields.

The "indigenous principle," as this movement became known, has had a profound influence on modern missions. While widely accepted today, ideas developed by Venn, Anderson, Nevius, and others were fairly radical for their time. They brought both biblical methodologies and cultural sensitivities to bear on the missionary task, hallmarks of twentieth-century missiology.

While the indigenous church movement influenced missiology and missionary practice, another movement grew that swelled the numbers of missionaries serving among unreached peoples. The Student Volunteer Movement (SVM), as it came to be known, was initially inspired by the "Cambridge Seven," students at the elite British university who forsook wealth and privilege to give their lives to missions in China. The best known of the seven was C. T. Studd, eventual founder of the Heart of Africa Mission, later the World Evangelization Crusade. Studd's controversy-laced career lasted for more than fifty years and touched both China and Africa.

Better known as a leader of the SVM was John R. Mott. Though never a missionary in the truest sense, Mott, through his involvement with the Young Men's Christian Association (YMCA) and the SVM, led thousands of young men and women to overseas ministry. Under the teaching of evangelist D. L. Moody,

Mott surrendered to missionary service while a student. At a meeting in 1886, Mott and other students (known as the Mount Hermon Hundred) signed a pledge to become foreign missionaries. Two years later Mott chaired the Student Volunteer Movement for Foreign Missions, a role he held for three decades.

Mott's motto was "the evangelization of the world in this generation." The movement spread from the United States to Europe and Asia, and more than 600 students attended the 1891 convention. By 1920, the meeting had grown to almost 7,000. The growth of SVM shifted the center of the missions-sending world to North America.

But numbers of missionaries was not the only contribution of SVM to missions history. Building on the foundations of missionaries like Hudson Taylor, student volunteers crossed denominational lines. Mott became the leader of a growing ecumenical missions movement that led to the World Missionary Conference at Edinburgh, Scotland, in 1910.

The Edinburgh conference was not the first missionary gathering of its kind. The Union Missionary Convention in New York, held in 1854, sought to address problems of missionary training and the overlap of missionary work with seminary missions courses and comity agreements that divided territories between agencies and denominations. In 1900, thousands attended the Union Missionary Convention to hear reports from a long list of missions agencies and speakers including Hudson Taylor and John Mott. Then-Governor Theodore Roosevelt was also among those who addressed the delegates.

The pivotal nature of the 1910 Edinburgh conference was its global reach and the wave of optimism spurred by movements like the SVM. While primarily (though not exclusively) composed of Western missionaries and missions leaders, the conference produced a statement that touched on many of the most important issues of the day. "This is a decisive hour for Christian missions," the report began.

> The call of Providence to all our Lord's disciples,
> of whatever ecclesiastical connection, is direct
> and urgent to undertake without delay the task
> of carrying the Gospel with serious purpose
> to discharge it. The opportunity is inspiring;

the responsibility is undeniable. The Gospel is all-inclusive in its scope, and we are convinced that there never was a time more favourable for united, courageous, and prayerful action to make the universality of the Gospel ideal a practical reality in the history of the Church.[6]

Conference participants were called upon to increase their emphasis on fields like China and Asia and to engage the "unoccupied fields." In addition, church leaders were reminded of the importance of health among sending churches as well as the primacy of evangelism in missions.

The Edinburgh meeting led to the formation of the International Missionary Council in 1921, then to the Commission on World Mission and Evangelism of the World Council of Churches. Further conferences in Jerusalem (1928), Madras (1938), and Willingen (1952) reflected declining optimism as the result of two world wars, as well as increasing theological liberalism within the ecumenical movement. By the 1960s, unfortunately, the heirs of the Edinburgh conference had embraced pluralism, and missions fervor had all but died out.

The Great Century had a tremendous impact on the growth of the Christian missionary movement. In 1800, approximately 200 missions-sending agencies (including both Protestants and Catholics) were around the world with about 25,000 foreign missionaries. By 1900, the number of agencies had increased to 600 with around 62,000 missionaries. Among these new organizations was the Foreign Mission Board of the Southern Baptist Convention (now the International Mission Board), formed in 1845 as the first act of the new convention of churches. The Foreign Mission Board's sister agency, the Board of Domestic Missions (now the North American Mission Board), concentrated on church planting and ministry in North America. By the end of the twentieth century, the International Mission Board, SBC, was one of the largest and most influential sending agencies in the world.

The movement continued to grow throughout the twentieth century, even in the face of war, economic depressions, and

---

[6] DuBose, *Classics of Christian Missions*, 331.

liberal theological movements. By 1970, 2,200 agencies supported some 240,000 missionaries. The global Christian population had grown from 23 percent of the world population to 33 percent. The number of evangelicals, the driving force behind the modern missions movement, tripled between 1800 and 1900.

The twentieth century also brought unprecedented opportunities for Christian missions. Improved transportation and communication technologies, globalization, medical advances, and the rise of volunteerism contributed greatly to the growth of missionary activity. Academic studies in anthropology and linguistics helped missionaries better understand their fields. In many ways the Great Century continued well beyond Edinburgh.

Ralph Winter, himself an important figure in missions history, identified three overlapping eras of the modern missions movement. The first, covering what we have called the Great Century, was characterized by the rise of missionary societies. Groups of churches and individuals, dominated by European leadership, focused on engaging new countries. The second era (1865–1980) witnessed a shift in dominance to American leadership and a move away from strategies based on political nations to people groups,[7]

Two of the most important figures during Winter's second era of missions history were Cameron Townsend and Donald A. McGavran. Townsend was born in 1896 and was influenced by John R. Mott and the SVM. He and a friend went to Guatemala in 1917 to distribute Spanish Bibles among indigenous peoples, but Townsend noticed that many did not speak or read the language. He spent the next years learning the Cakchiquel language and translating the Bible. Townsend became convinced that Bible translation was imperative for reaching non-Christian peoples. He also believed that linguistics and translation provided a means for missionaries to enter cultures hostile to missionaries.

In 1934, Townsend founded Camp Wycliffe as a training ground for translators, followed in 1942 by the birth of Wycliffe Bible Translators. While recruiting and preparing translators,

---

[7] Ralph D. Winter, Steven C. Hawthorne, Darrell R. Dorr, D. Bruce Graham, Bruce A. Koch, eds., 4th ed., *Perspectives on the World Christian Movement: A Reader* (Pasadena, CA: William Carey Library, 2009), 259.

Townsend continued his own work, serving among various language groups in South and Latin America. In 1969, at age seventy-two, he and his wife moved to Russia to launch translations of several languages in the Caucasus region. Townsend died in 1982, having drawn attention not only to Bible translation but also to the importance of language groups in missionary strategy.

Donald Anderson McGavran was born December 15, 1897, in Damoh, India. His parents were missionaries, as were his grandparents. As a child, the young McGavran attended the Edinburgh Missionary Conference of 1910 but did not give himself as a missionary until much later. He served in World War I then graduated from Butler College in Indianapolis. He became involved in the YMCA, eschewing missions, stating, "My father and grandfather were missionaries. My family has done enough for God. I am going to be a good Christian and make a lot of money."[8] In 1919, however, he attended the Student Volunteer Convention where he heard John R. Mott speak.

After ten years as a church planter in India, McGavran became a mission administrator in 1933. He studied the mission stations under his direction and found that only 11 of 147 were growing in any way. McGavran began to ask why churches in similar circumstances with faithful missionaries would grow or not. His studies led him to argue that the gospel traveled most easily across family and ethnic bridges, an idea he published in *The Bridges of God* in 1955. McGavran's teaching on people groups, missions strategy, and the priority of evangelism was controversial, but his influence grew. In 1965, he became the founding dean of the School of World Missions at Fuller Theological Seminary, long the largest missions training school in the world.

Both Townsend and McGavran were heirs of the SVM's passion for the evangelization of the unreached. Among their lasting influences was the growing shift from viewing the "nations" as political and geographical entities to groups of people tied together by ethnic, language, and social bonds. Ralph Winter brought this shift to the churches' attention in a presentation at the 1974 Lausanne Congress for World Evangelization. Trained as an engineer, Winter worked in Guatemala before McGavran

---

[8] Donald McGavran, "My Pilgrimage in Mission," *International Bulletin of Missionary Research* 10, no. 2 (April 1986): 53.

asked him to join the faculty at Fuller Seminary. At Lausanne, Winter gave a plenary paper titled "The Highest Priority: Cross-cultural Evangelism," in which he argued that modern missions had focused too much on political boundaries rather than people groups. The result, he contended, was that a small minority of missionaries were working among the vast majority of unreached peoples. His call to reach the unreached brought together McGavran's and Townsend's philosophies and applied them to future missionary strategies.

A second important feature of the Lausanne meeting was the debate over the priority of evangelism in Christian missions. Men like McGavran argued that, while ministry to social needs was an important task for the church, evangelism must retain priority. John Stott composed a definition of *evangelism*, the "Lausanne Covenant," that was approved by the delegates to the congress. It clarified the primacy of evangelism without negating the importance of human needs and justice ministries.

While individuals like Townsend, McGavran, and Winter worked to define and clarify missions strategies, innumerable missionary practitioners gave their lives to enact those strategies and get the gospel to the unreached. During the twentieth century dozens of specialized missions agencies arose that promoted the use of modern technologies like radio and television, medical advances, and indigenous church planting.

Jim Elliot, Nate Saint, Ed McCully, Roger Youderian, and Pete Fleming were missionaries from various organizations who joined together for "Operation Auca," an attempt to reach and evangelize the Waodani people in Ecuador. After making contact with the tribal group, all five were killed on January 8, 1956. Their story inspired reports and magazine articles in the United States and inspired countless missionaries, much as Brainerd's journal had two centuries before. Other missionary martyrs line the history of twentieth century missions. In China, men and women like Southern Baptist Bill Wallace and China Inland Missions' John and Betty Stam gave their lives. More recently, in 2002, three Southern Baptist hospital workers in Jiblah, Yemen (William E. Koehn, Kathleen Gariety, and Martha Myers) were killed by a gunman. Their witness is joined by countless of named and unnamed missionaries.

CONCLUSION

Across the 2,000-year history of Christian missions and the expansion of the church from Jerusalem to the ends of the earth, several key factors stand out. They serve both as a reminder and as an inspiration for our own work. First, we see the work of God throughout the ages. Luke tells us that after Pentecost, "every day the Lord added to them those who were being saved" (Acts 2:47). Paul, in speaking of his ministry of discipleship and church planting, wrote, "God gave the growth" (1 Cor 3:6). While faithful missionaries have given their lives to carry the gospel and make disciples, God is the primary worker who bears fruit through his people to accomplish the Great Commission.

A second factor throughout the history of missions is that when the gospel has gone forth, it has done so as a result of the ministry of the entire church. In the earliest days of the church, men and women shared their faith as part of their daily lives. During the Reformation the Moravians and the Anabaptists were entirely involved in the spread of the gospel. And in the modern era, even as specialized societies and sending organizations developed, their support came from the local churches who gave toward missions. When missions fervor has waned, it has often been because Great Commission ministry became the task of a specialized few.

Third, healthy missions has always involved the preaching and teaching of God's Word. The Antioch church studied and preached the Scriptures. The Celtic missionaries set up schools and churches to teach the Bible. Bible translation and teaching were important facets found in strategies throughout the modern missions era. Historically, missions has not only relied on the Bible for guidance but also for the content of its message and strategy.

Closely related to the third point, the history of missions teaches us that theology matters. The loss of a Christ-centered, grace-filled, biblically sound theology leads to a loss of missionary passion. The Reformation was a movement to return biblical theology to the church, and the fruit of the Reformation (even if not immediately among the Reformers) was missions. In the twentieth century, churches who held to a theology of biblical authority continued to emphasize the expansion of the church while others slipped into relativism and pluralism. Sound theology is the spark of active missions.

Sound theology also leads to passionate evangelism, a fifth mark of missions throughout history. Early believers knew that they had good news to share, and they did so. The purpose of Carey's "Enquiry" was to point British Baptists to both the reality of global lostness and the importance of evangelism. Evangelism was rarely separated from ministries to human needs, however. The early church was noteworthy for its care of widows, orphans, and the sick. Education and relief have often gone hand in hand with gospel proclamation.

Another factor in healthy missions has been that missionaries view their work not only as proclaiming the gospel but as the expansion of the church. Church planting and evangelism cannot be separated; making disciples takes place most naturally in local churches. From the time of Acts through every period of missions history, missionaries have entered new fields, shared the gospel, led people to faith in Christ, then gathered them into churches. While those churches may look different depending on culture and geography, they are always churches.

Effective evangelism and church planting require thoughtful contextualization. Whether one considers the Celtic monks, the Moravians, William Carey, or Donald McGavran, culture has been in important consideration in Great Commission ministry. Throughout history we have seen bad models (Roman Catholic missions in South America that opened the door to syncretism or Protestant missionaries in Africa who assumed that doctrine was accepted) and good. Of all the subject areas within this textbook, history perhaps has the most to teach us on this issue.

Finally, the history of Christian missions is the history of sacrifice. Scores of missionaries have given their lives in Great Commission work. Violence, disease, persecution, and war have cost the church dearly over 2,000 years. Families left their homes never to return. Jesus' words, "Greater love has no one than this, that someone lay down his life for his friends" (John 15:13), have been true countless times of those called out to proclaim the gospel across cultures and to the unreached.

RESOURCES FOR FURTHER STUDY

Baptist Missionary Society. *Periodical Accounts Relative to a Society Formed Among the Particular Baptist for Propagating the Gospel Among the Heathen*, no. 1. London: J. W. Morris, 1800. Available online: http://www.wmcarey.edu/carey/per-acct-vol1/bms-founding.pdf.

DuBose, Francis M. *Classics of Christian Missions*. Nashville: Broadman, 1979.

Duesing, Jason G., ed. *Adoniram Judson: A Bicentennial Appreciation of the Pioneer American Missionary*. Nashville: B&H Academic, 2012.

George, Timothy. *Faithful Witness: The Life and Mission of William Carey*. Birmingham, AL: New Hope, 1991.

McGavran, Donald Anderson. "My Pilgrimage in Mission." *International Bulletin of Missionary Research* 10, no. 2 (April 1, 1986): 53–54.

Terry, John Mark, Ebbie C. Smith, and Justice Anderson. *Missiology: An Introduction to the Foundations, History, and Strategies of World Missions*. Nashville: B&H Academic, 1998.

Winter, Ralph D., Steven C. Hawthorne, Darrell R. Dorr, D. Bruce Graham, and Bruce A. Koch, eds. *Perspectives on the World Christian Movement: A Reader*. Pasadena, CA: William Carey Library, 2009.

CULTURE AND GLOBAL MISSIONS

CHAPTER 7

APPLIED ANTHROPOLOGY
IN MISSIONS

"Good missionaries have always been good anthropologists." Thus missionary linguist Eugene Nida begins his classic work, *Customs and Cultures*.[1] In fact, all missionaries either learn anthropology in school or on the job. Relating correctly to other cultures is the basic element of the missionary task, and those who find success on the field are those who do it well.

What makes the study of cultural anthropology so essential to Christian missions is that thousands of cultures are in the world, and each is different from yours to one degree or another. Every people group has its own rules for living, including rules about such things as the "right" way to eat, work, communicate, show respect, worship, marry, and govern society. They also have their own values that define what they judge to be delicious food, melodious music, beautiful art, and the way they measure poverty or wealth. The reason their culture seems so strange to you when you first arrive is simply that it is not your own. Because you did not grow up there, you do not automatically fit in.

Enculturation is what happens when you grow up in a particular place learning to live appropriately in that society. You naturally learn the language, appreciate the music, enjoy the

---

[1] Eugene Nida, *Customs and Cultures* (Pasadena: William Carey Library, 1975), xi.

food and the rhythm of life, play the popular sports, use and relate to the common sense of humor, and consider to be second nature every other aspect of daily life that is natural to that place. Other people who did not grow up in your home culture do not know your particular patterns, just as you do not know theirs. The degree to which each culture is different means the missionary must adjust in that same degree to be effective in intercultural ministry.

In its broadest sense, *anthropology* simply means "the study of man." However, many divisions of anthropology are devoted to researching and understanding languages, biological distinctions, ancient societies, musical systems, and even the gastronomy of diverse groups. Our focus in this chapter is on cultural anthropology, the study of the cultures of mankind, and the implications for missions.

UNDERSTANDING CULTURE

Culture has existed since the garden of Eden; whenever two or three people interact, a culture guides them. As observed in chapter 2, as the discipline of cultural anthropology has developed, countless different definitions of *culture* have been proposed. You will recall that we showed, fortunately, they are all variations on the same theme of shared beliefs, values, and patterns of behavior of a group of people. Culture, then, is the learned and shared design or pattern of living for a group of people. It is not innate but learned as one grows up among a people, and then it is passed on to the next generation, giving them a basis for proper conduct, thinking, and interaction. Cultures are ever developing and evolving with new innovations in technology, the latest discoveries and inventions, the annual additions to the language's vocabulary and dictionaries; in turn, the next generation's culture will receive, adapt, and eventually pass on yet another cultural system.

Evaluating Culture Systems

Cultural anthropologists have devised terms to refer to the many aspects of their discipline. The work of the missionary faces the same challenges ministers in their home countries face, but it is complicated by cultural misunderstandings because a newcomer does not view life the same way the culture sees it. The way an insider thinks of his own culture is called the *emic perspective.* He knows intuitively why people act, believe, and speak as they do in his home culture. He knows to eat certain foods for breakfast and others later in the day, the proper volume to use, and the appropriate distance to stand from one another when speaking in a public place. The point of view of an outsider who comes to the culture from another is the *etic perspective.* The reasons and routines of the new culture's life that come naturally to the insider are a mystery to him.

The missionary's challenge is to avoid judging the culture as inferior before he understands it. This unfair critique of other cultures, considering them not as wise or as good as one's own, is called *ethnocentrism.* We tend to think our culture is the center of the universe and that everyone else should see life as we do. We all have this tendency because our own culture is all we know; thus, it seems "the right way to do it." We can never totally erase ethnocentrism, but being aware of it can help us delay critical judgment and learn to appreciate many aspects of other cultures.

We use the term *personality* to describe kinds of people. We may describe them as outgoing and funny or introspective and introverted. Sometimes we say we have a "personality clash" with a certain person because of his nature. Just as we use commonly understood terms to describe another's personality type, we can better understand other people groups, and do so more quickly, by referring to their *culturality* type.

Missionaries and cultural anthropologists have researched and categorized the cultures of the world in various ways. Sarah Lanier has described the cultures of the world as tending to belong to hot- or cold-climate cultures, having been influenced by the weather of their home region. While she allows for the anomalies of Inuit people in the cold Arctic zones or Eastern European peoples that live more as hot-climate cultures, she demonstrates that people of the hotter climates of the world tend to be group oriented, relational, inclusion minded, indirect in their communication, and think more of the event at hand than what the clock says. Those in the colder climates tend toward individualism, direct communication, and have a higher value of privacy. Lanier is only one of those who have helped missionaries with a system to understand the cultures of the world.[2]

Geert Hofstede and others believe cultures can be classified as more or less extreme in their particular position along five dimensions—identity, hierarchy, gender, truth, and virtue—resulting in ten different possible characteristics. Hofstede points out that no culture actually embraces any of the dimensions in their extreme but tends toward one end or the other. However, he uses the ten descriptors represented by the two extremes of each of the five dimensions to help us understand them. For instance, this helps us understand whether a culture's identity is individualistic or collectivistic.[3]

Sherwood Lingenfelter helps the missionary understand not only the culture to which he goes to serve but also his own. He includes an instrument the missionary may fill out and grade to understand his own preferences for living life—oriented by the clock or the event, thinking of life in dichotomistic[4] or holistic terms, anticipating crises in order to avoid them or simply living as if crises do not happen. He writes that cultures tend to be ascribed-status conscious or value personal achievement more. Like others, Lingenfelter recognizes that some cultures are more concerned with saving face and avoiding embarrassment at all costs, while others are happy-go-lucky, enjoying life as it comes.

Richard Lewis believes it is helpful to consider cultures relative to their position on a triangle. One corner of the triangle is *linear-active* people who are organized planners and do one thing at a time, such as North American and Western European cultures. *Multi-actives* are cultures in Latin America and much of Africa that are people oriented and may do several activities at once, moving freely back and forth among them. *Reactives* are respect-oriented, introverted listeners who prefer to

---

[2] Sarah A. Lanier, *Foreign to Familiar: A Guide to Understanding Hot and Cold Climate Cultures* (Hagerstown, MD: McDougal Publishing, 2000).

[3] Gert Jan Hofstede, Paul B. Pedersen, and Geert H. Hofstede, *Exploring Culture: Exercises, Stories and Synthetic Cultures* (Yarmouth, ME: Intercultural Press, 2002), 91–160. In addition to the system found in this excellent resource, iPad and iPhone apps are available that locate countries of the world on each dimension's continua.

[4] *Dichotomistic* refers to a binary, either-or approach to life (the thief is guilty or innocent), while *holistic* considers the whole of the matter (he only stole bread because his family was sick and starving).

respond rather than push their opinion first. Reactives are typically American indigenous peoples and Asian cultures. Studying any of these suggested systems is helpful to the missionary who wants to understand and be understood more quickly in another culture.

While there are great benefits to knowing your own *culturality,* with its tendencies and preferences, and how to anticipate the culture in which you will serve, this knowledge should not be used as a tool for choosing a culture for missionary service where you think you will fit in more easily. Rather, as God guides you to the culture of your missionary call, you will be able to anticipate and prepare yourself, your family, and your team for the challenges and tension points you know you will encounter.

There are many ways to study and understand the cultures of the world in addition to these systems. It has often been said that when Adam and Eve fell in the garden, three things entered the world: guilt, shame, and fear. While every culture has all three of these elements, they tend to emphasize one of the three. Many missionary anthropologists have found them to be helpful guidelines for understanding and relating to other cultures. We always find the cultures represented by each of these aspects with a partner characteristic.

The cultures of the world tend to live on a balance of guilt-innocence, shame-honor, or fear-power. Western cultures that are more dichotomistic in their orientation see people as either guilty or innocent. Asian cultures and most cultures embracing Islam have a high value of honor and avoid shame at all costs. Animistic cultures are constantly aware of evil spirits, ancestors' influences, magic, curses, and sorcery and live in fear of these or anyone who has the skill to manipulate their power. To understand and appreciate the beliefs, worldview, and behavior of fear-power or shame-honor cultures and how they differ from the guilt-innocence orientation of the West, missionaries are wise to learn about the basic life orientation of their target cultures regarding these three aspects.

Ethnographic research is the process of using skills and tools for investigating and learning about other cultures. The most basic tool in the missionary's toolbox is participant observation. Most missionaries use participant observation to some degree whether or not they call it by that term. It goes beyond merely observing daily life to asking why, when, how, and by whom something is done. As the missionary participates in life, the value and use of other ethnographic research tools become obvious. Skills necessary for informal, formal, and group interviews, interpreting data from surveys, recording life histories, bibliographic research, and many other tools constitute the ways missionaries can learn their people's worldview and culture. Computer programs that assist the missionary are valuable for streamlining the process, but living among the people, learning the language, eating the food, and living life as they do are essential in ethnographic research.

Intercultural Communication

Missionaries must learn how to effectively communicate the gospel in ways that are both culturally appropriate and biblically faithful. Achieving one or the other is difficult for anyone; achieving both requires study and application. It does not come easily, and the missionary's miscommunicating attempts, despite his best efforts, often lead to exasperation. The temptation is to say nothing at all unless he can do so with those who share his native language. However, as I often tell my classes, "You cannot *not* communicate." Even your silence communicates, sometimes more "loudly" than any words would convey.

All new missionaries recognize that they must engage in language learning before they can communicate with the people. This lifelong process involves two distinct perspectives. One is to learn the language as a necessary tool so you may do the work you were sent to do, whether you relish the task or not. The second approach is to love the language, not only because it is the key to heart-to-heart communication with those you seek to reach but for its beauty, complexity, rhythm, and unique expression. This latter approach results in the missionary who effectively and almost effortlessly communicates the gospel and love of Christ for his hearers. This is akin to the difference between a pianist who has the skill to mechanically play the notes of the music and the one who has the music in his heart and soul; it becomes a part of him and flows through him. Some missionaries fail to learn the language well for a host of reasons, but the degree to which they do not know it well often correlates directly to their ineffectiveness in ministry.

Learning the new language well is the first step, learning to use it appropriately is the second, and both steps are essential. This is easily illustrated in the dialect prejudice we find in our own cultures. Those who live in the deep South may pejoratively prejudge someone with a "Yankee" accent, while those from the northern parts of the USA may prejudge a person who speaks with a thick southern drawl or a "redneck" accent. Imagine the ministry implications of a person who comes to the USA to serve as a missionary among a highly educated population in the Northeast but who learns English among the heavily accented Cajuns of Louisiana or the southern drawl of those in the Mississippi delta.

In the same way, societal groups and cultures that consider themselves the highest class will be reticent to accept "truth" from an unknown person who speaks with an accent of the lower class. The rich and powerful influential classes of Latin America tend to look down on the indigenous peoples. Speaking Spanish with the accent of an indigenous person will negatively impact one's ministry among the elite classes. Where will you study the language when you get to the field? It should be as much of a factor as the language you need to learn.

Speaking at the appropriate volume, using idioms, humor, and turn-taking correctly in conversations will help the missionary fit in well. This is only learned in context and living life completely immersed in another culture. Students of Spanish throughout high school and college frequently only know how other gringos speak Spanish—not the unique colloquialisms and the rhythm of verbal expression of native speakers in the many and diverse cultures that speak Spanish.

As we have seen, each culture has its own worldview, beliefs, values, and systems of behavior. Culture is not synonymous with worldview; rather, they share a symbiotic relationship—each influencing (and being influenced by) the other. Whatever system we use to explain reality, where we came from, where we go when we die, where disease comes from, what the basic purpose of life is and so on, is our worldview, but we received it from others around us as we enculturated. This worldview in turn causes us to live in certain ways, embrace certain religions, marry, and bury in the ways that are part and parcel of our unique culture.

The point here is that, as Richard Weaver has insightfully observed, ideas have consequences.[5] What people perceive to be ultimate truth will determine the religions they develop and how they live. What they value as beautiful will guide their expressions of art, fashion, and music. All of these basic foundations will guide them in the rules of the game of life regarding behavior—ethical treatment of others—and they will continue to change as new developments require consensus behavior.

Intercultural communication refers to the skills that facilitate clear communication in a culture that is not your own. Think of culture and worldview as the operating system of a computer. You may have a "Mac brain" and find yourself serving as a missionary in a culture made up of "PC brains." The ways these computers operate both require electricity, programming, and software, and may seek to fulfill the same basic goals; but they do so differently. Unless some adjustment is made, there will not be a clear and successful outcome in the interchange.

Imagine someone encountering the problem $10 + 5 = $ _____ on a math test. If they answer $10 + 5 = 3$, it would be wrong and marked incorrect. However, if the student encounters the problem in a "Learning to Tell Time" class, his answer would be correct. How many colors are there in the rainbow? How many days of the week are there? Some cultures recognize only two colors, others four, six, or seven. Some cultures do not count above three and hence do not number the days of the week as seven. Communication in such cultures must take into account the worldview, not merely the language, as if we need only concern ourselves with grammar and vocabulary.

When medical missionaries arrive in new cultures, they find they are faced with challenges they never had to consider. Now, in addition to the diagnosis and treatment of disease and injuries that are scientifically quantifiable, the physician must consider how to persuade a patient with an infection to take one pill per day for ten days when the patient believes his disease is the result of his ancestors' anger or a curse from an enemy's shaman. The patient wonders why these pills will appease their

---

[5] Richard Weaver, *Ideas Have Consequences* (Chicago: University of Chicago Press, 1984).

great-grandfather or counteract the spirit darts of a long-distance curse. A prescription for guaranteed failure would be to send out medical missionaries who are totally unaware that these challenges exist, and without teaching them that these beliefs are just as real in the patient's mind as the conclusions of a lab's blood tests are in the doctor's mind.

Learning language well and learning to use it in culturally appropriate ways are essential, as we have seen. Yet learning to use it effectively in context requires learning all of the forms of nonverbal communication, which is simply all the ways that we can communicate without actually using words. Edward Sapir wrote that we respond to gestures "in accordance with an elaborate code that is written nowhere, known by none, and understood by all."[6] Just as silence communicates a powerful message, so does touching someone's shoulder while speaking. In some contexts this is a helpful gesture that communicates sincerity, while in others it is an unwelcome and inappropriate advance.

Edward T. Hall was one of the first to address this aspect of nonverbal communication and write extensively about it.[7] He realized that the ways we communicate are more powerful than the words themselves. Studies on nonverbal communication demonstrate how important it is that missionaries learn it in order to influence the culture most effectively. In two different studies, researchers found that the majority of information taken from human interaction is nonverbal, revealing its astonishing level of importance. They found that the majority of meaning is communicated through facial and vocal expressions, not only the words we use:

- Facial Expressions: 55 percent
- Paralanguage (the way the words are said): 38 percent
- Verbal (the words themselves): 7 percent[8]

[6] Edward Sapir, *The Collected Works of Edward Sapir: Culture, Society, and Individual* (Berlin: Mouton de Gruyter Publisher, 1999), 169.

[7] For additional information see *The Silent Language* (1959, 1981; repr., New York: Anchor, 1990), *The Hidden Dimension* (1969, 1982; repr., Anchor, 1990), and *The Dance of Life* (1983; repr., Anchor, 1984).

[8] See A. Mehrabian and M. Wiener, "Decoding of Inconsistent Communications," *Journal of Personality and Social Psychology* 6 (1967): 109–14; and A. Mehrabian and S. R. Ferris, "Inference of Attitudes from Nonverbal Communication in Two Channels," *Journal of Consulting Psychology* 31, no. 3 (1967): 48–258.

The words we speak communicate, but the specific word choice, facial expression, appearance, tone of voice (paralanguage), and accompanying gestures can strengthen or negate the surface meaning. You may strongly affirm your rights as a citizen, responding to a speech at a political rally by shouting, "Yeah. Right!" Or you may skeptically respond to a friend's remark that you have just won a million dollars by saying the same words but in a way that negates the meaning of both words. Short-term missions volunteers to Latin America sometimes will overhear the word *gringo* and ask if it is a derisive term. The answer usually depends, however, on the tone of voice and the facial expression of the person who said it. It could be a term of endearment or a pejorative term reserved for disliked North Americans.

Missiologist Donald K. Smith has a helpful insight to what he terms the Twelve-Signal System for communication.[9] You have learned how to use all twelve signals in your home culture, and you do so daily without even realizing it. Only one of the twelve signals is the language. As we have already seen, language is used differently, and dialects or accents may sometimes nuance meanings that are unintended. The reality of this, seen in the relationship of the USA and England, has been observed by many, including Winston Churchill, who is noted to have said, "We are two countries divided by a common language." Just as speaking English among non-English speakers will not communicate what you desire, each of the other eleven signals in the system must be studied to know how it is used in a new context. The twelve signals Smith recounts are:

1. Verbal—speech of the language itself (English, German, Spanish, Mandarin)
2. Written—symbols that represent speech (alphabets, Chinese characters)
3. Numeric—numbers and number systems (biblical numerology, police radio)
4. Pictorial—two-dimensional representations (No Smoking, Airport Exit)

---

[9] Donald K. Smith, *Creating Understanding* (Grand Rapids: Zondervan, 1992), 120.

5. Artifactual—three-dimensional representations and objects (uniforms, wedding rings)
6. Audio—use of nonverbal sounds and silence (school bells, alarm clocks)
7. Kinesic—body motions, facial expressions, posture (ballet, eye contact, slouching)
8. Optical—light and color (lighting in plays, white for weddings and black at funerals)
9. Tactile—touch and the sense of feel (touching another's shoulder or arm)
10. Spatial—use of space (distance apart in intimate, casual, or public speaking)
11. Temporal—use of time (making someone wait, being "on time")
12. Olfactory—taste and smell (perfume, scented candles)[10]

We may communicate using any one of these systems in isolation, but we rarely do. More often we combine them into communication complexes that require really knowing the cultural nuances to discern a meaning. We all know how to use them at home, but when we use them all that same way in other cultures, we will miscommunicate. Many new missionaries realize their immediate need to learn the language, but only after unfortunate and unfruitful struggles in their interaction with others in their new culture do they realize the power of these nonverbal communication systems.

Some of the most powerful and commonly misused forms of communication are hand gestures. It is possible to reinforce a spoken message with a gesture. For instance, "Come on, hurry!" may be more emphatically communicated by rapidly and repeatedly waving your hand toward you from the waist to the face, or you can ask someone to wait while holding your hand at shoulder height palm outward. You may say, "OK!" and complement the phrase with a hand gesture of making a circle with the thumb and index finger with other fingers outstretched. All of these could miscommunicate and may be greatly offensive in some other cultures. We use gestures to substitute verbal

---

[10] Ibid., 122.

communication at times. Each of the above gestures communicates even without the spoken word. "Come," "Wait," and "OK" are all commonly used gestures. In fact, we use them almost subconsciously, such as when the librarian hears a noise or whisper and almost reflexively raises her index finger to her lips.

Offensive gestures, such as the middle finger in our culture, communicate strongly and elicit an immediate unconscious visceral response. Imagine being in a culture that uses the raised middle finger to greet and wish you good health. Rounding the corner in an office building, you bump into someone who gives you a raised middle finger and continues down the hallway. You immediately experience anger, offense, indignation, or all of the above. Only when you remember that their intentions are completely innocent can you smooth your ruffled feathers.

The fact is, missionaries often unwittingly offend others through similar actions. Examples of such things are touching them with the left hand in countries where that hand is for personal hygiene and hence unclean, touching a Thai child on the head, which is a sacred part of their body, hugging people to greet them in nontactile cultures, or touching a member of the opposite sex in Muslim cultures.

Making eye contact when speaking in the West communicates honesty and frankness, but in other cultures it may be taken as a challenge to fight, indicate sexual interest, or communicate a lack of respect. Just as missionaries must learn the most adequate dialect of the spoken language, and learn to use it well, they must also learn the many nonverbal ways humans communicate and make the adjustments to their patterns of communicating when serving in another culture.

Using the language correctly in context is the key to clear communication. The contextual use of language is the key to being truly bilingual and bicultural. Learning the language is the key to learning the culture, and learning the culture is the key to language learning. Trying to learn one without the other will always fall short. The effective missionary learns the language and the culture and seeks to fit in. When the missionary does not fit in, especially in those situations where the missionary is all the culture knows about Christianity, nationals often assume that Jesus does not fit their culture either; to the degree that missionary is offensive to the culture, Jesus will be too. Remember, the missionary is the messenger and lives out Christianity before them. How do we make Christianity at home in the cultures of the world?

CONTEXTUALIZATION

The most basic explanation of *contextualization* is taking something from one place and putting it in another while retaining faithfulness and sensitivity to the original intent of the thing. For our purposes, contextualization is communicating the gospel, planting churches, discipling others, training leaders, and establishing Christianity in other areas of the world while being both faithful to God's Word and sensitive to the culture. Although a relatively new term in Christianity, the word has a turbulent history and is frequently the source of much controversy because different levels and theories of contextualization are found among missionaries today. Before we begin to explore some of the controversial forms, we should make sure we understand some ways we all contextualize without hesitation.

Traveling to other countries requires us to fit into the local culture to survive. My wife and I were recently in England, where visitors from the USA must adapt to the road rules quickly because cars drive in the left lane there. As I travel around the world, I find that every culture has its own form of "comfort food," eating at times of day dictated by a rhythm that everyone seems to accept as normal, such as the evening meal at 9:00 or 10:00 p.m. in Madrid, or enjoying foods common to me but strange to imagine on my plate at certain times of the day, such as minced fish and onions for breakfast in Trinidad. Even forms of greetings are quickly learned, and after a mistake or two, we thrill at the cultural surprises of a vacation abroad. Our response may be merely a shrug and a halfhearted, "Well, when in Rome . . . ," but these are all forms of contextualization to which we learn to adjust when traveling.

Many of you have made the transition from living at home and attending high school to living in a dorm and being away at college. Thinking back on the trials and difficulties, as well as the fun and excitement at times, all this transition required is another example of adjusting to a new culture. Your experience was probably streamlined by the fact that almost all of the people in your college were from your own cultural background, spoke your language, and were undergoing the same stress of adjustment as you. Still, it required an adjustment period and some new patterns of daily living as well. To one degree or another, such changes are required when we change jobs, eat with another family, or begin visiting a church of another denomination. In a new culture it is often difficult to know who is who or what to do without a life program with some explanatory information.

Pastors who are nervous about contextualization are actually involved in it to some degree all the time. When they preach the same message to different audiences, they are contextualizing the message to each setting. They may share Sunday morning's message in the children's sermon, in the preaching hour, to the shut-ins at the nursing home on Monday, and to a youth group on Friday; and every time they share it, the delivery style and perhaps even vocabulary should be nuanced to the particular group.

Contextualization in international settings requires us to consider worldviews, languages, legal matters, and a host of other factors that may require some adjustment to our delivery style. For instance, in countries where Christian church buildings are illegal or worship on Sunday is forbidden, churches may meet in homes on Friday or Saturday. Certainly the language of delivery would not be English in a country that speaks a different language, but as we have seen, the language is not all that must be adjusted for clear communication.

The biblical basis of contextualization is seen in 1 Corinthians 9:20–23. The apostle Paul stated:

> To the Jews I became as a Jew, in order to win Jews. To those under the law I became as one under the law (though not being myself under the law) that I might win those under the law. To those outside the law I became as one outside the law (not being outside the law of God but under the law of Christ) that I might win those outside the law. To the weak I became weak, that I might win the weak. I have become all things to all people, that by all means I might save

> some. I do it all for the sake of the gospel, that I
> may share with them in its blessings.

Here we see Paul's use of contextualization as well as the limits of such. He says he does it all for the sake of the gospel. If some aspect of your contextualization practices would bring offense or reproach to Christ and his Word, you must not do it. We contextualize so as to be faithful to the gospel while being sensitive enough to the culture as to help them understand it and to understand that they do not have to leave their own culture to embrace another to be saved. Darrell Whiteman recounted hearing a Thai Christian marveling after years of being a Christian and finally learning this truth: "I am realizing that I can be both Christian and Thai."[11]

The controversial aspects of contextualization begin where missionaries disagree on the extent to which they may make the gospel fit in the culture. Some missionaries evangelize Muslims using the Qur'an in the initial stages of evangelism because it speaks of the historical Isa (Jesus) and uses the name Allah to refer to the God of the Bible and because the local language has only that word as the name for God. Christian churches meet on Fridays, with worshippers who wash their face and hands at the door, leave their shoes outside, sit on rugs instead of pews, and call themselves Muslims who follow Jesus. This causes many to become uncomfortable and nervous about overcontextualization. However, the controversy does not stop there; indeed, it really only begins there.

In recent efforts to advance the kingdom among Muslims, some missionaries have begun referring to themselves as Muslims because the term simply means "one who submits," and they reason that they submit to God. When it is countered that *Muslim* means "one who submits to Allah," they respond that they use the name *Allah* to refer to the God of the Bible, so there is still no problem. Others will even recite the Muslim creed, "There is no God but Allah, and Mohammed is the prophet of Allah," defending this practice with the above argument and adding to it that a prophet is one who speaks *for* God,

---

[11] Darrell L. Whiteman, "Contextualization: The Theory, the Gap, the Challenge," accessed August 28, 2012, http://www.spu.edu/temp/denuol/context.htm.

and Mohammed certainly did, whether they accept everything he said as truly *from* God or not.

While it may not appear so at first, ecclesiology (the doctrine of the church) is crucial to understand and address this point for contextualization. Some have argued that the essence of a church is the social network of relationships in a society. They continue that this social network of relationships is what must not be disrupted if Christianity is ever to make any inroads in the non-Christian areas of the world. One missiologist has said, "The 'church' (i.e. committed community) is already there, they just don't know Jesus yet."[12] Their desire is to add Jesus to the existing religions of such peoples with the belief that this will complete the Muslim adherent.

Although there is certainly reason to be concerned and question some of these practices, we must acknowledge that missionaries of differing opinions champion their particular efforts because they love the Lord and want to see his kingdom advance and not from some sinister plot to undermine and overthrow Christian missions.

How can we clearly communicate the gospel without simply replicating our home church on one hand *or* letting the process go too far on the other? Eugene Nida and David Hesselgrave, among other missionary anthropologists, have suggested a tricultural model of communicating the gospel.[13] This model could also be applied in planting churches, training pastors, or living the Christian life before a watching world. After all, Jesus did not call us to take potted plants of churches to other countries but, rather, to plant the pure seed of the gospel in the soil of the target culture and allow the Holy Spirit to grow the plant or tree that he desires to see. The three cultures of the tricultural model of communication are the biblical cultures, the missionary's home culture, and the target people's culture.

The Holy Spirit inspired the Bible to be written through about forty human authors, over about 1,500 years, in at least three languages. Scripture represents many cultures in its

---

[12] Tim and Rebecca Lewis, "Planting Churches: Learning the Hard Way," *Mission Frontiers* (January/February 2009), 18.

[13] See David Hesselgrave, *Communicating Christ Cross-Culturally* (Grand Rapids: Zondervan, 1991), 107–8; Eugene Nida, *Message and Mission: The Communication of the Christian Faith*, rev. ed. (Pasadena: William Carey Library Publishers, 1990), 52–53.

pages: Egyptian, Roman, Babylonian, and all those of Asia Minor. The kinds of cultures, languages, styles of literature, and backgrounds of authors and recipients are all crucial to understand for rightly interpreting and applying the Word of God.

Likewise, the missionary must understand his own culture and how it has interpreted and applied God's Word as normative in his home church. Some churches in the United States wash one another's feet when they partake of the Lord's Supper; others do not, but they partake of the Lord's Supper every time they meet. Some Christian women wear a head covering while others do not, but they remain silent in church. Some greet male and female members alike with a holy kiss. All claim biblical warrant for the way they "do church," while others believe certain admonitions were cultural, and today we have different forms to mean the same things.

What a church practices as the proper interpretation and application of any passage is repeated around the world ethnocentrically by its missionaries unless they stop to examine the Bible's meaning and how and why their church has applied the teaching in their context. Indeed, it is not uncommon to see red-brick churches with stained-glass windows and pews in countries where everyone lives in mud huts with thatch roofs.

Paul G. Hiebert recounted the historical pendulum swings of Christianity's approach to contextualization.[14] He related that the early days of the modern missionary movement walked hand in hand with the age of colonialism. As nations staked their claim on the nations and territories of the world, establishing their rule and footprint in every land, they also established churches. Those nations with a state church—such as the Anglicans of England, Lutherans of Germany, and Catholics of Spain and Portugal—naturally established their churches, seminaries, and clergy in the countries they claimed. They did not study local cultures to understand them, as to be more equipped to persuade people to believe. Existing culture was rather something to be replaced so that civilization, commerce, and Christianity might reign in their "proper" forms. This era was obviously one of noncontextualization.

---

[14] Paul Hiebert, *Anthropological Reflections on Missiological Reflections* (Grand Rapids: Baker Academic, 1994), 75–92.

The second era was an overcorrection to this error. As the social sciences developed and taught the world to understand more about languages and the diverse peoples of the world, an infatuation with cultures began to swing the pendulum back the other way. In the new era the world was enamored with people groups and cultures. Anthropologists believed that if a culture considered certain kinds of murder to be good and culturally appropriate, then it was OK for them to do so, even though the same action would be condemned in another culture. Each culture was studied as a universe to itself; it was considered unjust and unfair to apply one system of ethics or religion equally to all. This extreme pendulum swing carried many into the heresy of pluralism, believing that all religions had equal value.

Hiebert explained that the best approach would be a critical contextualization. In his view many missionaries operated on a surface perception that either allowed or forbade practices that they did not even understand, only to learn later that they had embraced sinful practices while forbidding innocuous aspects. Hiebert presented a simple four-step process that missionaries could follow and find culturally appropriate expressions of Christianity that were faithful to God's Word.[15]

First, he suggests that the missionary study to exegete the culture; i.e., seek to know it and understand what they are doing and why they are doing what they do. Second, study the Word of God, note where God (not your home church necessarily) speaks to some cultural practice as sinful. Third, study the passage in the hermeneutical community of fellow believers and then lead them to see what God says about this practice and challenge them to face it in light of his Word. Finally, guide them into a new contextualized practice that will serve as a functional substitute for the sinful practice. In this way they will have ownership in the new practice, and it will be seen to be God's Word guiding them and not merely the foreign missionary. When this four-step process is not followed and the missionary simply dictates new practices, Christianity will seem to be a misfit in the target culture and that those within the people group must leave their culture to embrace Christ. When this four-step critical contextualization *is* implemented, the missionary may

---

[15] Ibid.

evangelize, disciple, plant churches, train leaders, and correct sinful patterns in society in effective ways that are faithful to God's Word and sensitive to culture.

CONCLUSION

Just as we began by acknowledging that missionaries *will* learn about the cultures they seek to reach, either by trial and error or careful study, we conclude by reiterating this foundational reality. We should always seek to ensure that Scripture informs culture and not the reverse, but we must carefully examine our own expressions of Christianity in light of the pure teaching of God's Word. When we do, we will likely find extrabiblical, cultural applications we have accepted as normative alongside firm biblical teachings that must not be compromised. Only through a careful and thorough understanding of God's Word, as well as the target culture, can we be sure we do not create unnecessary stumbling blocks to the cross. Jesus became man and walked among us. Paul became as the Jew to the Jew and the Greek to the Greek. Likewise, we must understand and identify with those we seek to reach. By doing so, we will witness more effectively.

RESOURCES FOR FURTHER STUDY

Hesselgrave, David. *Communicating Christ Cross-Culturally.* Grand Rapids: Zondervan, 1991.

Hiebert, Paul G. *Anthropological Insights for Missionaries.* Grand Rapids: Baker, 1985.

Hofstede, Gert Jan, Paul B. Pedersen, and Geert H. Hofstede. *Exploring Culture: Exercises, Stories and Synthetic Cultures.* Yarmouth, ME: Intercultural Press, 2002.

Nida, Eugene. *Customs and Cultures.* Pasadena: William Carey Library, 1975.

Smith, Donald K. *Creating Understanding.* Grand Rapids: Zondervan, 1992.

CHAPTER 8

WORLD RELIGIONS

INTRODUCTION

There was a time when most people in the Western world only knew other people within a narrow religious spectrum. Protestants might know Catholics, and in the larger cities Christians might know Jews, but that was as far as religious diversity went in the experience of most people. Adherents of other faiths were perceived as foreign, experienced vicariously through the media, but unknown personally. While American Christians have known the growing psychological pressure of secular materialism for decades, they have not faced the pressure of having friends whose deeply held religious convictions are entirely outside the Judeo-Christian stream of thought. Only a few decades ago, all American military chaplains fell into one of the three categories of Protestant, Catholic, or Jew, and the most exotic members of the chaplain corps were Greek Orthodox or Mormon. Today Muslim and Buddhist chaplains serve in the American military. Even an average-sized city like Louisville, Kentucky, in the American heartland, has a Hindu temple and multiple Buddhist temples and Muslim mosques. The small town of Somerset, in rural, southeastern Kentucky, has a population of a little more than 11,000, but now Muslims live in Somerset and work in the local regional hospital. Religious pluralism is now the normal experience of most American Christians.

Obviously the experience of living around people from different religious backgrounds has always been common to missionaries. In the evangelical sense of the word, a missionary is someone who crosses ethnic, cultural, and/or linguistic barriers to share the gospel of Jesus Christ with those who do not yet know him. Inside the Western world many of those who need to be evangelized come from a nominal Christian or secularized background. Most of the people in the world with no access to the gospel, on the other hand, are Muslims, Hindus, Buddhists, or animists. They are either active practitioners of these faiths or at least come from cultural backgrounds steeped in them. The cutting edge of the advance of the gospel lies within the context of the other great religions of the world.

What should Christians think of other religions? Popular culture in the West, dominated by relativism and desiring to be nice, shuns the truth question altogether. Committed secularists regard all religions as equally invalid. The more popular position is to regard all religions as somehow equally valid. Asserting that one is valid at the expense of others is regarded as arrogant, rude, indefensible, and potentially dangerous. Under pressure from this cultural orthodoxy, many evangelical Christians find themselves most comfortable with a form of inclusivism that maintains the truth of the gospel but finds room for adherents of other faiths to be saved. We have already argued that this position is biblically untenable.[1] At the other end of the spectrum, there are Christians who regard members of other faiths with suspicion and even hatred. What is the biblical way through this issue?

A BIBLICAL THEOLOGY OF NONBIBLICAL RELIGION

The Old Testament begins with the clear message that there is one, and only one, God. He existed before all things, and everything other than God was created by him. When God delivered his people out of slavery in Egypt and gave them his law on Mount Sinai, he began the Ten Commandments with a clear statement of his exclusivity.

---

[1] See chap. 4.

> I am the LORD your God, who brought
> you out of the land of Egypt, out of the house
> of slavery.
> You shall have no other gods before me.
> You shall not make for yourselves a carved
> image, or any likeness of anything that is in
> heaven above, or that is in the earth beneath, or
> that is in the water under the earth. You shall
> not bow down to them or serve them, for I the
> LORD your God am a jealous God. (Exod 20:2–5)

The first commandment forbids the worship of any god other than the Lord God who delivered Israel out of slavery. The second commandment prohibits using any images in worship, whether of the true God or of other gods. The people of God are strictly forbidden from any participation in any religious worship or allegiance other than the biblically prescribed worship of the one and only God who saved them.

Other warnings against worshipping other gods follow in the law. Exodus 20:23 says, "You shall not make gods of silver to be with me, nor shall you make for yourselves gods of gold." Worship of other gods was a capital offense: "Whoever sacrifices to any god, other than the LORD alone, shall be devoted to destruction" (Exod 22:20). God also told his people when he led them into the land of the Canaanites, "You shall not bow down to their gods nor serve them, nor do as they do, but you shall utterly overthrow them and break their pillars in pieces" (Exod 23:24). The sordid episode of the golden calf reinforced the prohibition against any worship other than worshipping the true God in the right way (Exodus 32). Afterward God made clear that his people were to have nothing to do with the religious practices of the peoples around them. Those religions were not alternate ways to know the real God, nor were they conduits of salvation. They were evil.

> You shall tear down their altars and break
> their pillars and cut down their Asherim (for
> you shall worship no other god, for the LORD,
> whose name is Jealous, is a jealous God), lest
> you make a covenant with the inhabitants of the
> land, and when they whore after their gods and

sacrifice to their gods and you are invited, you
eat of his sacrifice, and you take of their daughters for your sons, and their daughters whore
after their gods and make your sons whore after
their gods.

You shall not make for yourself any gods of
cast metal. (Exod 34:13–17)

The same message is repeated again and again in the law of
God. There is only one God, and he expects the exclusive worship, allegiance, and obedience of his people.

The prophets were sent by God to the people of Israel to call
them back to this exclusive relationship with God. In the book of
Kings, the rulers of the northern kingdom of Israel were all condemned for tolerating idolatry, and those of the kings of Judah
who came under censure were condemned for the same thing.
Exclusive loyalty to the Lord God and obedience to his law were
the criteria by which their reigns were judged. The prophets
consistently condemned the syncretism that characterized the
religious life of Israel. It was not enough to worship the true God
in company with other gods. He had to be worshipped alone. It
was not that the prophets regarded the gods of the nations as
real gods. The prophets were, after all, committed monotheists.
However, they did not regard nonbiblical religion benignly. They
recognized that idolaters attributed to their false gods the attributes and characteristics of deity. One of the most biting bits of
satire in the Bible is Isaiah's description of idol-worship:

All who fashion idols are nothing, and the
things they delight in do not profit. Their witnesses neither see nor know, that they may be
put to shame. Who fashions a god or casts an
idol that is profitable for nothing? Behold, all
his companions shall be put to shame, and the
craftsmen are only human. Let them all assem-
ble, let them stand forth. They shall be terrified;
they shall be put to shame together.

The ironsmith takes a cutting tool and works
it over the coals. He fashions it with hammers
and works it with his strong arm. He becomes
hungry, and his strength fails; he drinks no

water and is faint. The carpenter stretches a line; he marks it out with a pencil. He shapes it with planes and marks it with a compass. He shapes it into the figure of a man, with the beauty of a man, to dwell in a house. He cuts down cedars, or he chooses a cypress tree or an oak and lets it grow strong among the trees of the forest. He plants a cedar and the rain nourishes it. Then it becomes fuel for a man. He takes a part of it and warms himself; he kindles a fire and bakes bread. Also he makes a god and worships it; he makes it an idol and falls down before it. Half of it he burns in the fire. Over the half he eats meat; he roasts it and is satisfied. Also he warms himself and says, "Aha, I am warm, I have seen the fire!" And the rest of it he makes into a god, his idol, and falls down to it and worships it. He prays to it and says, "Deliver me, for you are my god!"

They know not, nor do they discern, for he has shut their eyes, so that they cannot see, and their hearts, so that they cannot understand. No one considers, nor is there knowledge or discernment to say, "Half of it I burned in the fire; I also baked bread on its coals; I roasted meat and have eaten. And shall I make the rest of it an abomination? Shall I fall down before a block of wood?" He feeds on ashes; a deluded heart has led him astray, and he cannot deliver himself or say, "Is there not a lie in my right hand?" (Isa 44:9–20)

With the rest of the prophets, Isaiah regarded the gods of the nations around Israel as no gods at all, but they were a malignant nothing, not a harmless one. Compromise with or participation in any religion other than that revealed in Scripture was a horrible evil.

The same themes run through the Psalms. Psalm 96:5 says, "For all the gods of the peoples are worthless idols, but the LORD made the heavens." Psalm 115 contrasts the living God with the false gods of the nations:

Our God is in the heavens;
he does all that he pleases.
Their idols are silver and gold,
the work of human hands.
They have mouths, but do not speak;
eyes, but do not see.
They have ears, but do not hear;
noses, but do not smell.
They have hands, but do not feel;
feet, but do not walk;
and they do not make a sound in their throat.
Those who make them become like them,
so do all who trust in them. (Ps 115:3–8)

The psalmist does not entertain any hopeful thoughts about nonbiblical religion. Instead, he contrasts true religion from false in uncompromising terms. Our God is in heaven, and he does whatever he pleases. In contrast, their idols are inanimate and useless. Idolaters are far from being saved by their religious sincerity; they become as lifeless as their gods.

In summary, exclusive fidelity to the Lord God of Israel is one of the huge, overriding lessons of the Old Testament. God is a jealous God, and he should be. He will not share his glory with another. Furthermore, his name matters. It is not a neutral, interchangeable symbol. It represents his identity and his character. The God of the Old Testament is not an abstract deity but a specific, particular, personal God. He must be worshipped and served on his terms, as he has made himself known. Other religions are deadly and must be rejected at all costs.

The New Testament assumes the Old and reaffirms it. Idolatry is condemned, not embraced. Paul denounced it as folly in his letter to the Romans: "Claiming to be wise, they became fools, and exchanged the glory of the immortal God for images resembling mortal men and birds and animals and reptiles" (Rom 1:22–23). In his first letter to the church in Corinth, he discussed the question of whether Christians may eat meat that has been sacrificed to idols. He acknowledged that idols have no real spiritual existence (1 Cor 8:4). However, he regarded participation in idol worship as deadly so that if someone thought of himself as participating in such worship by eating such meat, he could be spiritually destroyed. He actually regarded pagan religion as demonic.

> What do I imply then? That food offered to idols is anything, or that an idol is anything? No, I imply that what pagans sacrifice they offer to demons and not to God. I do not want you to be participants with demons. You cannot drink the cup of the Lord and the cup of demons. You cannot partake of the table of the Lord and the table of demons. Shall we provoke the Lord to jealousy? Are we stronger than he? (1 Cor 10:19–22)

It is no wonder he tells the Corinthian Christians to flee from idolatry (cf. 1 Cor 10:14).

Conversion, as Paul understood it, involved turning away from previous religious allegiances as well as turning to the gospel. He described the conversion of the Thessalonian Christians in exactly those terms: "You turned to God from idols to serve the living and true God" (1 Thess 1:9). Christ cannot be added to another religious system, nor can he be accessed through another religious system. He is Lord alone, and he is Lord entirely on his own terms.

All of this biblical data up to this point has been aimed at the grossly immoral polytheism of the ancient world. What about ethical monism such as found in Buddhism and some forms of Hinduism? What about Islam, which purports to worship the same God as Christians, which rejects all forms of idolatry, and which enjoins a high level of morality on its adherents? What about Judaism, which is rooted in the Old Testament Scriptures God inspired? The perspective of the New Testament on Judaism gives a definitive answer to these questions. If any religion could be regarded as having some level of ongoing validity before God, it would be Judaism. However, the New Testament is unapologetically Christocentric. Jews as well as Gentiles are under condemnation for sin and are saved by faith in Jesus alone (Romans 1–3). Judaism alone, of all non-Christian religions, can be completed in Christ without having to jettison its Scriptures because God inspired those Scriptures. However, the New Testament gives the authoritative interpretation of the Old Testament, and that interpretation finds the fulfillment of everything in the Hebrew Bible in Christ. That understanding of the Old Testament must be embraced. Rabbinic Judaism, as it has developed over the centuries, has gone far down other paths, and those paths must be abandoned on coming to Christ. Perhaps the most revealing portion of the New Testament on the question of other religions is the book of Hebrews. This letter was written to Christians who were tempted, under pressure, to revert to Judaism. Even that is out of bounds. Judaism has no meaning or value except as it is fulfilled in Christ, and now that he has come, the types and shadows of Jewish religion have lost all validity. If that is true of Judaism, how much more is it true of religions that are not rooted in God's self-revelation in Scripture?

The message of Scripture is consistent. God is a jealous, exclusive God. That jealousy is consistent with his identity as the only true God and as the ultimate good. His goal in creation, redemption, and judgment is his own glory, and it should be. Anything else is idolatry on his part.[2] He will not share his glory with another. His name matters. Nonbiblical religion is a result of the fall of humanity, not a fruit of common grace.[3] Even the truth that may be found in other religions is found in the context of unbiblical worldviews. Non-Christian religions are not sources of revelation or salvation. They are error that must be corrected and replaced by the gospel.

Does this mean that Christians should hate or fear members of other religions? No. Contemporary society finds it difficult to understand how it is possible to love someone and regard them as wrong at the same time, but Christians are called to exactly this posture. Christ commanded us to love our neighbors as ourselves, and the parable he told to illustrate what he meant involved a Samaritan, a follower of a false religion. He also commanded us to love our enemies, to pray for them, and to do good to them. God loves the world that is in rebellion against him, and we are commanded to be like him. Christians must love Muslims and Hindus and Buddhists and Jews and proponents

---

[2] John Piper, *Let the Nations Be Glad* (Grand Rapids: Baker Academic, 2003), 31.
[3] This is the contention of the inclusivist Clark Pinnock in *A Wideness in God's Mercy: The Finality of Jesus Christ in a World of Religions* (Grand Rapids: Zondervan, 1992), 23–33; but Todd Miles demonstrates the fallacy of this argument in *A God of Many Understandings?* (Nashville: B&H Academic, 2010), 215–17.

of all other religions. If they fail to do so, they are in sin. They must love them even if they are persecuting Christians. However, Christians must not love other religions, and they must never compromise with them.

This, then, is the biblical perspective on other religions. Everything the Bible teaches is true, and true knowledge of God is not possible except through what he has revealed in his Word. Salvation comes through the gospel of Jesus Christ and nowhere else. That gospel must be heard and believed for any sinner to be saved. Other religions may have remnants of truth within them. They may display some measure of beauty and dignity. They may serve to restrain some of the excesses of lawlessness. However, they are neither means of knowing God nor vehicles of salvation. Christians should love all people, including adherents of other religions. Christians should seek the welfare of those outside the body of Christ. At the deepest level, however, seeking their welfare means seeking their salvation. The teaching of the Bible on nonbiblical religion is a powerful motivation for missions. The most loving thing we can do for any non-Christian is to share the gospel with them and to pray for their salvation because without faith in Christ they are eternally lost.

THE GREAT RELIGIONS OF THE WORLD

What follows is a brief survey of the world's great religions. Obviously, in a book such as this, only a cursory treatment will be given, but at the end of the chapter resources are listed for further reading.

Judaism

Modern Judaism has its roots in the Bible. Jesus was a Jew, as were all of his apostles and most of the writers of the New Testament. Initially, Old Testament worship was focused on the temple in Jerusalem, and Mosaic law forbade offering sacrifices anywhere else.[4] The destruction of the temple in 586 BC, and the Babylonian exile that followed, forced a major shift in the religious practices of the Jews. Many of the features of modern Judaism began to emerge at this point in history. Unlike the exiles

---

[4] The failure to keep this requirement was a component of the indictment the prophets brought against Israel in the period leading up to the Babylonian exile.

from the northern kingdom who were deported by the Assyrians after 722 BC, the exiles from the southern kingdom of Judah resisted assimilation and maintained their religious identity.

One of the most important institutions they developed in this new environment was the synagogue. The synagogue was not a temple. No sacrifices were held in synagogues. Rather, it was a place of prayer and teaching. It became the centerpiece of Jewish community life. Synagogues developed during the period of the exile, which formally lasted until 538 BC, and they continued even after temple worship was resumed with permission from the Persians. A large population of Jews remained in exile, scattered across the ancient world, and for them the synagogue was absolutely central. Even the Jews who returned to Palestine, however, continued the practice of forming and meeting in synagogues. A synagogue requires a quorum (*minyan*) of ten Jewish men. The synagogue service became formal and liturgical over the years, with set prayers for various occasions. Reading and teaching from the Hebrew Scriptures are also a prominent part of synagogue worship. A new type of religious leader emerged: the rabbi. Unlike the temple priests, rabbis do not need to be descendants of Aaron, and, also unlike the priests, they do not have a sacrificial or mediatorial function. The rabbi was primarily a student and teacher of the Hebrew Scriptures, as he remains to this day.

The lesson of the exile was learned well. Exclusive loyalty to God and obedience to his law became hallmarks of postexilic Judaism. Numerous movements emerged within Judaism in the centuries between the return from Babylon and the time of Christ, such as the Sadducees, the Essenes, and the Zealots. The people who placed their lasting stamp on Judaism, however, were the Pharisees. The other groups died out or were exterminated when Jerusalem fell and the temple was destroyed again in AD 70. Pharisaic Judaism survived and became normative. The rabbis, out of concern for obedience to God's law, constructed a fence of rules and practices around the Commandments to guarantee that even inadvertent disobedience was impossible. Hence, the simple command of the law, "You shall not boil a young goat in its mother's milk" (Deut 14:21) became the complex set of rules for kosher cooking, including separate dishes, that completely separate meat preparation from all contact with dairy products. The full codification of this set of rules and practices became the Talmud, a multivolume work consisting of commentary on the law and application of it. The Talmud became the defining document of rabbinic Judaism from late antiquity to the modern period.

In the modern era Orthodox Judaism continues to be a significant force in the Jewish community. Orthodox Jews are often known for their distinctive dress, their strict adherence to kosher dietary laws, and their serious observance of the Sabbath. However, orthodoxy is no longer the sole expression of Jewish faith and practice. Reform Judaism is much more open to accommodation with the surrounding culture. Reform Jews place little emphasis on the Talmud, and they look to the Torah (God's Law) primarily for ethical instruction. Their synagogue worship is usually in the vernacular. They typically do not have a messianic expectation. Reform Judaism has a high level of concern for social justice issues, and they are often aligned with the political left. The middle ground between Orthodox and Reform Judaism lies in the Conservative Jewish movement. Conservative Jews do not hold to the rigid application of Talmudic regulations, but they feel that Reform Judaism has gone too far in the opposite direction. Conservative Jews study the Talmud. They tend to blend into the surrounding culture in matters of appearance, but they are far more traditional than Reform Jews.

Jewish belief is summarized in the *Shema* (Hebrew for "hear"): Hear O Israel: The LORD our God, the LORD is one! (Deut 6:4). It is a combination of ethical monotheism with the historical experience and cultural development of the Jewish people. Jewish boys are circumcised on the eighth day of life and confirmed (*Bar Mitzvah*) when they are thirteen. Reform and Conservative synagogues will also confirm their daughters (*Bat Mitzvah*). The weekly Sabbath begins at sundown on Friday and extends to the following sundown. The major holidays of Jewish life are Rosh Hashanah (The Head of the Year) and Yom Kippur (Day of Atonement) in autumn and Passover in spring. Because of the cultural pressure of Christmas celebrations in majority-Christian countries like the United States, Hanukkah (the eight-day Festival of Lights, celebrating the rededication of the temple after it was defiled by the Greeks in the second century BC) has become a major holiday as well. Other holidays include Sukkot, or the Feast of Booths, on the fifth day after Yom Kippur; Shavu'ot, or the Feast of Weeks (Pentecost), celebrated seven weeks after Passover; Purim, celebrating the deliverance of the Jews from Haman in the book of Esther; and Tisha B'Av, the fast commemorating the destruction of the temple, which occurs in late July or early August.

Approximately 15 million Jews are in the world, which is around 2 percent of the world's population. The largest concentrations of Jews are in Israel and the United States, with about 5.6 million each. The lowest concentrations of Jews are in sub-Saharan Africa, with around 100,000, and southern and eastern Asia, with about 200,000.[5]

Christians who seek to share the gospel with Jews should keep three things in mind. First, they should not assume that Jews will interpret the Old Testament in the same way as evangelical Christians. Over the course of centuries of exposure to Christian interpretation of the Hebrew Bible, distinctively Jewish understandings have developed that point away from the Christian interpretation and application of Jewish Scripture that point to Jesus. In particular, this is true of the necessity of blood sacrifice to atone for sin and of the expectation of the

Messiah. Second, do not assume that Jews obey the law of God to earn salvation or to escape judgment. Modern Judaism is basically universalist. In their own minds Jews obey the law out of love for God and out of a sense of heritage and identity. Third,

the horrible atrocity of the Holocaust was simply the worst of a long list of injustices visited on Jews by the ostensibly Christian world. That list includes the expulsion of the Jews from England in 1290 and from Spain in 1492. Repeated spates of persecution and even massacre occurred throughout the Middle Ages in Western Europe and into the modern period in Eastern Europe. For most of history, the Muslim world treated the Jews better than the "Christian" world did. Many Jews now regard Christian attempts at conversion as simply another attempt to rid the world of Jews, a form of cultural genocide. Jews need the gospel

---

5 Pew Forum, "The Global Religious Landscape," accessed May 29, 2013, http://www.pewforum.org/global-religious-landscape-jew.aspx.

of Jesus, and Christians need to share it with them. They need to do so, however, with sensitivity and humility.

Islam

"There is no God but Allah, and Muhammad is his prophet." This confession of faith, said in Arabic, with intent, is what makes a person a Muslim. *Islam* means "submission," and a Muslim is one who submits to God. Islam is the second largest religion in the world, and it is growing.

The roots of Islam are found in the Arabian Peninsula in the sixth and seventh centuries AD. The city of Mecca, in Western Arabia, was a major center for the caravan trade. The Arabs were idol worshippers, and a cubical shrine in Mecca, the Kaaba, housed hundreds of idols. It also contained a black rock, thought to be a meteorite, which had special significance in Arabic worship. The Kaaba was the focus of an annual religious pilgrimage that brought people from all over Arabia to Mecca. Even though Mecca is only a few hundred miles from Jerusalem, and this was centuries after the death and resurrection of Jesus, no one had bothered to translate the Bible into the Arabic language.

Around the year AD 570, a man named Muhammad was born. He was orphaned at an early age and raised by his uncle. As a young adult he joined the merchant trade and at least once went on a caravan to the Byzantine Christian city of Damascus. Eventually he married a wealthy widow named Khadijah and went into semiretirement. He began meditating in a cave on nearby Mount Hira. One day in AD 610, he came back from his meditations and told his wife that he had received a frightening visitation from the angel Gabriel (*Jabril* in Arabic). He was concerned that he had gone insane, but his wife and her Christian kinsman told him that he had been blessed with a revelation from God (*Allah* is the word Arab-speaking Jews and Christians already used for God before Muhammad was born). Muhammad continued to report receiving these revelations, although no one else ever heard or saw anything. At first the revelations were fairly short, and they concentrated on the proclamation that there is only one God, the denunciation of idolatry, and the command to live a moral and ethical life. These constitute the shorter chapters of the Qur'an, which fall at the end of the current arrangement. Muhammad began preaching to his fellow Meccans. Some were converted, but others felt that their way of life was threatened by the attacks on idolatry, and opposition grew.

In AD 622, Muhammad decided to emigrate from Mecca to the city of Yathrib, which had invited him to come arbitrate in their internal disputes. This emigration (*Hijra* in Arabic) was the beginning of the Islamic calendar, which designates its years *Anno Hijra* (AH). This also led to the change of the name of Yathrib to the City of the Prophet, Medina. Muhammad seems to have thought that he was a prophet in the line of the prophets of Judaism and Christianity, and he expected the Christians and Jews to flock to his cause. He even had his followers face toward Jerusalem to pray at first. When they largely failed to join his movement, he turned against them. The Jews of Medina (there were few Christians) were either killed or enslaved. The revelations that Muhammad reported after he arrived in Medina are longer and often spoke to issues that arose in his administration of the city or his controversies with his opponents. Medina became a Muslim city under Muhammad's rule. A simmering war developed between Mecca and Medina, and the Muslim forces of Medina won. In 630 Muhammad occupied Mecca, cleansed the Kaaba of all its idols (but left the black rock), and proclaimed amnesty to most of his opponents. By the time Muhammad died in AD 632, all of Arabia was part of the Islamic commonwealth.

Following the death of Muhammad, Islam swept out of Arabia and conquered a vast empire. Within a few decades Palestine, Syria, Mesopotamia, Persia, and Egypt were under Muslim rule. Within a hundred years, Islam had overrun North Africa and Spain and had penetrated into what is now France. Only in 732 was the tide stopped, when Charles Martel, the grandfather of Charlemagne, defeated the Muslim invaders at the battle of Tours and drove them back into Spain. In the east the Muslim Empire extended to the Indus River in the Indian subcontinent, and to the northeast it reached into modern-day Kyrgyzstan. The civilization built by the Muslims, largely on the scholarship and administrative abilities of their conquered Christian subjects, was one of the most brilliant in history. Islam was slowly pushed out of Spain, climaxing in the fall of Granada in 1492 to Ferdinand and Isabel. In the east, however, Islam advanced again through the Mongols and the Turks, who came out of central Asia. Russia was overrun by the Mongols in the thirteenth century, and that branch of the Turko-Mongolian confederation subsequently converted to Islam. Another branch of the Turkish family converted to Islam in central Asia, pushed through Persia, and defeated the Byzantine Empire in a major battle in eastern Anatolia in 1071. They quickly overran the area now known as Turkey, and in 1453 the great Christian city of Constantinople fell to the Ottoman Turks. Ottoman forces invaded southeastern Europe and twice besieged Vienna before slowly receding back toward modern-day Turkey after 1683. Meanwhile, Muslim armies out of central Asia established a series of Islamic empires in India, and the peoples of Malaysia and Indonesia became Muslim through Islamic missionary outreach. Today, Muslims are a majority in North Africa and much of the Sahel, all of the Middle East other than Israel, all of central Asia, and much of Southeast Asia. In Southern Asia the countries of Pakistan and Bangladesh are majority Muslim, and even though Muslims are a relative minority in India, the population of India is so large that it still has the fourth-largest Muslim population in the world.

A common misconception is to think that Arab and Muslim are the same thing. They are not. Arab is an ethnolinguistic term, referring to an ethnic group and to the language they speak. Islam is the name of a religion, and Muslim is the name given to a person who follows Islam. Not all Arabs are Muslims. Most indeed are, but ancient Christian populations are in places like Egypt and Lebanon who speak Arabic but who have resisted the pressure to convert to Islam for fourteen centuries. On the other hand, most Muslims are not Arabs. The Turks are almost entirely Muslim, but they are ethnically distinct from the Arabs, and they speak a language—Turkish—that is completely unrelated to Arabic. Likewise, the Iranians are ethnically Persian, not Arabic, and their language is Indo-European, more closely related to English than to Arabic. The peoples of Central, South, and Southeast Asia who profess Islam are also not Arabs in ethnic identity or in language. The four largest Muslim countries in the world are Indonesia, Pakistan, Bangladesh, and India, and none of them are Arabic.

Every Muslim must believe six things. The first of these is *God*. Islam teaches that there is only one God and that the worst sin imaginable is to ascribe equals or partners to him. The Qur'an explicitly denies that God could have a son or that Jesus is divine, and it even has Jesus himself rejecting the notion that he is the son of God. The second article of faith is in *God's Prophets*. God has sent thousands of prophets across the earth and throughout the ages. All of these prophets have taught the same religion—Islam, or submission to the one and only God. These prophets include Adam, Noah, Abraham, Moses, David, Solomon, John the Baptist, and Jesus. Muhammad is the last and greatest of the prophets, and what he taught completes what the other prophets taught; but even he is only a man and only a prophet. The third article of faith is in *God's Books*. A special category of prophets were given books for the instruction of humanity. These books include the *Taurat* (the *Torah*, or Law of Moses), the *Zabur* (the Psalms of David), and the *Injil* (the Gospel of Jesus). However, the Jews and Christians corrupted their books, so Muhammad was sent to set the record straight, and the Qur'an can never be corrupted. Muslims are taught that wherever the Bible contradicts the Qur'an, it does so because Christians changed the text from what it was originally. The fourth article of faith is *God's Angels*. Formal Islam has a high degree of awareness of the supernatural world, and this is even stronger in popular or folk Islam, where spirits and demons are a major concern of everyday life. The fifth article of faith is in *God's Decrees*. God is conceived as absolutely sovereign in Islam, to the point that he directly wills evil as well as good. The final article of faith in Islam is in the *Final Judgment*. Islam places great stress on the end of the world, the judgment facing everyone, the horrors of hell, and the pleasures of paradise.

Islam acknowledges the historicity of Adam and Eve and their fall into sin, but it denies that their sin had any lasting impact on themselves or their posterity. Children are born innocent but ignorant. Everyone is capable of obeying God's requirements fully. People need instruction, not redemption, so Islam has prophets but no savior. Who then will reach paradise? The teaching of the Qur'an combines four elements. One of these is belief, and many Muslims think that even Muslims who sin greatly only go to hell for a time of purgation, after which all who believe in Islam will go to paradise. Another is good works, and the accumulation of merit figures largely in Islamic thought. The third element is forgiveness, which may be obtained under certain circumstances but which is seldom guaranteed. The fourth is predestination, which is unknowable. What about the fate of non-Muslims? Some texts in the Qur'an seem to indicate that People of the Book (Christians and Jews) may have a chance to make it to paradise. Other passages seem to say otherwise and to assert that only Muslims escape hell. The world of Islam is divided on the subject.

The life of a Muslim revolves around the Five (or Six) Pillars of Islam. The first of these is the *confession*, recorded at the beginning of this section. This is repeated at every significant junction in life. The second is *prayer*. Every Muslim is supposed to face Mecca and pray at five set times of the day. The prayers are preceded by ritual washings. The prayers themselves are set forms in Arabic, whether the person praying understands Arabic or not, and they are accompanied by a prescribed ritual of bowing and kneeling. The third pillar is *almsgiving*. A Muslim is expected to give a percentage of his income to the poor and earns merit by doing so. The fourth pillar is the month of the *fast*. This month, called *Ramadan* in Arabic (*Ramazan* in Turkish and Farsi), is set to the lunar calendar, so it lasts twenty-eight days and it occurs ten days earlier every year. During that month no Muslim may eat, drink, or smoke anything from sunup to sundown. The meal after sundown to break the fast each day is a major celebration, as are the holidays that immediately follow the ending of the month. The fifth pillar is the *pilgrimage* to Mecca. Every Muslim is expected to do this once in his lifetime. The pilgrimage involves a series of rituals, many of which predate Islam, and it occurs at a set time of the Muslim calendar year. Some would call *jihad* the sixth pillar. *Jihad* literally means "struggle." The Greater Jihad is the internal struggle to submit to God in the life of the Muslim believer. The Lesser Jihad is the struggle to advance Islam politically and militarily.

Christians who reach out to Muslims should be aware that Islam prohibits eating pork or drinking alcohol. Muslims believe that Christians have changed the text of the Bible, so that the book we have is not reliable. However, long experience has shown that Muslims who come to faith in Jesus usually do so after consistent exposure to the Word of God and the lives of Christians. Show friendship. Extend hospitality. Pray openly for your Muslim friends in their presence. Salt your conversation with memorized Scripture. When they seem at all open to it, give them a Bible in their heart language and urge them to read the Gospels. Above all, pray that God will open their eyes and soften their hearts. Muslims can come to faith in Christ, and they are doing so today in unprecedented numbers.

Hinduism

The world of Hinduism is different from the world of Christianity, Judaism, and Islam. Hinduism is the indigenous religion of the Indian subcontinent, and it almost defies clear definition. Many distinct movements are within Hinduism, and there is no set creed or singular liturgy of worship that defines it. The history of the Indian subcontinent shows how it came to be as it is today.

An advanced civilization arose in the Indus Valley, in modern-day Pakistan, in the third millennium BC. It was culturally mature, but little is known today about its religion. The language of that civilization was probably from the Dravidian language family, related to the languages spoken in south India today. Somewhere around the year 1500 BC, a people called the Aryans invaded India from the Iranian Plateau, speaking an Indo-European language. They conquered the subcontinent over a period of time, starting in the northwest corner and primarily settling in the north. As a result, north Indians (along with the people of Pakistan and Bangladesh, which are modern creations) speak Indo-European languages, while south India still speaks Dravidian languages.

Over the next thousand years a new civilization developed from this invasion and blending of cultures. The roots of Hinduism emerged as the religious expression of this culture. During this period the *Vedas* came into being. These are four volumes of sacred writing in Sanskrit, the prototypical Indo-European language, and they are the oldest sacred texts of Hinduism. They were transmitted orally at first but eventually written down.

In the period between 500 BC and AD 500, the epic poems the *Mahabharata* and the *Ramayana* were written.

Meanwhile, a variety of other religious forces made themselves felt in India. Buddhism began in the sixth century BC as essentially a reform movement within Hinduism, but its rejection of the caste system made it inassimilable. For a time it seemed set to take over India, but today it is virtually unknown in the land of its birth. Jainism also was birthed in India and still exists there today. The Jains share much of the basic worldview of Hinduism, but they too rejected the caste system; and they remain a distinct religion. Eastern Christianity entered the subcontinent early in the Christian era and became an integrated part of society in south India, but their influence was not widely felt. The greatest external religious force to enter India was Islam. Islam was established in northwest India early in the Muslim era, and from the tenth century on much of India was ruled by Muslims out of central Asia. Islam is by far the largest non-Hindu presence in India, but it never came close to majority status except in the northwest and northeast corners. Western Christianity arrived around the year 1500, first with the Roman Catholic Portuguese and then with the Protestant British. Christians now constitute a small but respectable minority in India, and Christianity has influenced Hinduism. Still, the religion of India has shown a remarkable ability to absorb outside influences without changing its basic character.

Hinduism has a common base of beliefs that cut across the variety of sects and movements: respect for the *Vedas*, a hierarchical order of being that includes the caste system of human society but extends beyond it, *samsara* as the endless round of life, death, and rebirth in reincarnation, *dharma* as a way of life in acceptance of the caste system and as appropriate for one's place in it, and *karma* as the outworking of one's deeds. All Hindus regard the *Vedas* as inspired and authoritative, but those words do not necessarily carry the same meaning as in Christian theology, and interpretation and application can vary widely. All Hindus accept the caste system. Caste is based on karma from one's previous life, and it is unchangeable. There are four basic castes: the Brahmins, or priestly caste; the Kshatriyas, or warrior/ruler caste; the Vaishyas, or merchant caste; and the Shudras, or working caste. The first three are known as "twice born" castes, and they are allowed to participate fully in Hindu religious life. The fourth exists to serve the first three. Below the scale are the Untouchables. Your caste in your present life is the consequence of your karma from your last life. Karma is automatic and impersonal. In this life you get exactly what you deserve from your last life. Reincarnation is not regarded as a positive thing because life involves suffering, and the goal of Hinduism is to escape the cycle of reincarnation and achieve *moksha*, or release. Bad karma is worked off by accepting one's place in the caste system and living appropriately to one's caste status.

Hinduism is said to have 330 million gods. In some forms of philosophical Hinduism, these are simply manifestations of the One. For most Hindus these gods have individual existence. Three gods are found in all Hindu sects: Brahma the Creator, Vishnu the Preserver, and Shiva the Destroyer. Other gods are found only in specific locations. Hinduism has no problem with differing regional deities, and it has no problem with absorbing a new deity (like Jesus) alongside the ones it already has. Hindu practice involves the worship of idols, and these idols are generally regarded as more than simply representations of their deities. The gods are present in them. Hinduism does not have a weekly corporate worship service. The gods are worshipped daily, and anyone may worship anytime. A morning worship service, conducted by a priest who must be a Brahmin, may consist of ritually waking up the god, giving him or her a bath, clothing the god, feeding the god, and then worshipping him or her. Making offerings and participating in worship may induce the god to do something for you, and it may also help you accumulate merit.

Christians seeking to share the gospel with Hindus should recognize the vast distance between a Christian worldview and a Hindu worldview. Hindus do not want to be born again; they want to stop being born again in the endless cycle of suffering in life. Christians must be careful that the language they use is not misunderstood in Hindu terms. Hindus are more than willing to absorb a new god into their pantheon, but the concept of only one God who demands exclusive allegiance is new and strange to them. Still, the gospel is the power of God to salvation. Jesus is far more attractive than the varied deities of Hinduism, and when he is lifted up, he draws people to himself. Eternal life in the presence of an infinitely glorious God is a far more attractive destiny than the pale hope of eventual *moksha*. Many Hindus have come to faith in Jesus Christ, and many more yet can come.

Buddhism

Buddhism began within the world of Hinduism, and it reflects much of the same worldview. Indeed, Buddhism could be considered a reform movement of Hinduism. With its renunciation of the caste system, Buddhism is certainly far more exportable outside of India than classical Hinduism. It all began with a man who was born a Hindu in India. According to legend, Siddhartha Gautama was born a wealthy prince in what is now northeast India. His father tried to shield him from anything that might induce him to become religious, but when he was a young adult, he left his father's house and his wife and infant son to seek enlightenment. He engaged in extreme asceticism and finally attained enlightenment (Buddhahood) while meditating under a fig tree. He began to teach others, including the primary Hindu gods. After a number of years, he died and reached Nirvana.

Gautama taught that the physical world is *maya*, or illusion. Unlike Vedic Hinduism, however, he taught that behind the illusion is not some ultimate reality, but *sunyata*, or nothingness. In common with Hinduism, Gautama believed in *samsara*, the ongoing cycle of life, death, and rebirth, governed by karma, the automatic and impersonal consequence of one's deeds. Like Hinduism the goal is to escape this cycle. The final state of the enlightened is *Nirvana*, or the realization of self-extinction. Gautama taught the Four Holy Truths:

1. To live is to suffer.
2. Suffering is caused by an attachment to the physical world.
3. To eliminate suffering you must eliminate all attachment.
4. Attachment can be eliminated by following the Noble Eight-Fold Path.

The Noble Eight-Fold Path is, in essence, the agenda for Buddhism. It is sometimes represented by a wheel with eight spokes. The eight points are:

1. Correct view
2. Correct intention
3. Correct speech
4. Correct action
5. Correct vocation
6. Correct effort
7. Correct mindfulness
8. Correct concentration[6]

Neither Gautama himself nor any of the gods is necessary for Buddhism. Gautama attained Nirvana, and he brought the correct teaching; but it could have come through anyone else. It is possible to be an atheist and a Buddhist, as gods are not necessary to the system. It operates on its own.

Many varieties of Buddhism exist, and most fall within two main camps: Theravada Buddhism, which is the predominant version in Southeast Asia, and Mahayana Buddhism, which predominates in East Asia. Theravada Buddhism is a religion designed around the institution of monkhood and is perhaps Buddhism in its most basic form. Mahayana, or Great Vehicle Buddhism, is a broader movement. It includes such sects as Tantric Buddhism, Pure Land Buddhism, and Zen Buddhism. Mahayana Buddhism blended easily with Chinese and Japanese folk religion and became part of the popular religious mix in both countries. In Mahayana Buddhism, *sunyata* is redefined as absolute compassion, which is a far more attractive picture of the ultimate state. Mahayana Buddhism provides a way for lay-people as well as monks to achieve enlightenment. It also has more of a role for divine beings, such as Dhyani Buddhas and Boddhisattvas, in the process of attaining Nirvana.

In practice, many Buddhists treat the Buddha, the Dhyani Buddhas, and the Boddhisattvas as gods to be worshiped and to be entreated for help in this life, even though formal Buddhism denies that the Buddha is a god. Particularly in Theravada Buddhism, where enlightenment is only a possibility for monks, common

---

[6] Winfred Corduan, *Neighboring Faiths* (Downers Grove: IVP Academic, 2012), 329.

laypeople continue to express the needs, fears, and desires of popular religion through the forms of Buddhism. However, the concepts of *maya, sunyata, samsara,* and *karma* exercise a powerful effect on people from Buddhist cultures and make the worldview of the gospel strange to them.

As with Hindus, care must be taken in communicating the gospel with Buddhists. The worldview differences run deep, and expressions such as "born again" can be profoundly misunderstood. The idea that the physical world is both real and good is a direct contradiction of the concepts of *maya* and *sunyata.* Eternal life in heaven is far different (and far more positive) than Nirvana (although Pure Land Buddhism has a vaguely similar concept). Here again the Christian witness to Buddhists should love them, pray for them, expose them to the power of the Word of God, and lift Jesus up. He will draw Buddhists to himself.

Animism

Animism is the popular religion of the world. It is not an organized system, and it takes on a variety of forms around the world; but there are certain consistent features to popular religion everywhere. The most foundational of these is the perception of a multitude of spiritual beings in the world whose activities impinge directly on human life. Western materialists envision a one-level universe in which the physical world is all there is. Many Western Christians and Jews function in a two-level universe in which there is the physical world in which we live and a largely top level consisting of God and heaven. For most of the world, a third level is between those two, and it is the most important level of all. This third level is inhabited by a huge variety of spiritual beings—some perhaps good, many evil, many simply capricious—who directly impact the events of life in the material world. These spirits are generally feared, as they are responsible for sickness, crop failure, good luck, prosperity, and disaster. They must be appeased in order to survive and have success. Some of these spirits are located in a place, such as a sacred grove or mountain, or an object, such as a rock, a tree, or a stream. Others are free to roam at will. Also intrinsic to most forms of animism is a concept of mystical power, which can be held and used by persons of power, such as witchdoctors or shamans, and can be channeled through rituals, spells, and talismans. Animistic societies may or may not have the concept of a God or gods who are somewhere above the ordinary spirits in the hierarchy of the universe. Many do, in fact, believe in a Creator God but hold that he is distant or that they have lost contact with him.

In such a system illness and misfortune are usually held to come from either the spirits or from the activities of people of power—magic, witchcraft, or the like. Therefore, the solution to these ills is either propitiation of the spirits or counteracting magic. In either case people of power play a huge role in ordinary life. These people wield enormous power over those around them, and they are usually both respected and feared.

In animistic societies people are also usually regarded as possessing spirits, and those spirits continue in some form of existence after death. Many, if not most, animistic societies practice some form of care for the spirits of the dead. This may mean bringing either real or token offerings of food and drink to their graves. It often takes the form of veneration of ancestors, which is a feature of societies all over the world. Ancestors who are not properly cared for may visit bad fortune on their neglectful descendants. Ancestor veneration or worship is part of the glue that holds society together in many cultures.

At the heart of animism is fear. These spirits are not loved but feared. Their behavior is unpredictable. Animists always have something to be afraid of, and they spend their lives doing all they can to assure that the spirits are for them and not against them.

Animism is the heart of traditional religion the world over. This is true in Africa, in the jungles of the Amazon in South America, and in the rain forests of Southeast Asia. It is also true of Chinese traditional religion. At the same time, animism has blended itself in syncretistic fashion with every religion on earth. Its presence is clearly seen in folk Islam, where a thin veneer of formal religion covers a deep well of animism. The same is true of popular Hinduism and Buddhism. It is also true of popular Christianity in many places around the world.

Contrary to Western materialism, the Bible teaches that the spirit world really does exist and that it directly impinges on the material world. The Bible takes the presence of demons and angels for granted. However, these spirits are never to be propitiated or manipulated. The use of magic is strictly forbidden. Instead, the gospel brings the good news that Jesus Christ has absolute power over the spirit world. This is a major theme of the Gospels that Western believers largely overlook (as they pay little attention to the spirits), but it is a source of joy to those who fear the power of spirits they can neither control nor predict. The gospel is good news indeed to animists, and it is no wonder they have proven highly responsive to it globally.

CONCLUSION

Many other religions are in the world, including Confucianism and Taoism in China, Shinto in Japan, and Zoroastrianism in Iran and India. Wherever Christians go with the gospel, it is important that they study the religious beliefs of the people they are trying to reach. Given the level of syncretism with animism that exists in most religions, it is necessary to explore what people actually believe and do, not what their formal religion says they ought to believe. The purpose of this research is not disinterested scholarship or pluralistic dialogue but effective communication. People hear new information through the filter of their existing worldview. Cross-cultural evangelists need to know what their listeners actually hear when the gospel is presented to them. They need to know what background needs to be filled in for their listeners before the gospel makes sense. They also need to understand what issues must be addressed in discipleship once a person has come to Christ out of another religion. There is a clear and sharp distinction between biblical Christianity and all forms of nonbiblical religion. Christians should love adherents of all of the other religions of the world. They should seek to understand them, and they should treat them with respect. There is no place for bigotry or demagoguery in the attitudes, words, or actions of Christians toward non-Christians. At the same time there is no salvation apart from hearing and believing the gospel of Jesus Christ. Saving faith includes repentance, including repentance from all forms of nonbiblical religion. People who come to faith in Christ should be urged to remain in their community as much as possible, but they must never be urged to remain within the structures or allegiances of any non-Christian religion. It is right and necessary that we call people out of non-Christian religions when we call them to faith in Christ.

RESOURCES FOR FURTHER STUDY

Bowker, John. *World Religions*. New York: DK Publishing, 1997.

Breen, John, and Mark Teeuwen, eds. *Shinto in History: Ways of the Kami*. Honolulu: University of Hawai Press, 2000.

Child, Alice B., and Irvin L. Child. *Religion and Magic in the Life of Traditional Peoples*. Englewood Cliffs, NJ: Prentice-Hall, 1993.

Corduan, Winfried. *Neighboring Faiths*. 2nd ed. Downers Grove, IL: IVP Academic, 2012.

Durkheim, Emile. *The Elementary Forms of Religious Life*. Translated by Karen E. Fields. New York: The Free Press, 1995.

Fine, Lawrence. *Judaism in Practice: From the Middle Ages Through the Early Modern Period*. Princeton, NJ: Princeton University Press, 2001.

Flood, Gavin. *An Introduction to Hinduism*. New York: Cambridge University Press, 1996.

Flood, Gavin, ed. *The Blackwell Companion to Hinduism*. Malden, MA: Blackwell, 2003.

Harvey, Peter. *An Introduction to Buddhism*. New York: Cambridge University Press, 1990.

Neusner, Jacob. *Judaism in Modern Times: An Introduction and Reader*. Cambridge, MA: Blackwell, 1995.

Picken, Stuart D. B. *Essentials of Shinto: An Analytical Guide to Principal Teachings*. Westport, CT: Greenwood, 1994.

SECTION 4

THE PRACTICE OF GLOBAL MISSIONS

CHAPTER 9

STRATEGIES FOR DISCIPLE MAKING

"Go, therefore and make disciples . . . teaching them
to observe everything I have commanded you."
Matthew 28:19–20

"The great tragedy of the world is not that it
is unreached but that it is undiscipled."
—Bill Ogden, *South America Mission*

Jesus commanded his followers to go and make disciples of all
the people groups of the world. Missionaries have learned the
difficult lesson that undiscipled people do not understand the
full implications of Christianity in their own lives, and, sadly,
they are therefore unable to pass the faith along to others. What
is discipleship? Why is it so important? How should we go about
it? These are excellent questions for the missionary when considering the essentials for effective and fruitful ministry.

Several related terms share a common root to refer to the
process of growing in Christlikeness. The noun *disciple* refers to
the believer who is a committed student of Christ. *Discipleship*
is a related word, referring to the process by which one learns.
The same word has a verb form, *to disciple* or *discipling*, which
refers to mentoring and educating another in the process of
growing in godliness and pursuing holiness. Oswald Chambers

wrote, "Discipleship means personal, passionate devotion to a Person, our Lord Jesus Christ."[1] Although the term *disciple* is rare in the Old Testament, the concept is clearly present in the relationships of Moses and Joshua and Elijah and Elisha. In the New Testament era, students followed rabbis, learned from them, memorized their teachings, and were committed to passing their knowledge along to others. Followers of Jesus were called disciples for similar reasons. When we consider the term *disciples* in the New Testament, we normally think of the twelve disciples and the seventy he sent out, but really all of those who were born-again followers of Christ were considered disciples. They were people whose lives had been changed by Jesus, who were committed to him, who learned from him, and who would be commissioned to tell others about him. The terms *discipleship*, *discipling*, or *disciple making* all refer to the process of making disciples, and a disciple is simply one who loves and learns from Jesus.

Every born-again believer is a disciple to a certain degree; that is why some missiologists and evangelists have often used the term to speak of bringing people to faith for the first time. In *Understanding Church Growth*, Donald McGavran used the term in this way when he referred to *discipling* as a verb, meaning "helping a people . . . turn from non-Christian faith to Christ. Discipling [is] followed by perfecting, that is, by the whole complex process of growth in grace, ethical improvement, and the conversion of individuals in that first and succeeding generations."[2] McGavran went on to write,

> The new English verb *to disciple* proved attractive. Shortly after 1970 it began to be used for the process by which individuals in any society (Christian or non-Christian) first became Christian, and then it was used for the entirely different process by which existing Christians become illuminated, thoroughly dedicated followers of Christ.[3]

---

[1] Oswald Chambers, *My Utmost for His Highest*, deluxe ed. (Uhrichsville, OH: Barbour, 1963), 132.
[2] Donald A. McGavran, *Understanding Church Growth*, 3rd ed. (Grand Rapids: Eerdmans, 1990), 123.
[3] Ibid.

While McGavran preferred to use the words *discipling* to refer to bringing someone to faith in Christ and *perfecting* for what we routinely mean as discipleship, this is confusing to modern ears. The commonly accepted usage of the term *discipleship* today refers to the process by which believers are taught to obey all Christ has commanded.

Every person who places faith in Jesus Christ is not automatically his disciple in the stricter sense of word. A disciple is at the very least a Christian who is committed to serve him as a bond slave, learn from him, follow him, serve him, and obey all he has said. Francis Cosgrove summarized a biblical profile of a disciple in the following eleven facets, demonstrating that a life of discipleship is neither automatic nor the path of least resistance in daily life.

1. A disciple is a learner—open and teachable.
2. A disciple puts Christ first in all areas of his life.
3. A disciple is committed to a life of purity in all areas of his life.
4. A disciple has a daily devotional time and is developing in his prayer life.
5. A disciple demonstrates faithfulness and a desire to learn and apply the Word of God through hearing it preached and taught, reading it frequently, Bible study, Scripture memory, and meditation on the Scriptures.
6. A disciple has a heart for witnessing, gives his testimony clearly, and presents the gospel regularly with increasing skill.
7. A disciple attends church regularly to worship God, to have his spiritual needs met, and to make a contribution to the body of believers.
8. A disciple fellowships regularly with other believers, displaying love and unity.
9. A disciple demonstrates a servant heart by helping others in practical ways.
10. A disciple gives regularly and honors God with his finances.

11. A disciple demonstrates the fruit of the Spirit by an attractive relationship with Christ and his fellow-man.[4]

WHO IS A DISCIPLE?

Jesus taught that the decision to be a disciple should not be taken lightly. He said that when we consider becoming his disciple, we should first count the cost.

> If anyone comes to Me and does not hate his own father and mother, wife and children, brothers and sisters—yes, and even his own life—he cannot be My disciple. Whoever does not bear his own cross and come after Me cannot be My disciple.
>
> For which of you, wanting to build a tower, doesn't first sit down and calculate the cost to see if he has enough to complete it? Otherwise, after he has laid the foundation and cannot finish it, all the onlookers will begin to make fun of him, saying, "This man started to build and wasn't able to finish."
>
> Or what king, going to war against another king, will not first sit down and decide if he is able with 10,000 to oppose the one who comes against him with 20,000? If not, while the other is still far off, he sends a delegation and asks for terms of peace. In the same way, therefore, every one of you who does not say good-bye to all his possessions cannot be My disciple. (Luke 14:26–33 HCSB)

Notice that Jesus says we must love and be more committed to him than we are to our own family members, bear whatever cross he assigns to us, be willing to pay any price, and renounce all possessions. Oswald Chambers wrote, "Whenever our Lord talked about discipleship, He always prefaced it with an 'IF,'

---

[4] Francis M. Cosgrove Jr., *The Essentials of Discipleship: What It Takes to Follow Christ* (Dallas: Roper, 1988), 15–16.

never with an emphatic assertion—'You must.' Discipleship carries an option with it."[5]

Discipleship is a commitment to the Lord Jesus Christ that requires effort, sacrifice, and surrender. Imagine a man who is an accomplished musician. When his friends tell him they wish they could play like he does, he responds, "No, you don't." Then to comfort the sting, he explains that if they did, they would dedicate long hours of practice day in and day out, sacrifice personal time with friends, stay away from their books, television, and computer so they could repetitively practice the same piece over and over until it became second nature to them, until their fingers performed the notes effortlessly, and until they felt that the instrument was an extension of their own body. When such dedication is revealed to be necessary, many change their mind. Consider becoming an Olympic athlete and imagine the years of dedicated training, special diets, early morning runs, weight-lifting workouts, and total commitment necessary in order to stand on the platform listening to your country's national anthem while receiving the gold medal. That is total commitment. Are you that committed to Jesus Christ? To be a disciple is to strive for holiness. A. W. Tozer wrote that every Christian is as holy as he or she wants to be.[6] It is hard work and requires self-discipline, especially on those days when we would rather do something else. The Puritan William Secker's words concerning fasting could describe the self-discipline required: "By fasting, the body learns to obey the soul; by praying, the soul learns to command the body."[7]

PERSONAL SPIRITUAL DISCIPLINES

Personal spiritual disciplines are the habits of a disciple's life in order to grow in Christlikeness, pursue holiness, and practice godliness. Don Whitney has written to teach modern disciples of Christ how to grow in godliness, admonishing that practicing spiritual disciplines is a biblical instruction: "Discipline yourself for the purpose of godliness" (1 Tim 4:7 NASB).[8]

---

[5] Chambers, *My Utmost for His Highest*, 82.
[6] See A. W. Tozer, *Born After Midnight* (Camp Hill, PA: Wingspread, 1959), chap. 1.
[7] I. D. E. Thomas, comp., *A Puritan Golden Treasury* (Carlisle, PA: Banner of Truth, 2000), 79.
[8] See Donald S. Whitney, *Spiritual Disciplines for the Christian Life* (Colorado Springs, CO: NavPress, 1991).

Missionaries would be wise to develop these disciplines in their own lives for many reasons. Missionaries who are deployed overseas, often in gospel-hostile places, find that a walk with God is harder when separated from fellowship with believers back home in the sending church. Additionally, many missionaries serve in areas where all the people know about Christ and Christianity is what they see in the missionary. To the degree the missionary is unethical, lazy, rude, harsh, unspiritual, or sinful in any way, so is Jesus Christ in their minds. Many will follow Christ as the missionary does.

Another crucial reason that profound experience in practicing these spiritual disciplines is so helpful is because the missionary is responsible for training new believers to walk in holiness and become disciples of Jesus Christ. In discipleship one cannot truly teach what one cannot model. The biblical guideline is for those who know to teach the ones who do not know, whether it is parents teaching their children (Deut 6:6–10; Eph 6:4), trained men training other faithful men (2 Tim 2:2), or older women teaching younger women (Titus 2:3–5).

Personal spiritual disciplines guide the missionary in discipleship and growth in holiness, even when isolated from other believers or Bible study groups for a time. Don Whitney identified these disciplines as Bible intake, prayer, worship, evangelism, serving, stewardship, fasting, silence and solitude, journaling, and learning.[9] The Puritans practiced spiritual disciplines and taught the importance of striving after holiness to their congregations. Bishop J. C. Ryle, who followed in the Puritan tradition, illustrates the importance of such a life in his classic *Holiness*.[10] The contemporary scholar J. I. Packer wrote of the Puritans in *Quest for Godliness*, demonstrating the importance they placed on discipleship for Christlike holiness.[11] Charles Spurgeon said of the Puritan John Bunyan that he was so saturated with the Bible when you cut him he bled "Bibline."[12] John and Charles Wesley and George Whitefield were members of a group that was

---

[9] Ibid., 17.

[10] J. C. Ryle, *Holiness* (London: Clarke, 1952). Available online at the Christian Classics Ethereal Library: http://www.ccel.org/ccel/ryle/holiness.toc.html.

[11] J. I. Packer, *Quest for Godliness: The Puritan Vision of the Christian Life* (Wheaton: Crossway, 1990).

[12] Quoted in David L. Larsen, *The Anatomy of Preaching* (Grand Rapids: Kregel Academic, 1999), 173.

derisively called "The Holy Club" at Oxford University. The term grew from their reputation for zeal for God, pursuit of holiness, visiting the sick, and daily hours in prayer. The list of greatly used men and women who were committed disciples of Christ could go on and on. Others ridiculed them, but their holiness gave them spiritual strength and the hand of God's favor to accomplish great things for him and the advance of his kingdom.

DISCIPLING OTHERS

The Bible is clear that we are to disciple new believers who come after us. The missionary's responsibility to disciple is the primary focus of this chapter and should be the primary focus of the missionary on the mission field. Paul wrote to Timothy, "And what you have heard from me in the presence of many witnesses, commit to faithful men who will be able to teach others also" (2 Tim 2:2 HCSB). The context of the passage makes clear that Paul was telling Timothy to prepare biblically qualified leaders to serve the church, but this teaching must include training in godliness and discipleship. Discipling for new converts is similar to feeding and nurturing newborn babies. It should never be assumed, for it is not automatic or guaranteed to occur at all without someone to help. If it is neglected, there is great danger to life and health.

The roles of missionaries change throughout their careers. When a missionary first enters an unreached mission field, the role of evangelist is primary, sharing the gospel with the lost and guiding them to know and embrace Christ. However, after the believers are won, the task of discipleship takes on significance. This is like parents with a new baby, feeding him and changing diapers. Then the parents must teach the toddler to walk and talk. Next comes training and guiding the young child through adolescence until the maturing young person leaves home and becomes a responsible, independent adult. The parents' role will change throughout the child's life, yielding more control and decision making to the child as he grows and is able to handle it well.[13] The missionary must guide and disciple new believers to

---

[13] See M. David Sills, *Reaching and Teaching: A Call to Great Commission Obedience* (Chicago: Moody, 2010), 41–44.

enable them to achieve this same level of responsible maturity in their Christian life.

The process of discipling new believers also assists in identifying those whom the Holy Spirit is calling to places of leadership. The believer begins to sense this inner call and desire to serve the Lord in his church, finding that those around him in his church body recognize the gifts, abilities, and anointing to serve the Lord in Christian ministry. The process of discipling results in churches with trained leaders who are spiritually mature and faithful. This is not to intimate that discipled people never sin, but carnal leadership is more typically found among those who were left to mature on their own when they were saved. Discipled leaders are more likely to lead faithfully and set a Christlike example for others to follow. We need trained leadership for biblically sound churches—a discipling church is preparing its own leadership.

When well-trained godly men who are biblically qualified and thoroughly discipled lead the church, it has a built-in protection system. Mark Dever has described the nine marks of a healthy church as:

1. Expositional Preaching
2. Biblical Theology
3. A Biblical Understanding of the Good News
4. A Biblical Understanding of Conversion
5. A Biblical Understanding of Evangelism
6. A Biblical Understanding of Church Membership
7. Biblical Church Discipline
8. Biblical Discipleship and Growth
9. Biblical Church Leadership[14]

Each of these marks grows out of the previous one and leads to the next; i.e., preaching through the Bible faithfully will produce biblical theology, and so on. The last two in the list are the ones that stand out to us most in this chapter, but notice that they do not exist in isolation. A desire for biblical discipleship, spiritual growth, and mature church leadership cannot neglect to practice the other healthy practices as well.

---

[14] Mark Dever, *What Is a Healthy Church?* (Wheaton: Crossway, 2007).

MULTIPLICATION DISCIPLESHIP

Most missionaries want to start New Testament churches as an essential part of their ministry. Indeed, some missionaries focus on church planting as their top priority. It has been said that when church growth outstrips trained leadership, troubles multiply quickly. In the history of the expansion of Christianity, the efforts that resulted in a rate of church growth greater than the rate of discipled leaders also resulted in carnal leadership, strife, and division. Missionaries who are intentional and persistent in producing mature church leadership through discipleship programs may produce fewer numbers of new churches in the beginning. However, discipled members and leaders will endure longer, reproduce other disciples and healthy churches, and be best equipped to faithfully teach the faith once for all delivered to the saints to the next generation of believers.

The argument could be made that the need for more churches and leaders is too great and traditional discipling takes too long. However, if a missionary were to concentrate on discipling six believers for six months and challenge each of them to win six more believers to disciple on their own, and then teach them to disciple others just as they were taught, he would learn the valuable principle of multiplication. Those six disciples can repeat that process in the next six months, discipling their own new converts, and encouraging them to win and disciple still others in similar fashion. Should this process continue and multiply every six months, and if no one fell away or was unsuccessful, in five years there would be millions of discipled believers—do the math!

Obviously, this is only an example to show the principle of multiplication; it would not succeed as designed in a fallen world where people fall away, where there are varying levels of commitment, and where real life complicates the consistency of the results. However, it serves to demonstrate the power of multiplication. With those possibilities in mind, imagine on the other hand that same missionary discipling two or three believers every year and then merely adding two or three more each successive year, and so forth. After five years he would only have fifteen disciples. Conversely, the multiplication process allows the missionary to continue mentoring his original six, supervising their instruction, discipling, and mentoring the next generation while developing a discipled church. These models help us see the exponential value of a discipleship process.

Because discipleship is simply the process of growing in holiness, Christlikeness, godliness, and a host of other nearly synonymous terms, it should not be surprising that serious Christian leaders and writers have admonished Christians to grow in this way for centuries. Many use different words, but they seek to exhort all believers to walk faithfully, ever narrowing the gap between what they know and the level they have actually attained. At their core, books on developing godly church members, teaching evangelists to evangelize, mentoring leadership, training pastors, and teaching theologians can all be said to be about discipleship at different levels. It is an unfortunate truth that its ubiquitous presence leads Christians to assume it and take it for granted.

How many of you were intentionally discipled, one-on-one or in a small group, when you were saved? We have asked this question in many contexts and rarely seen more than one hand raised, no matter the congregation. Church and mission leaders assume new believers will join the youth group, a Sunday school class, or a Bible study group or read good Christian books to grow in Christ. Many assume they will ask the pastor if they have questions, follow Christian friends to learn the faith, and spend lots of time in prayer and Bible study as they grow—so no one ever disciples them. Sadly missionaries who never received any intentional discipleship also fail to disciple others. We perpetuate our own experiences.

Discipleship is often relegated to the realm of stuff we will do when we get "caught up," and we calm the sting in our conscience with quasibiblical comfort such as, "They have the Bible and the Holy Spirit; He will lead them into all truth."[15] However, that is not a proper understanding of Jesus' words, and it runs counter to what he and the rest of the Bible teach us about discipleship and teaching those who come behind us. If people in our Judeo-Christian culture need to be discipled to live godly

---

[15] See Sills, *Reaching and Teaching*, which addresses the fallacy of assuming growth in biblical fidelity and practical holiness and provides examples from missiologists and mission fields to demonstrate the need to teach them all that Jesus has commanded.

lives and grow in holiness, how much more do those who have lived all their lives in cultures steeped in the lies of false religions, the fear of animism, and the worldview poison Satan uses to dull the hearts and minds of the nations? The lies they have always embraced as truth and the false explanations they have used to interpret the phenomena of daily life do not evaporate upon praying a prayer to receive Jesus as Lord and Savior. These erroneous demonic deceptions must be discipled out of people when they come to faith. There are both biblical and practical reasons for discipling people when they come to faith.

Jesus' Command and Example

Most missionaries want to disciple new believers, if for no other reason, because Jesus told them to do so. As the Great Commission states, the church is to go to all the people groups and make disciples, teaching them to observe all that Jesus commanded. Additionally, if Jesus is to be our Model and Example for all we do in his name, we would be wiser to ask, "What *did* Jesus do?" rather than speculating, "What *would* Jesus do?" Jesus was always teaching his hearers, guiding them in application of God's truth, using parables and illustrations from daily life to make sure they could understand his instruction. Even in showing compassion, he taught them. Mark 6:34 shows this: "He saw a huge crowd and had compassion on them, because they were like sheep without a shepherd. Then He began to teach them many things." Virtually all of the Gospels are replete with evidence of the teaching and discipling ministry of Jesus.

Gary Kuhne wrote about Jesus' discipleship principle of concentration, demonstrating the idea with concentric circles. Kuhne explained that Jesus spent most of his discipling and teaching time with the three disciples who are sometimes referred to as his inner circle: Peter, James, and John. Going out from there, Jesus spent much time with the twelve, then the seventy whom he sent out on mission. Kuhne then listed the masses that followed him and learned from his example and teaching.[16] Missionaries would be wise to remember that they cannot pour their lives into everyone to the same degree. Jesus

---

[16] Gary Kuhne, *Discipleship: The Best Writings from the Most Experienced Disciple Makers*, ed. Billie Hanks (Grand Rapids: Zondervan, 1981), 125.

spent three years pouring his life into committed disciples when he could have focused on the crowds and amassing a worldwide following. Jesus knew he would not be with them forever, so he prepared men to lead the church. Yet Jesus is not alone in this pattern of ministry.

The Early Church

The early church sought to live out the Christian life and to teach others to do the same. They did so without the benefit of 2,000 years of biblical scholarship, theological reflection, and missionary heroes who have learned the hard way and taught us through their lives. The love they showed for one another and the Lord Jesus Christ sheds light on the process they used. A perusal through the pages of the book of Acts reveals that the early church was committed to growing in Christ, loving one another, and learning to pray, give, learn from others, worship, and keeping a pure testimony before those around them. Francis Cosgrove wrote that this cycle of discipleship is seen most clearly in Acts 2:41–47 (HCSB).

> So those who accepted his message were bap-
> tized, and that day about 3,000 people were
> added to them. And they devoted themselves
> to the apostles' teaching, to fellowship, to the
> breaking of bread, and to prayers.
> Then fear came over everyone, and many
> wonders and signs were being performed
> through the apostles. Now all the believers were
> together and held all things in common. They
> sold their possessions and property and distrib-
> uted the proceeds to all, as anyone had a need.
> Every day they devoted themselves to meeting
> together in the temple complex, and broke
> bread from house to house. They ate their food
> with a joyful and humble attitude, praising God
> and having favor with all the people. And every
> day the Lord added to them those who were
> being saved.

Cosgrove pointed out eight key aspects of that early church in this passage.

1. They accepted the message, v. 41.
2. They were baptized, v. 41.
3. They were added to the church, v. 41.
4. They devoted themselves to instruction, v. 42.
5. They were part of the fellowship, v. 42.
6. They were trained to become reproducers, v. 47.
7. They reached out to the community, v. 47.
8. People were added to the church, v. 47.[17]

As previously noted, in areas where there is no strong church, new believers need to be folded into a fellowship of loving believers, fed the pure milk of the Word of God, and taught to feed themselves and others as they grow in Christian maturity.

Paul's Example and Exhortation

Paul wrote almost half of the New Testament in the thirteen epistles that are clearly attributed to him. This is important to note because his writings largely guide us in knowing what we are to do as believers and churches in the world. Indeed the New Testament could be divided into four general categories: the four Gospels teach us about the life of Jesus; the book of Acts teaches us about the expansion of Christianity; the Epistles teach us about how to live in this world as individuals and as Christ's church; and the Revelation teaches about the end times. Paul wrote in 1 Timothy 3:15, "But if I should be delayed, I have written so that you will know how people ought to act in God's household, which is the church of the living God, the pillar and foundation of the truth." He told Timothy, "Pay close attention to your life and your teaching; persevere in these things, for by doing this you will save both yourself and your hearers" (1 Tim 4:16 HCSB). He also gave one of the clearest commands for missionaries to know what to do when he told Timothy, "And what you have heard from me in the presence of many witnesses, commit to faithful men who will be able to teach others also" (2 Tim 2:2 HCSB).

Paul was one of our best biblical models of a mentor and discipler. He kept an eye out for promising protéges in his ministry to recognize which ones the Lord had gifted for ministry,

---

[17] Cosgrove, *The Essentials of Discipleship*, 124.

the ones who felt called, and those who would be helpful to him in his missionary service. Names such as Timothy, Titus, Silas, Onesiphorus, and Tychicus quickly come to mind as those into whose lives he deeply invested. However, we could also add Luke, John Mark, Priscilla, Aquila, and Apollos. The pattern of encouraging other believers and helping them to reach their potential for Christ's sake was a characteristic of the apostle Paul in his practice and teaching. Paul exhorted believers to discipleship, and, thankfully, the Bible gives us illustrations of his discipleship in action.

Acts 14:21–28

Many portions of Acts could be unpacked to show people coming to know the Lord, leaving behind paganism, and seeking to grow in godliness. In Acts 14:21–28, Paul and Barnabas are ministering on their first missionary journey. They struggled to make themselves understood in Lystra because of a language difference. Then Jews from places where they had already preached followed them and stirred up the crowds against them. They dragged Paul out of town and stoned him, leaving him for dead. Although he had encountered violent opposition to the gospel of Jesus Christ and those who thought they had killed him would be eager to correct what was lacking in their first attempt, Paul got up and went back into the city to be with the disciples again. Rather than letting a gospel-hostile mission field cut short or reduce his efforts to disciple the new believers, persecution seemed to fuel them. He and Barnabas went to Derbe next.

> After they had evangelized that town and made many disciples, they returned to Lystra, to Iconium, and to Antioch, strengthening the disciples by encouraging them to continue in the faith and by telling them, "It is necessary to pass through many troubles on our way into the kingdom of God."
>
> When they had appointed elders in every church and prayed with fasting, they committed them to the Lord in whom they had believed. Then they passed through Pisidia and came to Pamphylia. After they spoke the message in

Perga, they went down to Attalia. From there they sailed back to Antioch where they had been entrusted to the grace of God for the work they had completed. After they arrived and gathered the church together, they reported everything God had done with them and that He had opened the door of faith to the Gentiles. And they spent a considerable time with the disciples. (Acts 14:21–28 HCSB)

Paul and Barnabas were actively involved in evangelism; unreached people desperately needed to be reached with the gospel of Jesus Christ, but they needed more than that. Paul and Barnabas returned to those they had previously reached, even the areas where they had suffered persecution, to encourage the disciples, reminding them that followers of Jesus must pass through suffering on the way home.

When disciples hear faithful teachers explaining what it is to be a disciple from God's Word, it is instructive. When they see it lived out by their teacher, it is instructive *and* powerful. Discipling new believers and teaching them to be faithful in times of persecution and opposition is most powerful when it is lived out before them. Oswald Chambers said, "Discipleship is built entirely on the supernatural grace of God. Walking on water is easy to impulsive pluck, but walking on dry land as a disciple of Jesus Christ is a different thing."[18] The Bible contains commands and examples about the importance of discipling those who come behind us in the faith. Missionaries who seek faithfully to obey all that God's Word admonishes and exhorts them to do also quickly learn that there is a pragmatic reason for their ministries. God's ways work always and in all the ways God intends for them to work.

PRAGMATICS OF DISCIPLESHIP

Missionaries are limited in the number of people they can evangelize, churches they can plant, disciples they can train, and pastors they can teach. After arriving in India at the end of the eighteenth century and seeing the vast numbers of people in

---

[18] Chambers, *My Utmost for His Highest*, 215.

India's masses, a stunned William Carey remarked that if India would ever be reached for Christ, the Indians would have to do it. He knew there would never be enough missionaries to reach so many people. He also knew such an effort was not Jesus' plan anyway. The Bible teaches that we must prepare others to join in the work, and they in turn will train still others to train others. When asked how he would reach a city of millions if he knew he would be required to leave in only a few years, one student humbly replied, "I think if I had such a large task and so few years, I would pick out eleven guys and pour my life into them." The point was well made and well taken. We are not to accomplish the work alone.

Missionaries realize new believers need to be taught many things, but many languages have not yet been reduced to writing; and others that have been still do not have the Bible translated. Many people are coming to know the Lord in areas where there is no strong national church. The effort to evangelize in areas that are unreached and unengaged means there are few if any believers when the missionary begins the work. In addition to needing well-taught helpers, the missionary realizes that discipleship is needed because there is no other way for them to know the truth. Someone must teach them the truth and guide them in its application to daily life. How else would they know?

The pioneer missionary who plants a church experiences frustration when the church he planted begins to take most of his time and he is hindered in pioneer efforts. Who will plant other churches? He cannot send the new converts to do so because they do not know what to teach, how to preach, or where to start. He cannot go and work elsewhere because there is no one to pastor the church he would leave behind. Where would leaders come from? Quickly he realizes the pragmatic value of discipleship in missionary work. He prepares a workforce from the new believers, discipling them, teaching them, and mentoring them as they engage in the work of evangelism, discipling, church planting, and leadership training in areas he has never even been. The quantity of discipled workers should walk hand in hand with the number of new works attempted.

The pragmatic benefit of discipleship among the leadership is seen in the quality of new leaders as well as the quantity. We have always sought to avoid those models of pastoral training and theological education that resulted in churning out pastors in a program that merely concentrated on head knowledge. It is important that pastors and leaders have knowledge of the Old and New Testaments to know what God has actually said, Christian doctrine to know what we are to believe and what heresy looks like, church history to know how Christianity expands, where heresy happened and why, and what the heroes of the past have taught us. Many other components of head knowledge are essential in a pastoral training program; however, the hands and heart must be taught as well.

Pastors and leaders need to have their "hands" trained in the "how-to" of preaching, counseling, evangelism, church administration, and even ethics in finances. The heart must also be taught and prepared—this is the element that is often overlooked in traditional training programs. Indeed, this aspect is difficult to develop in Western educational models, and the result is often carnal leadership leading from business books or models from the political world.

The biblical model of discipleship, which includes the preparation of believers in personal spiritual disciplines and encourages them to practice them, results in hearts after God's own heart and the characters that we pray to see in the lives and testimonies of those we bring to the work. It also incorporates mentoring that facilitates accountability, teaching that is contoured to the believer, and feedback as needed for clarification. The biblical admonition to disciple both new converts and future leaders addresses the danger of overlooking the hands and heart. Much of the traditional method results in ordination ceremonies that Spurgeon described as "placing empty hands on empty heads."[19]

METHODS OF DISCIPLESHIP

As we have seen, the most basic understanding of discipleship is the believer growing in Christlikeness. Chambers said it is like God making us his instruments to do his work: "Our Lord makes a disciple His own possession, He becomes responsible for him. . . . The secret of the missionary is—I am His, and He

---

[19] Lewis A. Drummond, *Spurgeon: Prince of Preachers* (Grand Rapids: Kregel, 1992), 205.

is carrying out His enterprises through me. Be entirely His."[20]
The traditions of Christianity reveal many diverse models for
discipleship such as emphases on Bible study, prayer, missionary biographies, small groups, mentoring, and individual study
of workbooks. Some methods are more appropriate than others
for certain people groups. For instance, missionaries serving in
contexts of primary oral learners must avoid methods that are
dependent on high literacy, underdeveloped areas of the world
should not lean on technology, and the places with great persecution of believers must be careful with any open model.

Consistent and profound Bible study and prayer is one of
the most commonly found methods of discipleship in all eras of
Christian history and in virtually every area of the world. What
would we know about God if he had not revealed himself? Precious little. Psalm 19 and Romans 1 tell us that we would know
that he is—that there is a Creator—but we would not know
much about him, his Son's name, the work of Christ, or what
he wants from us. The best way to know him is through reading
what he has revealed about himself in his Word. As we read his
Word, we should pray asking for illumination, guidance in life,
assistance in sanctification, protection, provision, and so much
more. The more time we spend in the Bible and in prayer, the
better we know him; the more we know him, the more we seek
to be like him and pleasing to him. Walter Henrichsen wrote
that Dawson Trotman, the founder of the Navigators,

> developed an illustration to show how the Word
> can be implemented in the Christian life. There
> are five main ways: hearing (Rom 10:17), read-
> ing (Rev 1:3), studying (Acts 17:11), memoriz-
> ing (Ps 119:9, 11), and meditating (Ps 1:2, 3). All
> five must be functioning if one is to have a firm
> grasp on the Word.[21]

Bible study may take place in a church setting after a literate person reads the passage for discussion, as a well-educated
scholar reads it in the original languages, in isolated pockets of

---

[20] Chambers, *My Utmost for His Highest*, 180.
[21] Walter A. Henrichsen, *Disciples Are Made Not Born: Helping Others Grow to Maturity in Christ* (Colorado Springs, CO: David C. Cook, 2002), 108.

the Andes via a radio listening group, or in small groups like a college dorm, a Sunday school class, a youth group, a workplace break room, a home, or even under a tree on the African savannah. Some groups even operate online in a chat room or on a Web-based Bible study forum. There are countless ways to study God's Word, and the study of it guides his people to holiness and personal piety.

Small groups or same gender, one-on-one discipling relationships are effective. In larger groups or online, anonymity can be the enemy of spiritual growth. The saying, "You can run but you cannot hide," is often applied to small groups and one-on-one mentoring because the absence of even one member is immediately noticed and also because honest answers to accountability questions are unavoidable. Mentoring allows the one discipling to adjust and enhance his discipleship plan to the person rather than to execute a one-size-fits-all approach.

Countless discipleship resources are available today, in most major languages, and in print form as well as CD-ROM and online digital formats. The challenge for missionaries is finding a model that will suffice for the specific literacy level and the topics to be addressed. Additionally, taking 2 Timothy 2:2 into account, missionaries must consider not only what they are able to provide and teach but what their disciples will be able to continue on their own. For instance, glossy workbooks the mission agency or home church donates may be helpful and accessible for the missionary, but when the nationals are discipled in such a program, they generally have learned that "this is the way to disciple." In the absence of more workbooks, they will not be able to disciple others. The discipleship program must be reproducible, which may simply mean affordable for future discipling efforts.

Challenges face the missionary discipler that would not routinely be true for a pastor in his home culture. Missionaries must learn the language of the target culture much better than is required for basic communication. The missionary needs to be able to detect subtle nuances that would be missed by someone new in the language or who is using an interpreter to effectively speak to heart matters central to discipleship. Too often a missionary has the unfortunate and frustrating experience of discipling someone who breaks down with weeping and confession before the missionary's language skills are strong enough to know what the young believer is saying in such an emotional moment.

In a similar manner missionaries must know the target culture well enough to recognize cultural elements, such as tribal animistic tendencies, being incorporated into the growing Christian's worldview, Christian beliefs, or practices. Missionaries must know the culture well if they are to avoid the ever-present danger of simply adding a cross to the top of whatever complex religious system the disciple adhered to before embracing Christ. When those being discipled ask for wisdom and advice about whether it is OK to practice some cultural tradition or ritual, it is essential to know what is being prohibited or allowed and whether it would be the equivalent of killing a turkey at Thanksgiving or sacrificing a chicken on Halloween.

Additional tensions that often develop when missionaries are discipling in other cultures include relationships, privacy, time, and other intercultural issues. For instance, relationships between older and younger people in some cultures govern the types of relationships that are possible or the way the exchange of information should flow. A Western missionary may be perceived as wealthy, powerful, and dominant by a poor indigenous person of a lower-class people group within the socioeconomic structure of his own country. The missionary may be seen as a patron, and the "answers" to his questions will always be what the one answering thinks the missionary wants to hear or what will make him happy. If this dynamic is not recognized at the outset, many wasted hours may be spent in discipleship relationship before it truly is discipleship.

Privacy is not measured simply by being alone when you want to be; it also has to do with such things as what is yours and what is public, how close people sit to you, what topics are off limits in a conversation, and what information is too personal to reveal. Other cultures are surprisingly diverse in this area, and the most insulting behavior or the rudest question may be totally innocent and sincere. A missionary who has studied his target people group to know and understand culturally appropriate limits will be more effective in intercultural discipleship.

The view of time is also an area for consideration in discipling those of other cultures. Westerners tend to measure time by the clock on the wall, and making someone wait is rude and disrespectful; being "on time" refers to what can be measured by the clock. Other cultures tend to measure life by events rather than the clock. For instance, it is time to start a meeting when everyone who should be there gets there, and it is time to stop when we have done everything we came to do. An effective missionary can recognize subtle messages when they are intended and not take offense when they are not.

CONCLUSION

The effective missionary should seek to disciple new converts because the New Testament commands believers to do so, gives examples of Jesus, Paul, and others discipling those who came behind them, and shows that the early church was eager to grow in discipleship. There are many models for discipleship, and certain ones will be more effective in some areas, depending on need, ability, availability, and reproducibility.

Missionaries must know the culture and language where they are working to be the most effective, but more than that, they must know their Lord and his Word. A person can only teach, mentor, and disciple as much as he has been prepared. A shepherd can only lead his flock as high on the mountain as he has gone. When he stops, those following can go no higher. Oswald Chambers wrote, "Jesus Christ did not say—Go and save souls (the salvation of souls is the supernatural work of God), but—'Go and teach,' i.e., disciple, 'all nations,' and you cannot make disciples unless you are a disciple yourself."[22] Missionaries must seek to be discipled—whether by someone else or through personal spiritual discipline—if they hope to have a well deep enough to drink from for the rest of their lives and allow others to drink.

Discipleship does not occur automatically in the lives of new converts in a fallen world; they must be taught and mentored by one who has been discipled. In the same way a lifetime of ongoing discipleship is a decision that is made every day for the rest of a disciple's life. Even in areas of Christian leadership,

---

[22] Chambers, *My Utmost for His Highest*, 218.

some accept Christ, grow in the early days of their discipleship, and then back off of the hard disciplines to run on momentum. When their momentum loses steam, they begin to run on their own gifts, favors from friends, worldly models of leadership, or good old-fashioned manipulation and fear power. When new believers come to the Lord under such leaders, they learn what is modeled, and then they perpetuate what they have learned. It is essential that missionaries practice personal spiritual disciplines to get as close to Jesus as they can for the rest of their lives, disciple new converts in their ministries, and challenge them to continue (2 Tim 2:2). The next generation is watching. What will they learn? Chambers said, "The great essential of the missionary is that he remains true to the call of God, and realizes that his one purpose is to disciple men and women to Jesus."[23]

RESOURCES FOR FURTHER STUDY

Cosgrove, Francis M., Jr. The *Essentials of Discipleship: What It Takes to Follow Christ*. Dallas: Roper, 1988.

Henrichsen, Walter A. *Disciples Are Made Not Born: Helping Others Grow to Maturity in Christ*. Colorado Springs: David C. Cook, 2002.

Kuhne, Gary. *Discipleship: The Best Writings from the Most Experienced Disciple Makers*. Edited by Billie Hanks. Grand Rapids: Zondervan, 1981.

Sills, M. David. *Reaching and Teaching: A Call to Great Commission Obedience*. Chicago: Moody, 2010.

Whitney, Donald S. *Spiritual Disciplines for the Christian Life*. Colorado Springs: NavPress, 1991.

---

[23] Ibid., 219.

CHAPTER 10

CHURCH PLANTING

The heart of Christian missions is evangelism—proclaiming the gospel publicly and privately with a view toward persuading men and women to reject their idols and put their faith in Christ for salvation. But evangelism is not the end of the Great Commission task. Jesus commanded his followers to "make disciples," and making disciples means gathering the converted into congregations. J. D. Payne has said it well: "The advancement of the kingdom is significantly dependent on the multiplication of churches across people groups and population segments, across villages, towns, and cities."[1] Missions revolves around church planting.

WHY PLANT CHURCHES?

The primary support for church planting comes from the Bible itself. Jesus first pointed to the church in Matthew 16:18, when he said to Peter, "You are Peter, and on this rock I will build my church, and the gates of hell shall not prevail against it." The Greek word *ekklesia* signified a group assembled for a specific purpose. Luke and the New Testament writers picked up Jesus' word to identify the assembly of believers in Acts 5, the same group described in Acts 4:32–35:

---

[1] J. D. Payne, "Mission and Church Planting," in *Theology and Practice of Mission: God, the Church, and the Nations,* ed. Bruce Riley Ashford (Nashville: B&H Academic, 2011), 200.

> The full number of those who believed were of
> one heart and soul, and no one said that any of
> the things that belonged to him was his own,
> but they had everything in common. And with
> great power the apostles were giving their tes-
> timony to the resurrection of the Lord Jesus,
> and great grace was upon them all. There was
> not a needy person among them, for as many as
> were owners of lands or houses sold them and
> brought the proceeds of what was sold and laid
> it at the apostles' feet, and it was distributed to
> each as any had need.

It was only natural for believers to gather into churches, as most of the activities listed in this passage take place most appropriately in the context of a local church. Even more impor-tantly, the two central ordinances of the church, baptism and the Lord's Supper, are best practiced by a church body.

As believers were added to the church, and especially as the church expanded geographically, new local bodies of Christians were founded. Luke reports in Acts 9:31 that the church had moved into Judea, Galilee, and Samaria, saying, "And walking in the fear of the Lord and in the comfort of the Holy Spirit, it mul-tiplied." After the martyrdom of Stephen (Acts 7:60), believers scattered outside of Jerusalem, gathering a group in the city of Antioch. Acts 13:1 refers to that gathering as a church. The nat-ural result of men and women turning to Christ was a church.

The best-known examples of church planting in the New Tes-tament come through the ministry of Paul. One instance took place at Philippi when Paul met Lydia outside the city wall. After this businesswoman became a believer, she invited Paul to visit in her home, and a church was launched. Paul started churches in other cities, and many of his letters in the New Testament were directed toward those churches. Most of the churches met in homes. Paul's church plant in Corinth likely began in the home of Titius Justus (Acts 18:7). In other letters Paul indicated that churches met in various cities in the homes of Aquila and Priscilla (Rom 16:3–5; 1 Cor 16:19), Nympha (Col 4:15), and Philemon (Phlm 2).

While the Scriptures do not contain an explicit command to plant churches, the practice of gathering believers into churches is implied and testified to throughout the New Testament. As the gospel went forth from Jerusalem, churches appeared in cities throughout the Roman Empire then beyond, toward the ends of the earth.

Missionaries and leaders have identified a multitude of practical reasons for church planting in addition to the biblical model. New churches provide ways for believers from various people groups and languages to gather for worship and discipleship, even where they are the minority. The multiplication of churches allows for broader evangelism as implanted groups spread throughout a geographical area. Local churches also provide the means by which believers can be "salt and light" in a community, leading to cultural impact and transformation.

In spite of the multitude of good biblical and practical reasons to start churches, many church planters face significant opposition to their missionary efforts. Where churches exist, they may consider new churches a threat to their stability or health. Pastors of established churches sometimes argue that resources would be better spent to rehabilitate and rejuvenate existing congregations. Sometimes there might be a legitimate argument against starting a similar church in close proximity to a healthy church. In most communities, however, new churches will reach people not touched by existing congregations, leading to overall kingdom growth. Obviously, where the church does not exist, new congregations are absolutely necessary.

PREPARING TO PLANT A CHURCH

Church planting is an integral part of Great Commission ministry that is tied directly to evangelism and discipleship. The starting place for any church-planting effort should be in prayer. Planting is in many ways spiritual warfare as the church engages lostness, and prayer is a primary tool in that battle. A second important piece of preparation is developing a solid biblical and theological foundation, which is the purpose of chapters 3 and 4 of this volume. In addition to the basic biblical framework for missions, however, church planters must have a solid understanding of what they are planting. Before engaging church planting, missionaries must ask, "What is a church?"

Throughout church history various cultures have attached certain practices and forms to churches that, while they may not be unbiblical, are not required by the Scriptures for church planting. For example, many Western churches have an organ or a drum set as an important part of worship. Neither of these is prohibited by the Bible, but neither is required, either. Worship is necessary, but the exact forms of worship are not dictated.

While the term *church* encompasses the universal church made up of believers across all ages, church planting is concerned with local churches—the geographic, cultural expression of the universal church. Gregg Allison describes congregations in this way:

> Local churches are led by pastors (also called elders) and served by deacons, possess and pursue purity and unity, exercise church discipline, develop strong connections with other churches, and celebrate the ordinances of baptism and the Lord's Supper. Equipped by the Holy Spirit with spiritual gifts for ministry, these communities regularly gather to worship the triune God, proclaim His Word, engage non-Christians with the gospel, disciple their members, care for people through prayer and giving, and stand both for and against the world.[2]

This definition encompasses what some missiologists have referred to as the "irreducible ecclesiological minimum," describing what must be present, in general, for a group to be considered a church.

The International Mission Board of the Southern Baptist Convention, looking at the issue from the viewpoint of a denominational missions agency, defines "church" according to the Southern Baptist confession of faith, The Baptist Faith and Message. To clarify specific criteria for missionaries, the IMB added ten "guidelines" for church planters:

---

[2] Gregg R. Allison, *Sojourners and Strangers: The Doctrine of the Church* (Wheaton: Crossway, 2012), 30.

1. A church is intentional about being a church. Members think of themselves as a church. They are committed to one another and to God (associated by covenant) in pursuing all that Scripture requires of a church.
2. A church has an identifiable membership of baptized believers in Jesus Christ.
3. A church practices the baptism of believers only by immersing them in water.
4. A church observes the Lord's Supper on a regular basis.
5. Under the authority of the local church and its leadership, members may be assigned to carry out the ordinances.
6. A church submits to the inerrant word of God as the ultimate authority for all that it believes and does.
7. A church meets regularly for worship, prayer, the study of God's word, and fellowship. Members of the church minister to one another's needs, hold each other accountable, and exercise church discipline as needed. Members encourage one another and build each other up in holiness, maturity in Christ, and love.
8. A church embraces its responsibility to fulfill the Great Commission, both locally and globally, from the beginning of its existence as a church.
9. A church is autonomous and self-governing under the Lordship of Jesus Christ and the authority of His Word.
10. A church has identifiable leaders, who are scrutinized and set apart according to the qualifications set forth in Scripture. A church recognizes two Biblical offices of church leadership: pastors/elders/overseers and deacons. While both men and women are gifted for service in the church, the office of pastor/elder/ overseer is limited to men as qualified by Scripture.[3]

---

[3] "International Mission Board, Definition of a Church, January 25, 2005," accessed June 2, 2013, http://www.imb.org/main/news/details.asp?LanguageID=1709&StoryID=3838.

While these guidelines reflect certain aspects of Baptist doctrine and practice, they are helpful for church planters. Churches are bodies of baptized believers in Jesus Christ covenanted together for accountability and ministry, including proclamation of the Word, celebration of the ordinances, discipleship, missions, and having biblical leadership.

Biblical ecclesiology is important for church planters because of the importance of contextualization. When a planter knows what is vital to a New Testament church, he will be better able to determine what forms and expressions can be adjusted to culture. For example, worship is necessary, but the Scriptures do not dictate forms and modes of worship. Biblical leadership is a key to church life, and terminology (pastor, elder, etc.) might change. Yet we are not at liberty to adjust the scriptural requirements for elders and deacons set out in 1 Timothy 3. Whoever is functioning in these offices, regardless of the title of the office, must meet the biblical requirements for the office.

Another factor in planning for church planting is models. There are several ways to view church-planting models depending on your viewpoint. In terms of planter leadership, two models generally surface. In the apostolic model, a church planter raises up leaders quickly from the new church itself with a view toward moving on to other fields after the church is established. This model is most appropriate for missionary church planters, as one of the goals of intercultural church planting is indigenousness in leadership and form (see below). When a planter is working in his own culture (or a close culture), the planter pastor model might be suitable. There the planter becomes the pastor (or elder) with an intention to remain in the church long-term.

Either the apostolic or planter-pastor model can be led by individual planters or by a group working as a team. The advantages of church planting as a team are evident: mutual support and encouragement, combination of gifted individuals, or larger base of financial support. The team may look like a traditional church staff with a lead pastor, worship leader, student leader, and so on. Or the team might be made up of the core of the future church members. Either is a healthy model for church planting where possible.

Models can also refer to church structure. Structures should be guided by cultural factors rather than planter preferences. The "traditional" model is characterized by buildings and programs. Churches may meet in a permanent church building, or the congregation may gather in a school, commercial building, or the like. Traditional church plants are most appropriate for settings where churches are historically present and where there is a general cultural expectation of certain forms.

Two less traditional models are the "cell church" model and "house churches." In the cell church model, a church is decentralized into small groups that may meet in homes, businesses, or other so-called "third places" (neither in traditional church buildings nor in homes). The church is composed of all of these groups and usually has one pastor or elder board, as well as a somewhat hierarchical structure of group leadership. Cell churches might gather occasionally for large worship services. Often cell groups will hear a sermon or message from the central pastor.

The house church model is just as it sounds: churches are small, simply structured, and meet in homes. The key difference between cell churches and house churches is that in cell churches the groups are seen as part of a larger congregation. In the house church model, each group is autonomous (though they are often part of a larger, loosely organized network of house churches). Occasionally churches may follow the house church model but meet outside individual homes. They maintain the same general philosophy of simplicity while gathering in a third place.

While some house church advocates argue that their model is the best model based on historical and biblical grounds, any of these models (as well as variations on all three) are appropriate depending on context. The advantage of the cell church and house church models is their flexibility and low cost. Without the burden of buildings, these churches can reproduce more easily. In fact, one key factor in both models is intentional reproduction of groups or churches. Cell churches are often found in areas where real estate is expensive, as are house churches.

House churches are common in regions where Christians are persecuted.

One important development in twentieth-century missions related to church planting models is the church planting movement (CPM). Simply defined, a CPM is "a rapid and multiplicative increase of indigenous churches planting churches within a given people group or population segment."[4] While David Garrison, the author most frequently identified with CPM, would argue that they are not a model, he does describe several factors present in most CPMs:

1. Extraordinary prayer
2. Abundant evangelism
3. Intentional church planting of reproducing churches
4. The authority of God's Word
5. Local leadership
6. Lay leadership
7. House churches
8. Churches planting churches
9. Rapid reproduction
10. Healthy churches[5]

While these factors present healthy guidelines for church-planting models, they are best understood with context in mind. For example, the meaning of "rapid" varies from culture to culture, and church planting that is too rapid may lead to churches led by pastors/elders unprepared (or unqualified) for leadership. As mentioned above, house churches may not be appropriate in every culture. With thoughtful application the characteristics seen in CPM are helpful guides for church planters thinking about their task.

STAGES OF CHURCH PLANTING

Once general factors such as theological foundations and models are considered, church planting involves three basic stages. The first and most vital stage of church planting is *evangelizing.* Church planting cannot be separated from the

---

[4] David Garrison, *Church Planting Movements* (Richmond, VA: WIGTake Resources, 2004), 172.
[5] Ibid., 172.

proclamation of the gospel with a view toward persuading men and women to follow Christ. While many new churches have been the result of division or relocation (and God can use both of those means to accomplish his purposes), church planting is best defined as *evangelism leading to new congregations among unreached people groups, population segments, and communities*.

An important consideration of church planting during the evangelizing stage is *indigeneity*. The word *indigenous* comes from botany and horticulture and refers to plants that are "of the ground" or are native to a particular location or climate. Indigenous plants thrive, grow, and reproduce well in their native environment. In the same way, indigenous churches reflect culture and are "at home" among a people without accommodating or taking on unhealthy or unbiblical aspects of that culture. The "Indigenous Principle" of church planting developed in the nineteenth century with the work of Rufus Anderson and Henry Venn (see chap. 5). They argued that churches should be self-governing, self-supporting, and self-propagating (reproducing). Later missiologists added "self-theologizing" to emphasize the importance of a people-group church thinking biblically about its own worldview and culture.

The second stage of church planting is *gathering*. Once some have become Christians, they must be gathered into groups (congregations). At first this may mean only a few individuals meeting together in a "third place" for the purpose of accountability and Bible study. The heart of gathering is discipleship, which may take many forms, especially in the early stages of a church plant. During the gathering phase the seeds of biblical ecclesiology must be planted into the lives of new believers. Worship, proclamation (whether in preaching or in Bible study), and celebration of the ordinances may take place during this period, especially once the believers have agreed (covenanted) together to be a church. In this context the Great Commission admonition about teaching all that Jesus commanded takes form.

The third stage is *reproducing* and may overlap with the second stage. The reproducing phase has both inward- and outward-focused components. First, planters should seek to raise up leaders from within the people group or community the church represents. Take the opportunity to disciple men in such a way that they can find their spiritual gifts and learn to lead, especially in intercultural settings. As this group multiplies, a church will find its future pastors and deacons. Remember to keep the biblical qualifications of 1 Timothy 3 and Titus 1 in mind.

The reproducing stage should also point the church plant outward to consider planting new churches. Just as the Antioch church came from Jerusalem, then sent Saul and Barnabas to plant new churches, missionary churches in the twenty-first century should reproduce, planting new congregations among the unreached. The most natural form of reproduction is for a congregation to evangelize within a group of similar culture but in a different geographical area. When churches reproduce, growth is exponential and spreads throughout a people. Regardless of the model or methodology of church planting, churches should have reproduction as a core value.

Each of the three basic stages of church planting may have several components within, but all three should be present in a church-planting strategy. Leading up to evangelizing, planters must consider culture and people group, as described in chapter 7. Indigenous churches are most at home in their host culture, facilitating evangelism and reproduction. The goal of church planting is spreading the gospel among a people group or community.

If the heart of missions is evangelism, then missions must include church planting. C. Peter Wagner once wrote, "The most effective method of evangelism under heaven is church planting."[6] Missionaries may do more than church planting—agriculture, teaching, medicine—but all of the other activities should move toward church planting. Even short-term missions should work alongside missionaries or existing churches with a view toward evangelism that results in new congregations. Such is certainly the most effective means of "making disciples of all nations" (Matt 28:19).

---

[6] C. Peter Wagner, *Church Planting for a Greater Harvest* (Ventura, CA: Regal, 1990), 11.

RESOURCES FOR FURTHER STUDY

Hesselgrave, David, and Earl Blomberg. *Planting Churches Cross-Culturally: An Introduction to the Whats, Whys, and Hows of Global Church Planting.* Grand Rapids: Baker, 1980.

Ott, Craig, and Gene Wilson. *Global Church Planting: Biblical Principles and Best Practices for Multiplication.* Grand Rapids: Baker, 2011.

Sinclair, Daniel. *A Vision of the Possible: Pioneer Church Planting in Teams.* Waynesboro, GA: Authentic Media, 2005.

CHAPTER 11

THE INDIVIDUAL CHRISTIAN
AND GLOBAL MISSIONS

It is our prayer that this book has thus far introduced you to the universe of global missions and shed some light on the high calling of being a missionary to proclaim the glories of the gospel around the world today. We turn our attention now to practical matters for those who find themselves burdened to join God on mission in his world. This chapter will guide you through several key issues related to going, settling in, and fruitful ministry in your place in God's plan for the world.

GOING

We learned early on about the missionary call, what it is, and how to discern whether God is so calling you. At this point in the book, you may sense that God indeed has such a plan for your life and you long to be in his place for you somewhere around the world. As exciting as this sounds, you may also have some butterflies as you think about new languages to learn, strange foods you will eat, and many other aspects of adjusting to a new culture. Perhaps you also recognize some gnawing fears and anxieties as you consider such things as the necessities of life in the new place or headlines reporting unrest in the area where God is calling you. When you are as thoroughly prepared as you can be in all that can be known in advance, you will be more at ease as you learn other aspects of living life abroad when you arrive.

All of the authors of this text remember well the joy of discerning God's will and his missionary call on our lives. When he made clear the place and opened the door to go, the excitement was joined by a myriad of emotions: joy to join him on mission, thankfulness to be so chosen, sorrow to say good-bye, anxiety of the unknowns, contentment in knowing life's purpose, peace of resting in his will, and many more. It is a big decision to embrace God's missionary call on your life and go to live in another culture, but it is only the first of many. Countless decisions must be made after that, such as what to sell, give away, or store until you return. You soon learn that great freedom is in downward mobility—granted, when you are the one choosing it for Christ's sake and it is not being thrust upon you without warning. You will need to make decisions about who will handle stateside business and personal matters while you are gone. Of course, a major group of decisions surrounds the agency with which you choose to serve, the city in which you will live, where you will go to language school, whether to home school your children or place them in an MK school or national school, and so on. Embracing your call and the process of going to the field is a major life decision that will impact the rest of your life, but it is only the first of many more to come.

CHALLENGES OF KNOWING AND GOING

Confusion surrounding the missionary call is likely the primary cause of people not going to the mission field. Believing the call must be some mysterious, supernatural phenomenon, such as seeing your name in the clouds accompanied by the name of some exotic locale, or believing that every missionary's call must match another's call can create much tension. Sadly many feel that a deep desire to go to the nations to live, preach, teach, and serve must indicate that God has *not* called you, mistakenly thinking that if it sounds like something you would enjoy then it cannot be God's will. For this reason we addressed the missionary call early on in this book to dispel such notions and provide the components to consider when discerning a call.[1]

---

[1] For a broader understanding and further investigation, see M. David Sills, *The Missionary Call: Find Your Place in God's Plan for the World* (Chicago: Moody, 2008).

When the call is unmistakable, there is great peace in knowing your life direction, but doubts may remain about which path to walk to get there. Many wonder which agency they should serve through, where exactly they should go, and whether to go single or wait until they are married. Try to remember in the midst of website research and talking to agency representatives at missions conferences that the same God who has made your call plain will make all of these details clear as well. In the beginning of your exploration of how to fulfill your missionary call, two words of advice are in order.

First, guard your heart. Many know with profound certainty that God has called them to missions, and perhaps even the place, worldview, or language they are to serve. Yet, in the passage of time, the call is relegated to a back burner of life while in college, during dating, or beginning a career. They accumulate debt while obtaining education or fall in love with someone and marry without having the "missions" talk. Then they wake up one day and remember the call that was so plain years ago, but now life circumstances—debt, an unwilling spouse, or some other situation—preclude the possibility of leaving it all to go serve overseas. Many tears have been shed over the reawakening of a missionary call only after life has developed in such a way as to make its fulfillment difficult or virtually impossible.

Second, as you choose your agency and team for missionary service, make sure you know them as well as they know you. Just as you would not want to marry someone simply because they are willing to marry you, so you should ask as many questions of the agency (in person or in your investigation) as they ask of you. The agency and team with which you serve is as important a decision as the person you marry—at least with regard to your missionary service. Your contentment on the field, joy in serving the Lord and his people, and how long you remain on the field as a missionary are largely determined by agency and team fit. Many missionaries have returned after—or during!—a term of missionary service broken, depressed, and disillusioned. Perhaps the returned missionary questions whether he truly heard God's call or is personally lacking in some way spiritually. It could have been that his view of biblical interpretation, missionary methodology, or even interpersonal issues in the agency were at such odds that long-term service was simply too problematic. Missionaries serve on a team in most agencies, and teams are like family—you do not get to choose whom you get. It is worth the effort and expense to get to know the people on the team with whom you would serve and the mission agency's beliefs and methodologies before signing on the dotted line. Otherwise you may be a thorn in their side, and they will be one in yours.

CHALLENGES OF LEAVING AND CLEAVING

The challenge of knowing and actually going are related closely to the missionary candidate's willingness to leave and cleave. Just as a young bride and husband leave their families of origin and come together to begin a new life together as a family—still loving their mother, father, and siblings, but now cleaving primarily to each other—so missionaries must mentally, emotionally, and physically leave their home culture to be fully incarnate in the new culture. Failure to do so, whether due to being unprepared or being unwilling, results in deeper and longer-lasting culture shock. An ancient proverb teaches, "To sail to new and foreign lands one must be willing to lose sight of the shore."

The need to leave and cleave was patently obvious to earlier generations, but modern technology makes this increasingly problematic in our day. Missionaries in former days departed from their homelands, giving a reluctant last embrace and farewell to beloved family members, and then waved good-bye as the ship sailed out of port. Wiping away tears of sorrow, knowing they would likely not see many loved ones again in this life, they began the painful grieving of leaving. Over subsequent days they understandably mourned the loss of these relationships and life in their home culture. However, they soon turned their thoughts to their missionary call, the land where they would live, the language they would speak, and the gospel they would proclaim. With every nautical mile left in their wake, they were adjusting mentally, emotionally, and even spiritually to the missionary life they were beginning.

In our day many missionaries hug a tearful good-bye at the airport and walk toward the door to board the airplane, shouting to Mom, "I'll text you when we land. Then, we can Skype when we get to the guest apartment." And sure enough, within hours they are texting about the news of their arrival, or Skyping, e-mailing, updating Facebook pages, tweeting, and chatting online on one of the various Internet-based telephone services. Each day brings new challenges, of course, but these are tempered by three to four hours online, reading news from home and messages from friends, staying active long distance in church fellowships, keeping up with politics, and being swallowed up by the voracious, insatiable, time devourer that the Internet is. They never really have the chance to embrace the new culture because they never really leave their old one; they rarely venture out into the new and unknown. We have spoken with missionaries who talk by phone with their moms eight to ten times per day. And why not? They did so when they lived in the USA, and, with Internet-based telephone services, it is still a local call for them. One missionary still watches the same television show with her mom every week that she had watched with her before she left. The only difference now is that she is on the phone with her for the entire show instead of on the couch. A missionary administrator was visiting a missionary family on the field and asked the time. The missionary stared at her watch for so long that the administrator asked whether her watch was broken. She replied, "No, but I have to make the time zone adjustment in my head because I leave my watch set on the time of my hometown in the USA." It is hard to cleave to the new without leaving the old.

Sherwood Lingenfelter wrote in *Ministering Cross-Culturally* that missionaries must strive to incarnate as much as is humanly possible in the new culture, understanding that the most of it anyone will ever be able to attain is probably 75 percent because the missionary grew up in another culture. However, he stresses that in order to make this adjustment, you must be willing to lose about 25 percent of who you were before going. The goal is to be a 150 percent person—75 percent of the new and 75 percent of the old. Be forewarned that willingness to let go of the old is often the most difficult part.[2]

---

[2] Sherwood Lingenfelter and Marvin Mayers, *Ministering Cross-Culturally* (Grand Rapids: Baker Academic, 2003), 24.

CHALLENGES OF CULTURE SHOCK AND ADAPTING

Adapting to a new culture is not as easy you may think, especially if you are anticipating a missionary career in a place where you traveled on a one- or two-week mission trip. Rather than introduce you to new aspects of the culture, repeated trips to a country you really like tend only to confirm your initial impression, especially if you reunite with friends you made on the first trip or return to the same places. The eventual drain of culture shock will not set in on such a short trip, especially if you are staying in a nice hotel and eating meals prepared for you in restaurants or in others' homes, isolated from the harsher realities of life there.

The experience can be similar to visiting one of those all-inclusive resorts where everything is arranged and you do not even have to think. They pick you up at the airport in an air-conditioned van, take you to the hotel, wait on you the entire time, prepare your meals, and then return you to the airport at the end of your stay. You never really see the country itself or get to know the culture. Some mission trips are not far from such a scenario. When missionaries are commissioned to serve in the country and finally arrive to fend for themselves in everyday, mundane life, they often are disillusioned and disappointed.

Culture Shock[3]

Culture shock is a dark valley through which every intercultural worker must pass. Seasoned travelers sometimes naively think they will not really suffer it so much. While the peaks and valleys of the experience may not be as extreme for some as for others, everyone must go through the cycle of adjustment. Culture shock sneaks up on you to catch you when you least expect it. Missionaries are fortunate to be prepared to recognize the various stages of culture shock and the way through them.

Culture Surprise of the Tourist Stage

After the long process of discerning God's will for your life and embracing a missionary call, you begin the appointment

---

[3] Portions of the sections on culture shock and language learning are excerpted from chap. 10 of M. David Sills, *The Missionary Call: Find Your Place in God's Plan for the World* (Chicago: Moody, 2008).

process or sharing your vision for missions to raise your support. As you complete each necessary step, you are more excited and eager as you anticipate arriving on the field to begin your ministry. At last the day comes when you receive clearance to travel to the field. As you board the plane, knowing that thousands of prayers are finally beginning to find fulfillment, your excitement knows no bounds.

The first weeks in the country are like a honeymoon. You feel like you were born for this culture and that nothing could go wrong. We refer to this as the tourist stage because this is the deepest level of involvement that most vacation travelers reach. The culture engagement at this level is really more culture surprise or culture delight than culture shock. All of the sights are new and beautiful, and the colors are brilliant in the fields and village markets. You find that words fail you to describe in letters home how the fragrances of the restaurants, fields of flowers, and bakeries perfume the air. The money is like the money of some board game—all different sizes and colors! The food, music, customs, and hospitality of your new home make you wonder why everyone has not moved here. Even the challenge that you cannot speak the language yet is more of a novelty than a bother. Enjoy this stage; it will last only a few weeks.

The Deep Pit of the Rejection Stage

The next stage is the deep pit of the rejection period. This occurs because everything that once was normal is now abnormal, and you cannot function as you once did; though at first it was fun, now it is exasperating. No one speaks your language, which means you cannot speak it either. The delicious fragrances that once enchanted you have become a stench. What happened; did something change? The food you once thought so delicious now seems too bland—or too spicy—and you miss your mom's cooking. Much of the beauty you once saw is now an eyesore. You never really noticed the litter and graffiti before, but now it seems to be everywhere. You are constantly doing the math in your head to convert the local prices into "real money." The once beautiful music is now a racket to your ears and played much too loudly. You become paranoid and believe the nationals are out to get you, to take advantage of you in every transaction, and are thieves in waiting. You wonder what is happening and why you ever came here. A key to staying sane is to adopt the life motto that our family used: It's not wrong; it's not stupid; it's just different. Another member of our writing team reports that his family had the saying: There is a reason they do it this way; we will probably never know what that is, but surely there is a reason.

Telltale signs characterize the missionary's home during this rejection stage. The smell of hamburgers cooking or empty pizza boxes are in the kitchen on a daily basis. The music heard will be worship songs from the home church. The television will feature a favorite DVD brought from home. The jeans, sneakers, and ball caps will all be from home, and the T-shirt will probably have an American flag on it or a slogan in English. None of these things are evil or earmarks of a failed missionary. Yet, when they begin to describe and dominate his or her life, culture shock is usually at work.

The inability to speak the language results in frustration in daily life, like ordering at a restaurant or paying a utility bill. Self-esteem gives way to despondency. When two nationals are speaking their language and they begin to giggle, you are sure they are laughing at you. If you have just tried speaking in their language, they probably are! However, when your child is ill and you need to take him to the doctor, it is terrifying not to be able to speak the language. A friend of ours had recently arrived in a new country for language school. After someone from the language school dropped them off at the apartment that would be their home for the next year, their child suffered an epileptic-type seizure for the first time in her life. She was unconscious, and they did not know what was wrong with her, how to speak the language, how to work the phones, or whom to call if they had known. He took his child in his arms and walked to the street. A passing motorist realized that he was in dire need of help, motioned for him to get in the car, and took him to an international hospital where English-speaking doctors could care for her.

Crime is a reality all over this fallen world. When you are in a new country and going through culture shock, any crime seems personal. What often makes it worse is when the more-seasoned missionaries, forgetting how hard their own adjustment was, do not appreciate your hardships. When you are in culture shock and any crime occurs, you are angry, dwell on negative events, and unfairly characterize everyone you see on the streets as the potential thief. The nationals are not trusted, and you begin to paint all of them with the same brush.

In order to compensate for your inability to traffic in the educated, polite society of the new culture, you may begin to spend time with fellow English speakers. Perhaps you join the American Club or a country club, ostensibly because it has a pool where your kids can swim or they can take tennis lessons. Soon you are there several days of every week where you join with your ex-patriot friends, making one another feel better by ridiculing the nationals. You begin to retell all the ethnic jokes you heard as a child, but now the nationals are the idiots in the story. Some of you reading this now may find such unchristian behavior from missionaries hard to understand or even believe. That shocked perspective is what adds to your shame and conviction one day when you find yourself joining in. You may begin to question your sanity or salvation.

You must be intentional about avoiding the sticky trap of ex-patriot exclusive friendships and get involved in the culture. In order to be salt and light in the world, you must be in the world. Sherwood Lingenfelter and Marvin Mayers have described the reason we persevere past this point in our adjustment.

> Although we cannot reach perfection, we still can strive for the lesser goal of becoming incarnate in the culture of those we serve. . . We need to move from a position comfortable to us and our culture to a position approximating the goals of the culture to which we are sent. Wherever we serve, our objective should be to live in such a way that we respect, love, and share our very lives (including our priorities and goals) with those to whom we seek to minister.[4]

---

[4] Lingenfelter and Mayers, *Ministering Cross-Culturally*, 88–89.

This is because, no matter how hard it gets, a joy flows from obedience that overcomes the struggle.

Another cause of this difficult time of cultural adjustment is role deprivation. You may have been an important pastor, doctor, or teacher in your home culture, and now you cannot even communicate at the level of a first-grader, much less fulfill your accustomed role in life. In addition, the routines of your life are gone. You can no longer jump in the car to run an errand as you always have, you can't ask where the milk is in the grocery store, or you can't glance over a menu and decide what you'd like to eat. Life just seems difficult, and it drains you dry. Frustrations are present that you never knew at home, or even if similar situations did bother you there, you had ways of recharging your emotional or mental batteries at home that are impossible in the new culture: hanging out with friends, indulging at a favorite restaurant, visiting in a coffee shop, or going to see the latest movie. Additionally, little annoyances may be easily dealt with one at a time, but they usually come in waves of overwhelming numbers that wear down your cultural shock absorbers after a while. From then on, you are metal on metal, crashing through the terrain of a new culture and wondering whether this will ever become easy.

Emerging from the Valley of Despair

This rejection stage can last from a few months to a couple of years. The length of time you spend in this deep valley depends on how well you bond with the culture, learn the language, and make friends. Language skills are crucial for understanding cultural experiences and events. Once you learn the language, you can overhear two nationals laughing in their conversation and realize it is in response to a joke's punch line and not you. The comfort that comes with ability to communicate easily also brings a greater sense of security.

Making friends in the culture is crucial. As you make friends, you can attend cultural events with your own personal guide and cultural interpreter and learn to appreciate the food, music, humor, and rhythm of life. If the national foods seem strange to you and your children, make a family rule that you will try one new national dish every week. This is manageable for almost anyone, and you will identify national foods you really like. The nationals will be happy and proud to see you enjoying their delicacies—which makes it less offensive when you avoid those you find less palatable. You can experience and learn to appreciate other aspects of the new culture in bite-sized chunks as well. The resulting benefit is that what was so abnormal to you only a few months ago will begin to be normal. In fact, you will soon find yourself preferring some of the cultural peculiarities to your own home culture.

Coming out of the valley of despair can take one of several routes; two are unhealthy and one is the ideal. The first unhealthy route is assimilation, where some missionaries attempt to "go completely native." Some have tried to delete their past and attempt to forget English and their family back home, totally embracing the new culture as if they had been born into it. This might sound like the correct attitude, but it is not. God made you who you are, and all of your life experiences are his gifts to you—even the bad ones are worked together for your good and his glory (Rom 8:28). Total suppression of your past is the recipe for a psychological and emotional breakdown. Imagine getting married and attempting to delete your family of origin and all your previous life experiences; you would no longer be the person with whom your spouse fell in love. If you can embrace your past and the best of the new life, you will be better able to minister to the ones you came to evangelize and disciple and stay healthy in the process.

The second route is the other unhealthy extreme of nonacceptance. Some missionaries never get used to the new culture but only grudgingly acquiesce to the reality that they now live in it and cannot escape. They see no way out, either because of the shame that would accompany resigning and returning home, or perhaps their spouse loves the new country, and they do not wish to impede the family from fulfilling God's call. For them missions is a life sentence. The result is that they feel culture tension or culture stress, and they never accept the nationals as equals. They will never really trust them, never sit next to them in a meeting if they can avoid it, and never invite them into their home. Of course, they never say this aloud and often feel guilty for such an attitude. The effect on the family's missionary effectiveness is devastating. Culture-tension's actions speak much more loudly than its words.

The healthy way out of the pit of the rejection stage is cultural adaptation. This occurs when the new way of life that seemed so abnormal begins to feel normal, when it is hard to remember not soaking vegetables and fruits in a bleach solution to make them safe to eat or buying meat in outdoor markets or driving on the left side of the road. Life in the new culture gets easier; it seems normal. The sense of having routines returns; they are different, but a sense of normalcy is back, and you feel good about life again. You cannot wait to visit with your friends back home and tell them all about this new life as you enjoy a few of your favorite things back home again.

A Counterintuitive Shock

When you return home again is when you experience the real counterintuitive shock. Most missionaries are anxious about going to live in a new country and culture; they expect to experience some culture shock. Almost all the way through their first term on the field they daydream about how sweet it will be to go to their favorite fast-food restaurant whenever they wish or enjoy the candy bars, cereal, Dr. Pepper, or bacon they may not be able to get in the new country. They imagine enraptured friends listening to their every utterance as if they were Marco Polo returning from his travels. There is great shock upon finding that their friends' interest only lasts for a few polite conversations, and then they prefer to change the subject. They simply have no framework of reference for relating to the missionary's new culture. Most people want to talk about themselves or at least something they know.

You will also be shocked by the priorities and preferences of churches back home as you view them with a new perspective. How could they spend $10,000 to replace the upholstery on the pew cushions so they will match the new carpet? Do they not know about the tens of thousands of children dying of starvation and the millions who need to hear the gospel? The sick feeling you get from the waste and wealth of churches back home lets you know that you have changed. It is true; you cannot go home again—you are not the same person you were when you left. You are increasingly a citizen of a third culture, not the one of your birth or your target culture but some mixture of the two. You feel that you just do not have a home. Because you do not expect this sense of displacement and loneliness, it blindsides you as a returning or furloughing missionary.

The culture shock cycle is one all missionaries will go through, but culture shock is not a "one and done" proposition. While certainly some aspects you work through will not impact you as negatively as they did the first time around, every day finds the missionary and family members at differing levels of the cycle in repeated waves. In fact, it is more helpful to think of culture shock as endless cycles of culture fatigue and stress. The initial experience of culture shock and reverse culture shock will shake your emotional and mental world. Subsequent cycles are more like waves that will return again and again in times of stress and fatigue when living in a culture that is not your culture of origin.

CHALLENGES OF LANGUAGE LEARNING

Learning the language of your new country is both absolutely necessary for a successful missions experience and a significant contributor to your culture shock. There is much more to learning another language than simply memorizing vocabulary, learning grammar rules, and practicing pronunciation. One of the most beneficial things you can do is to begin making friends as quickly as your limited language skills will allow. Spend time with them and constantly ask what people are doing, why they are doing it, and in what ways the practice has changed over time in the country. In this process you will deepen the friendship because everyone enjoys introducing others to their country—just ask your grandfather how something used to be done back in the day. You will also be learning the colloquial ways of speaking, regional vocabulary, and likely some aspects of culture you would never have known otherwise. Be aware that learning another language is much easier when you know your own. When we teach Spanish or French, we recommend students purchase and use the books like *English Grammar for Students of Spanish* or its companion for French.[5] With such a

---

[5] Emily Spinelli, *English Grammar for Students of Spanish* (Ann Arbor, MI: The Olivia and Hill

resource you will be able to make quick work of understanding what your language teachers are talking about when teaching about past-perfect or present-progressive tenses.

Another great help in language learning is to accept the fact that you will be laughed with and laughed at. Craig Storti spoke of the gaffs you will inevitably make when starting out in a new culture when he said, "You can laugh them off to a point—they're all quite petty in the grand scheme of things—but most people tire quickly of making fools of themselves."[6] When you make a mistake in the language and others laugh, simply laugh along with them. It will show them your humility and joy in life that they will find refreshingly attractive. You will also be showing others that you want to learn their language. Those uptight folks who never open their mouths for fear of using the wrong word, tense, or conjugation do not learn the language as well or as fast and miss half the fun of living in another culture. A Spanish proverb says that one who speaks two languages has two souls. They do not mean this literally; the proverb simply means that you can express yourself deeply in each language in ways that would be much more difficult to say in the other.

Perhaps you already know the area of the world you will serve and want to begin now learning the language. You definitely should because every bit you learn now will not have to be learned later, and you are also developing your ear to "hear" the language and become comfortable in its sounds and rhythm. Even if you are not exactly sure which language you will eventually need to learn for missionary service, you can begin learning a language you could use in your community or on mission trips. The process of learning another language will serve you when learning other languages in the future because your brain will have developed a process of learning verb systems, modifiers, articles, and grammar. Faced with the daunting prospect of paying tuition or purchasing expensive software, some wonder about other options. An ESL-language exchange model is a good option for some. It involves teaching English to local immigrants or refugees for an hour or so each week, and then the

---

Press, 2007); Jacqueline Morton, *English Grammar for Students of French* (Ann Arbor, MI: The Olivia and Hill Press, 1997).

[6] Craig Storti, *The Art of Crossing Cultures* (London: Nicholas Brealey Publishing, 2001), 14.

tables are turned so that the student teaches the English teacher the student's language. Not only does the teacher learn another language; the student is able to give back and learns English from a native speaker without having to pay for the opportunity or begin life in the USA by losing face as a "charity case."

Perhaps the greatest advantage you could give to your language learning is a love for the language you are learning. When language learning is considered to be a necessary evil and as a chore to get out of the way so you can do your job, the language will not come easily, and what little does come will be used in a wooden fashion with a strong English accent. Make friends using the language, and learn to love its sounds and unique idioms. Learning the language is the key to learning the culture, and learning the culture is the key to learning the language. When two people fall in love, the effort to learn as much as possible about each other is not tedious. Your love drives you to learn more, and all you learn plunges you deeper in love. Strive to make that true with the language, and you will speak it well. Speaking the language well gives you credibility. It will also give to others a higher opinion of both you and what you have to say than if you butcher their language and make it painful for them to hear you out.

Some want to bypass language school, or shorten it greatly, thinking, *I'll get the basics in language school over a few months and then head out and polish my language skills when I get on my mission field.* That is a bad plan. You will learn crutches for communicating in the few months you are studying in language school, such as using present tense verbs but making hand motions to indicate you are referring to something in the past or sloppily using feminine articles with masculine nouns. Your brain learns these patterns, and you never polish them away because they sound correct to your brain. Others will think you are as unintelligent as you sound, and your gospel will seem fitting only for country bumpkins and simple-minded folks. Remember that all some will ever know about Jesus is what comes out of your mouth, and unfortunately they will judge him by the way you present him. Just as getting a good seminary education prior to missionary service whenever possible is not time wasted, so language school is not time in neutral, treading water when you could be on the field. You are digging a well that you and others will drink from for the rest of your life.

Language school is a stressful experience for everyone in the family. It hits each of your family and team members in unique ways because of the differences in our needs and desires. For instance, husbands tend to need significance in their lives, and wives tend to need security (I say "tend to" because both genders need both). However, total immersion language school threatens both spouses in both ways. The husband and father may feel his significance threatened when his wife picks up the language faster and scores better on language exams than he does and when his kids are fluently chattering away with national neighborhood children. It is difficult for him to find significance when he cannot even ask for a glass of water in the new language, much less preach, teach, or share a simple plan of salvation. The wife and mother may feel her family's security is threatened when she cannot communicate with a neighbor, doctor, taxi driver, or police officer. This sense of helplessness is not imagined; it is real. One positive result of this frustrating period of missionary life is that it throws us completely on the Lord for help and we live in constant dependence on him.

The trials of language school are many but well worth the effort. In some cases the husband may have an unfair advantage over his wife if there are young children in the family and Mom must stay at home with the babies or toddlers, relying on a tutor. She may feel unfairly hampered in what God has called her to do. However, some moms interact during the day with maids or neighbors who provide valuable practical tutoring, helping Mom gain fluency and ease with the language. No matter how you learn the language, make sure you do. Swallow your pride and learn to laugh at yourself. You will be a better speaker for Christ's sake as a result. The greatest missionaries had to begin learning the language sometime and had to overcome the discouragement that all of us feel in the process. Concerning his own feelings of inadequacy, envy, and frustration, Jim Elliot wrote in his journal,

> July 26—Marveled at my inner weakness yesterday. Felt miserably unworthy to be here as an "administrator of the mysteries of God." Strange

that I should—evidently for life—be put to such close contact with Pete and Betty whom I feel are far my intellectual superiors. . . . They are both able to correct my grammar and pronunciation, and seem to be able to apply tense rules so much easier than I. Felt weepy and useless yesterday at noon, swept with waves of envy and defeated wonderings about such things.[7]

INTERCULTURAL COMMUNICATION

Just as living in a world of many persons requires interpersonal communication skills, living life in a world of other cultures requires intercultural communication skills. This is evident in the root of the word *communication* that is seen in words such as *commune, community*, and *communion*. Sharing life together requires clear communication. When men and women, parents and teenagers, or management and labor try to communicate, sometimes miscommunication occurs. This typically happens when a speaker or writer sends a message, and the receiver assigns a meaning to it that was not intended by the sender. This could be caused by facial expressions, tone of voice, or other perceived signals that were never intended.

Communicating clearly in another language requires those involved to use a common language, but the words of written and spoken languages are only a small part of the process. Missiologists stress the importance of learning the language of the target people group in order to engage people's worldview, beliefs, and even thinking processes at profound levels in other cultures. It is crucially important that the missionary communicator knows the spoken language, but that is only one piece of the intercultural ministry puzzle.

Nonverbal Communication

There was a time when missionaries did not bother to learn the languages of the lands where they served; rather, they focused on teaching English so that the nationals could worship, learn, and serve with the missionaries. Fortunately, this cultural

---

[7] Jim Elliot, *The Journals of Jim Elliot*, ed. Elisabeth Elliot (Grand Rapids: Revell, 2002), 402.

imperialism has largely been left behind. However, just as it is wrong to expect people of other lands to learn your language in order to hear the gospel, so it is wrong to expect them to use nonverbal communication in the same way your home culture does. Nonverbal communication is both powerful and present everywhere.

Effective missionary communication requires culturally appropriate methods. Communicating in a new culture using the same system with the same intended meaning that you used at home is a guaranteed recipe for miscommunication. We cannot afford to miscommunicate when we are another culture's best, or only, hope for hearing the gospel, without which no one can be saved.

CONCLUSION

When a person is convinced of a missionary call and clear guidance from the Holy Spirit about where, when, and with whom to fulfill it, many emotions ensue. Following God's call on your life is the most exciting adventure, fulfilling endeavor, and rewarding life you can possibly imagine, but it will require you to step out of your comfort zone. You will learn languages, eat new foods, suffer bitter disappointments, meet lifelong friends, work hard, pray long, and grow in many ways. As you go out, go forth boldly but not arrogantly, and be clear as crystal, pure as the driven snow, and as innocent as doves, but do not be naïve. Study to show yourself approved, to know God's Word, to know as much of the language and culture as you can, and strive to be as active in Christian witness as you possibly can before you go.

RESOURCES FOR FURTHER STUDY

Elliot, Jim. *The Journals of Jim Elliot*. Edited by Elisabeth Elliot. Grand Rapids: Revell, 2002.

Lingenfelter, Sherwood, and Marvin Mayers. *Ministering Cross-Culturally*. Grand Rapids: Baker Academic, 2003.

Sills, M. David. *The Missionary Call: Find Your Place in God's Plan for the World*. Chicago: Moody, 2008.

Storti, Craig. *The Art of Crossing Cultures*. London: Nicholas Brealey, 2001.

CHAPTER 12

THE LOCAL CHURCH
ON MISSION

One of the most important developments in the recent history of Christian missions is the revival of local church involvement in missions. James Engel and William Dyrness, in *Changing the Mind of Missions*, noted that one of the areas where Western missions efforts had "gone wrong" in the twentieth century was the division of missions from the local church.[1] This separation has continued into the twenty-first century. Theology has not led to practice. While local church leadership in missions is nothing new (and not necessarily something lost), churches are in need of a recovery of a biblical and practical methodology for sending missionaries.

The purpose of this chapter is to consider how local churches—and their members—should and can be involved in the missionary task. In some sense it builds on all of the preceding chapters because the Great Commission was given to the church, which is a body of gifted and called followers of Christ. Therefore, the why and how of missions applies to churches and church members. In the New Testament we see the ministry of Jesus, the calling of the church, and then (for the majority of

---

[1] James F. Engel and William A. Dyrness, *Changing the Mind of Missions: Where Have We Gone Wrong?* (Downers Grove: IVP, 2000), 57.

237

the New Testament) the way the early church understood and implemented that calling.

The missionary call of the local church comprises several factors. Among these, first of all, is the call to *leadership*. Local churches must lead in the missionary task, but leaders within the church must also guide that missionary involvement. How do pastors and lay leaders help a church to think globally? What is necessary for a church to be "on mission"? Also, the missionary call to the local church is a call to *submission* and *service*. Most of the readers of this book will come from relatively affluent and educated contexts. It is easy within our culture to develop (usually unintentionally) a sense of superiority and paternalism, but this is not the example of Christ or the early church. Before considering the missionary call, followers of Christ must grasp his call to humility and sacrifice. In this chapter we will consider six general keys to thinking globally about the missionary call in the local church.

KEY 1: BIBLICAL UNDERSTANDING

The first section of this book deals with the biblical and theological foundations for Christian missions. The first key to an accurate view of the local church and missions is a biblical understanding of the Great Commission and missiology. Strategies and cultural studies are not the appropriate place to start, but the Bible is. Churches have the unique responsibility and opportunity to teach and preach the Bible, which is the starting place of missions.

Contemporary biblical theologians have identified a missional theme throughout the Scriptures: that God is a *sending* God. Along the same lines theologians, pastors, and leaders have long recognized the centrality of the local church in missions, even if that theology has not always been shown in practice. Johannes Blauw said that a theology of mission must, by necessity, be a theology of the church. For Blauw the biblical description of the church is the people of God called out of the world, placed in the world, and sent to the world. His definition is instructive in that it places missions as a foundational characteristic of the church from the beginning. George Vicedom contended that churches do not have the option to decide whether or not to do missions. Their decision is whether or not to be the church. The implication of this idea is that a gathering of believers is not the church unless they are taking part in God's mission to the world.

Local Church Missions in the Scriptures

Alongside these general statements of the centrality of the local church in missions, scholars have pointed to the Scriptures for support. Edmund Clowney, in his influential text called simply *The Church*, reminded readers that before the Great Commission came the "Great Constitution." In Matthew 16:13, Jesus asked his disciples, "Who do people say that the Son of Man is?" Upon Peter's confession of Jesus as the Christ, Jesus responded that God had revealed that fact to Peter and "on this rock I will build my church, and the gates of hell shall not prevail against it" (Matt 16:18). In this moment Jesus constituted the church, the people of God. Clowney described this people as "the gathered" but also as those who are sent to be "gatherers." Clowney recognized the integral role of missions in the life of the church.

Two other passages important to a biblical understanding of the role of the local church in mission are the "Great Commandment" and the "Great Commission." In Matthew 22, Jesus named as the greatest commandment, "You shall love the Lord your God with all your heart and with all your soul and with all your mind" (v. 37). Alongside that command is the second, You shall love your neighbor as yourself" (Matt 22:39). The Great Commission is recorded in all four Gospels and Acts, but the best-known version is Matthew 28:18–20:

> All authority in heaven and on earth has been given to me. Go therefore and make disciples of all nations, baptizing them in the name of the Father and of the Son and of the Holy Spirit, teaching them to observe all that I have commanded you. And behold, I am with you always, to the end of the age.

One historical question related to the Great Commission is that of audience. While some in church history, such as Martin

Luther, argued that the commission was given only to the apostles, the consensus today is that the entire church throughout history is the true recipient of Jesus' final commands. This question has important implications for this discussion. As William Carey and others later pointed out, if the command to "go" was only for the early church, then so would be the commands to baptize and teach.

John records a version of the commission more simply, with Jesus saying to the apostles, "As the Father has sent me, even so I am sending you" (John 20:21). The concept of "sentness" is critical to an accurate biblical understanding of the relationship between the local church and missions. God is a sending God— he sent his Son (John 3:16)—and the Son has sent the church to carry on his mission of redemption. It is no overstatement to say that the church, God's people as Christ's body, is God's plan for fulfilling Matthew 24:14: "This gospel of the kingdom will be proclaimed throughout the whole world." Christians are sent with the good news of Jesus Christ to be his body among the nations.

Antioch

Acts is Luke's account of the birth and expansion of the church. Several passages point to the involvement of the local church in missions, beginning with the commission in Acts 1:8. In Acts 8:4, the church is scattered following Stephen's martyrdom. According to Luke, "Those who were scattered went about preaching the word." This preaching resulted in churches, including the church at Antioch (Acts 11:19–25).

As the first "sending" church, the first-century Antioch congregation demonstrated several characteristics that should also be true of churches in the twenty-first century. Antioch was the third largest city in the Roman Empire—the Chicago of its day. It was a trade center and, as such, had a busy and diverse population. The believers who settled there encountered Jews and Gentiles, speaking first to those most like them (the Jews; Acts 11:19). Luke recorded, however, that some of the believers moved quickly to witness to Greeks, seeing "a great number" turn to Christ (Acts 11:20–21).

A first characteristic that stands out about the church at Antioch is its passion for God's Word. Luke recorded in Acts 11

that the Antioch church was "speaking the Word" (v. 19) and
that the members were "preaching the Lord Jesus" (v. 20). Barnabas came to the city and "exhorted" the people with God's Word
(v. 23). After he asked Saul to join his ministry, they spent a full
year teaching the Scriptures (v. 26). A church that is founded
on the Scriptures will know the Scriptures, and a church that
knows the Scriptures will be a sending church.

The Antioch congregation not only knew and understood
God's Word; it also put it to work by caring for those who needed
to hear the gospel. After speaking the gospel to their own, the
Christians broke down physical and ethnic barriers to preach
across cultural boundaries. Antioch was a diverse city, which
meant it was also a divided city. Hostility between ethnic groups,
including between Jews and Gentiles, was ingrained. The Christians, full of the Holy Spirit, gladly reached across those divisions to share the gospel.

Biblical foundations and evangelistic passion made the way
for the church at Antioch to become a sending church. As the
leaders of the church were gathered for worship, fasting, and
prayer, God spoke to *the church* (Acts 13:2). The Holy Spirit
called, "Set apart for me Barnabas and Saul for the work to which
I have called them." And the Christians responded, sending the
two preachers who had taught them to teach others. It is surely
significant that it was the church at Antioch that discerned the
call of Barnabas and Saul.

The sending of Barnabas and Saul was an important turning
point in the history of Christian missions, and it is exemplary of
the sending church. From Antioch the gospel went forth toward
the "ends of the earth." The departure of these two missionaries
was not a separation, however. Saul and Barnabas remained connected to the church at Antioch. Acts 14:25–28 explains:

> And when they had spoken the word in Perga,
> they went down to Attalia, and from there they
> sailed to Antioch, where they had been com-
> mended to the grace of God for the work that
> they had fulfilled. And when they arrived and
> gathered the church together, they declared all
> that God had done with them, and how he had

opened a door of faith to the Gentiles. And they
remained no little time with the disciples.

Both the Antioch church and its missionaries knew the
importance of reporting back to the sending church. Saul and
Barnabas felt accountable to their sending church, and they told
all that God had done as a result of the prayer meeting in Acts 13.
In turn the church celebrated and encouraged its missionaries.

In Paul's own writings, one need only look to 1 Thessalo-
nians 1:8 for evidence of local church involvement in missions.
There Paul commended the church at Thessalonica because
"the word of the Lord sounded forth from you in Macedonia
and Achaia." This verse is similar to Romans 1:8, in which Paul
rejoiced in the fact that the Roman church's faith had spread.
While these passages are not commands to local churches, they
give evidence that these churches were involved in the expansion of the church outside their own communities.

Finally, Ed Stetzer points[2] to 1 Peter 2:9 as evidence of
Peter's belief that the local church must be involved in missions:
"You are a chosen race, a royal priesthood, a holy nation, a people for his own possession, that you may proclaim the excellencies of him who called you out of darkness into his marvelous
light." Stetzer argues that the first part of the verse identifies
the church (a "chosen race, a royal priesthood, a holy nation,
a people for his own possession"). The second part of the verse
builds on that identity, showing that the reason God has called
out the church is that it "may proclaim the excellencies of him
who called you out of darkness into his marvelous light." The
church is called out of darkness and gathered together in order
that it might proclaim the gospel to the ends of the earth.

The local church, a body of redeemed and gifted individuals
joined together by the Holy Spirit, is God's chosen tool to get
the gospel to the nations. God's sent people send their own to
proclaim good news and be good news among both those who
have never heard and those who have not been discipled. Paul's
words in Romans 10:13–15 are a worthy call to the church and
her members: "'Everyone who calls on the name of the Lord will

---

[2] Ed Stetzer, "The Missional Nature of the Church and the Future of Southern Baptist Churches,"
in *The Mission of Today's Church: Baptist Leaders Look at Modern Faith Issues,* ed. R. Stanton
Norman (Nashville: B&H Academic, 2007), 79.

be saved.' How then will they call on him in whom they have not believed? And how are they to believe in him of whom they have never heard? And how are they to hear without someone preaching? And how are they to preach unless they are sent?"

KEY 2: A GLOBAL VISION

With a solid foundation of biblical understanding, churches will be ready to get a clear vision of the local, national, and global context of missions. In some sense missions begins at the door of the church. Jesus' last words before his ascension to the Father gave an outline for the spread of the gospel and the church as recorded in Acts: "You will be my witnesses in Jerusalem and in all Judea and Samaria, and to the end of the earth" (Acts 1:8). The image here is of the movement of the gospel from local to global. A vision of that movement from neighborhoods to nations is critical for local churches.

Though the number changes almost daily, there are just under 7,000 people groups around the world considered unreached (less than 2 percent evangelical population). That number represents more than 4 billion people. Almost half of those people groups have no missionaries working among them. A global vision for missions begins with an understanding of the reality of lostness.

Two "great migrations" have taken place in recent history. The first is urbanization—the move of populations from rural to urban. Much of that migration took place in the past century, at the turn of which less than 15 percent of the global population lived in urban contexts. The second wave of migration is that of individuals, families, and peoples moving away from their places of origin to a new locale. Enoch Wan, a leader in the study of missions and global migrations, cited statistics that 3 percent of the global population—some 214 million people—are now living away from their countries of birth.[3]

According to the United Nations, two-thirds of international migrants have settled in "developed" countries. Wan identified several "push and pull" factors affecting migration. Poverty, natural disaster, and political or religious persecution are forces

---

[3] Enoch Wan, "Diaspora Missiology," *Occasional Bulletin of the Evangelical Missiological Society* 20, no. 2 (Spring 2007): 3.

that often drive individuals and families from their places of origin. More positively, quality of life, opportunity, and religious freedom tend to draw migrants and refugees to developed countries.[4] These factors bring about great opportunity for Christian missions as millions of people move from unchurched lands to nations where the church is much stronger. A special study group formed by the Lausanne Committee for World Evangelization celebrates:

> Many previously presumed to be "unreached" people from the 10/40 windows are now accessible due to the global trend of migrant populations moving "from south to north, and from east to west." Congregations in the receiving countries (i.e. industrial nations in the West) can practice "missions at our doorstep" . . . i.e. reaching the newcomers in their neighborhoods without crossing borders geographically, linguistically and culturally. *When God is moving the diasporas geographically* making them accessible, the Church should not miss any opportunity to reach them with the gospel, i.e. *"missions to the diasporas."*[5]

The overlap between global migration and urbanization is the central concern for urban missions. A significant portion of urban population growth is ethnic.

As the nations described in Matthew 28:18–20 move to our cities and towns, the opportunities for evangelism are boundless. For migrants moving internally from villages to cities and for those emigrating to other nations, the overwhelming change of social life will provide opportunities for believers and churches to reach out with ministry and the gospel. Healthy, church-centered evangelism and missions will have a significant message for those who have left their homes for new ones. In addition, many immigrants and refugees will maintain contact

---

[4] Ibid., 2.

[5] Lausanne Committee for World Evangelization, *Scattered to Gather* (Manila: LifeChange Publishers, 2010), 27; emphasis in original.

with those back in their home villages, providing an additional opportunity for gospel missions.

Casting a global vision for the local church involves research in the community. Pastors and leaders must ask who are the unchurched in a neighborhood or who are the unreached who have moved there. Numerous resources exist, such as missions agencies, refugee programs, and local governments. If the nations are coming nearby the local church, then churches must consider how to reach out among them.

KEY 3: UNDERSTANDING MISSIOLOGICAL PRINCIPLES

In order to reach out across cultures, whether across the street or around the world, Christians must develop a basic understanding of missiological principles. Much of this book can contribute to that knowledge, but churches must consider how best to train potential missionaries well. While pastors might be able to preach on some topics during worship services, most such training will take place in small groups in specific settings. All church members should understand the concepts of people groups and intercultural communication. Those called out to share the gospel with those of other cultures should be trained in the basics of contextualization, evangelism, and the importance of church planting.

One way to develop training is through an ongoing missions "fellowship" within local churches. Many denominations offer programs focused on missions, but local churches can tailor materials to people groups and needs in their own communities. Missions agencies and missionaries on furlough can be excellent resources.

KEY 4: PRAY!

In Luke 10, as Jesus sent the seventy-two out to preach the kingdom in many villages, Jesus said, "The harvest is plentiful, but the laborers are few. Therefore pray earnestly to the Lord of the harvest to send out laborers into his harvest" (Luke 10:2). A couple of notable things stand out in this passage. First, Jesus commands clearly that his followers must pray in response to the needs in the harvest. Once a church grasps a clear vision of the mission field around them and to the ends of the earth, they must pray. Jesus specifically said to pray for *workers*. That is the second notable (and eye-opening) thing: as Jesus was telling his followers to pray, he was sending them out as the answers to that praying. A people praying for the harvest must consider the possibility that they will be called to go.

Many excellent resources exist to support a church's prayer for the nations. Missionaries and missions agencies often publish prayer letters and websites to keep churches informed of needs and opportunities on the field. *Operation World* is a book designed to inform praying Christians of the need in every country on earth and gives specific prayer requests according to a calendar of prayer.[6] Social media offers opportunities to hear from missionaries and agencies. Pastors have long noted that giving a time in weekly worship to praying for the nations not only raises missions awareness but also causes Christians to consider their involvement in Great Commission ministries.

KEY 5: CONNECT YOURSELF TO MISSIONS

Whether you are a pastor, staff member, or layperson in the local church, if you lead, you must connect yourself to missions. Setting the example in intercultural evangelism and missions involvement will make your teaching and mobilization more urgent and more real. The best place to start connecting is while you are in college or seminary, if that is part of your education. It is possible that some of your fellow students will be missionaries, and you can begin now to support them with prayer and other means of help. If your church already supports missionaries or agencies, contact them to find out how you can be more involved in their ministries.

One way to get more connected to missions is by joining a short-term team to see intercultural evangelism and church planting firsthand. The next section of this chapter will deal more thoroughly with short-term missions, but you should lead by example by getting involved. If you are not a pastor, then encourage (and provide for) your pastor to go.

---

[6] The most recent edition is Jason Mandryk, *Operation World*, 7th ed. (Colorado Springs: Biblica, 2010).

KEY 6: CONNECT THE CHURCH TO MISSIONS

A final key to leading the local church in missions is to *connect* the church to what God is doing around the world. This task certainly begins with prayer, as mentioned above. The more a church family is exposed to prayer needs for people groups and missionaries, the more deeply they will see opportunities to be involved. From there the possibilities are almost endless.

Churches have approached the missionary task in different ways. One possibility too frequently seen is the church that merely *supports* missions. That church gives regularly to missions agencies, perhaps through its denomination, but the agency is the driving force. The church provides financial and some people resources, but that is the end of its involvement.

A second model is the independent *sending* church. There the church has caught the vision of the local church as missionary, but it feels as if the entire task is up to one congregation. The leadership develops its own strategies, sends its own missionaries, and supports them fully. The *sending* church is connected to missions, but it is limited to its own resources.

A better vision is a combination of both models. Churches should support missionaries and missions agencies financially. Many churches working together can do much more than each church working alone. Dozens, if not hundreds, of missions-sending agencies have appeared over the past decades that can provide strategy, logistical support, and training for missionaries; these need support. But churches must also develop for themselves a broad missions strategy that addresses the local, national, and global fields. Such a strategy will include partnership with agencies and denominational organizations, but churches must not delegate the entire missionary task away. Southern Baptists have exemplified this principle since the formation of the Cooperative Program in 1925. The Cooperative Program is a funding mechanism through which thousands of churches join together to support missions internationally and in North America. Partnership allows the broader body of Christ to work together in Great Commission ministry.

There are many ways for churches to connect to the mission field. Most missions agencies have ways for pastors or missions leaders to communicate with field personnel, and many missionaries are more than happy to share with churches and ministries. Putting a missionary face with the facts and figures of a missions vision can strengthen a church's focus.

SHORT-TERM MISSIONS

The most common way for a church to connect is through short-term missions (STM). The STM movement is a relatively recent phenomenon—one that Ralph Winter referred to as the most surprising mutation in modern missions in the late twentieth century. Jerry Rankin, past president of the International Mission Board (IMB), outlined a major paradigm shift away from sending only long-term career missionaries to more and more short-term personnel. At the same time, Rankin recognized that this shift also represented a change in the IMB's vision. That organization, the largest sending agency in the world, is making the shift from sending missionaries with the support of churches to supporting churches in their involvement in missions—a significant transition.

The rise of STM began in the 1960s due to a combination of increasingly easy travel and awareness of the overseas context fostered by veterans of World War II. Most STM took place through missions agencies such as Youth with a Mission (YWAM) or the IMB's student programs (launched in 1965). Increasingly, however, local churches began to send teams to work for a period of days or weeks. From around 120,000 short-term missionaries in 1989, the movement grew to more than 2 million in 2006.

The first challenge in a discussion of STM is definition. The IMB defines a short-term missionary as one who serves less than four years, although these might be volunteer or be appointed and receive a salary. Roger Peterson offers what is perhaps the most valuable definition: short-term missions is the God-commanded repetitive deployment of swift, temporary, nonprofessional missionaries.[7] This definition has several facets that are worth unpacking.

First of all, STM involves a time element. The length of service might be from a few days to a few years. For Peterson, the key question is the missionary's intention. He argues that

---

[7] Roger Peterson, Gordon Aeschliman, and R. Wayne Sneed, *Maximum Impact Short-Term Missions* (Minneapolis: STEMPress, 2003), 110.

short-term missionaries go with the intention of returning to their previous work or ministry. Career missionaries, on the other hand, go to the field with no intention of returning before retirement. This distinction of short-term missionaries as "temporary" is valuable.

Second, short-term missions is the *repetitive* deployment of missionaries. Short-term missions should only be part of a larger strategy that must involve repeated deployments by either the same missionaries or a different group. Advocates of STM recognize that in most contexts short-term missionaries can only complete a part of the overall task of evangelization or church planting. Short-term missionaries must see their work as part of a bigger task undertaken both by field missionaries and local churches.

Peterson emphasizes that STM must be *swift*. Short-term missionaries can go where they are needed quickly. Whether the task be disaster relief, medical care, event-based evangelism, or some other time-sensitive project, short-term missionaries can be mobilized and sent quickly.

The idea of short-term missionaries as "nonprofessional" is perhaps the most controversial element of Peterson's definition. By this he means two different things. First of all, short-term missionaries are often highly skilled but are not professional missionaries. Many are doctors, engineers, agriculturalists, or construction workers. They are professional, but their profession is not missions. A second facet of that definition is that short-term missionaries may not have formal training in missiology or theology. Peterson sees this as an advantage because short-term missionaries are not restricted by degree programs or qualifications. He argues that short-term missionaries do not need such training. Others worry about this trend, saying there must be a balance between long-term missionaries with appropriate missiological training and short-term missionaries. This "amateurization" of missions is not necessarily an advance.

STM offers many opportunities, but it also brings potential problems. In terms of opportunities, short-term missionaries can provide much-needed support that multiplies the ministry of career missionaries. Short-term missionaries can free others for tasks that only long-term missionaries can perform. And many argue that STM is an excellent recruiting tool for future career missionaries.

One critical issue in short-term missions, especially when missionaries are sent directly from the local church, is cultural acquisition and missiological problems. If missionaries do not recognize the potential problems in cross-cultural ministry and communication, they can do more harm than good. One example is in human need projects. Too often local churches see needs overseas and recruit short-term personnel to help meet those needs. Instead of helping, churches and short-term missionaries build unhealthy dependency that causes long-term problems.

Another potential problem is expense. Many have questioned whether short-term missions is a good use of resources. Kurt Ver Beek is one such scholar.[8] He studied recovery efforts in Honduras following Hurricane Mitch, analyzing reconstruction work funded from outside of Honduras but performed by local workers and work performed by short-term construction teams. He found that it usually costs about $2,000 to rebuild a house, but short-term teams were spending an average of $30,000 to come work on the field. Local believers and those whose homes were rebuilt were thankful for the relationships with Americans and for their homes but often questioned whether it was best for them to come.

A common response to arguments like Ver Beek's is that short-term missions has a significant impact on future career personnel, on giving to missions organizations, and on personal devotion. Ver Beek found that the short-term projects in Honduras had no long-term effect in any of those areas. His study is supported by further research in other parts of the world.

In 2005, Ver Beek and Robert Priest participated in an online forum on ChristianityToday.com. While Priest recognized the validity of Ver Beek's research, he argued that any impact, even short-term impact, is valuable. Speaking mainly of student missionaries, Priest argued that part of the problem is short-term missions must be done properly, with appropriate training and follow-up, in order to have a long-term impact.

---

[8] See Kurt Alan Ver Beek, "The Impact of Short-Term Missions: A Case Study of House Construction in Honduras after Hurricane Mitch," *Missiology* 34, no. 4 (October 2006): 477–95.

DOING SHORT-TERM MISSIONS WELL

Leaders in the short-term missions movement have attempted to answer some concerns related to its rapid growth. A list of "Standards of Excellence in Short-term Missions" outlines important considerations including training, stewardship, and partnership.[9] The document advocates the practice of allowing the field (whether missionaries or nationals) to guide strategy and planning. These standards, which have been adopted by many sending agencies, should have an impact on short-term missions practice.

First, STM leaders and participants must keep the focus on the glory of God and the expansion of his kingdom. The purpose of STM is the same as for missions in general. While researchers have shown that STM does have at least some impact on personal discipleship and missions support after a project, those must not be the primary motivation behind STM. Secondary benefits must remain secondary.

A second key to STM done well is that it is field driven. Sending churches and leaders must not develop strategies and plans without the input of field missionaries and national believers. An important word to remember is partnership. In a good partnership, participants will consider both the gifts and the abilities of the short-term missionaries and the needs of the field. Too often churches have "decided" to send a team to do some type of work (construction, vacation Bible school, medical teams) without consulting the field to find out if such work is really needed. Even more dangerous are projects that build dependency or do more harm than good.

Short-term missionaries must also be well trained. Many resources exist for team preparation, but most cover the same basic areas that are parallel to good missionary training in general. First, missionaries should have a basic understanding of the biblical foundations for missions. Second, teams should receive general preparation for intercultural evangelism. A project-specific cultural orientation is important, as well. Much of the team training should take place before departure, but some can take place on the field. Missionaries can share evangelism tools and cultural cues, for example.

---

[9] See http://www.soe.org for more information.

Finally, short-term missionaries and sending churches benefit from a thorough follow-up process. Debriefing should begin while on the field, even daily during the project. Many teams have found journals helpful in keeping track of thoughts during the project. Following the project, short-term missionaries should share with one another and with the sending church. Accountability to those who supported the project financially and through prayer will strengthen a church's future work. In addition, debriefing solidifies the discipleship growth that takes place during the project.

STM is one way local churches connect to missions. Others include traditional models such as visiting missionaries and missionary conferences. Some churches are creating dedicated areas in high-traffic areas of the church building to focus on missionary connections. Churches are "adopting" unreached people groups for prayer and STM focus. Once a congregation and its leaders catch the vision for engaging in missions, the possibilities for connection are almost limitless.

Missions was the task of the church in the first century, and it remains so in the twenty-first. From the time of William Carey's call to the Northhampton Association to "expect great things from God and attempt great things for God," healthy congregations have been involved in the Great Commission task. A revival of missions involvement today is a good sign, and your leadership (whether as a pastor, church member, or missionary) is as important as ever.

RESOURCES FOR FURTHER STUDY

Horner, David. *When Missions Shapes the Mission: You and Your Church Can Reach the World.* Nashville: B&H, 2011.

Mandryk, Jason. *Operation World: The Definitive Prayer Guide to Every Nation.* 7th ed. Downers Grove: InterVarsity, 2010.

Peterson, Roger, Gordon Aeschliman, and R. Wayne Sneed. *Maximum Impact Short-Term Mission: The God-Commanded Repetitive Deployment of Swift, Short-Term Non-Professional Missionaries.* Minneapolis: STEM-Press, 2003.

Stiles, J. Mack, and Leann Stiles. *Mack and Leann's Guide to Short-Term Missions.* Downers Grove: IVP, 2000.

CHAPTER 13

THE TWENTY-FIRST-CENTURY PRACTICE OF GLOBAL MISSIONS

THE CONTEMPORARY ENVIRONMENT

The gospel never changes. However, global conditions change constantly. As a result, the context and conditions for missionary advance are always in flux. Still, many elements in a good missiology are valid everywhere and in every age. These include bold and faithful gospel proclamation, the necessity of translating the Bible into the heart language of the people, the imperative of making disciples and planting churches, the importance of cultural understanding and effective cross-cultural communication, and the urgency of leadership training and appropriate theological education. These elements of good missiology also include the importance of the missionary's own life as a disciple of Jesus and such personal skills as language learning, cultural adaptation, and effective teaming. Just as a wise sailor checks the weather forecast to learn what conditions lie ahead on the sea, a wise missions strategist should be alert to changing conditions in the world and in the church, as these may constitute new threats or opportunities and may require new tactics.

One such changing condition is the growing secularization of the West. This has been obvious for a long time, but it continues to accelerate in its pace. Fifty years ago missionary service was respectable in the eyes of Western society. In the decades since, that attitude has moved to indifference and then on to open hostility. Missionary service that has religious conversion as its goal violates the most cherished cultural value of the contemporary West: tolerance. This has several significant implications for the missionary enterprise. First, many parts of the West have become so completely de-Christianized that they must be reevangelized, and the effort will be an uphill battle. The post-Christian West thinks it has tried Christianity and outgrown it. Although spirituality is popular, formal Christian faith carries a stigma of backwardness and intolerance. Second, missionaries cannot count on the assistance of their home governments while laboring overseas. Secular Western governments now often think missionaries have no business trying to convert others, and when trouble comes, they may either turn their backs on their own citizens or actively use the opportunity to get the missionaries out of the way. They certainly will not do anything to ease the access of missionaries into other countries. The missionary enterprise is now completely severed from Western state sponsorship for the first time since the fourth century. Third, this spirit of secularism has affected Western churches. There is no longer any motivation for nominal Christians to continue to go to church or even to affiliate with any organized religion at all. "No religion" is now the second largest religious identity in America, after Christianity, and it is growing rapidly. This is already resulting in a drop in church attendance. In itself this post-Constantinian environment is good for the health of the church, but it also means a drop in church income. There is simply less money to spend. Churches that do not have a firm grasp on gospel exclusivism are subtly influenced by the spirit of the age and increasingly spend their resources on themselves and their immediate environment. Christians who have syncretized with secular values are also much less likely to give up comfort and safety and embrace potential suffering as missionaries for the sake of the gospel.

Another changing condition is the resurgence of world religions. In the heyday of Western colonialism, Western and Christian triumphalism went hand in hand, and the other great religions of the world seemed to be stagnant and demoralized. However, under pressure from the West, Hinduism, Buddhism, and Islam have all been revitalized. Islam has always had a built-in apologetic against Christianity. It now has a renewed sense of self-confidence against what it perceives to be the immoral West, and it has taken an increasingly aggressive stance against Christian proselytism in those countries where it constitutes a majority. Islam is now engaged in active efforts to spread its faith in Europe and North America, with some success. Buddhism and Hinduism have also experienced internal renewal. They have developed their own responses to Christian witness, and they have gained a respectful hearing among the elites in Western societies. (The first Buddhist chaplain in the US Army began his career as a Southern Baptist pastor.[1]) There are also significant numbers of Buddhists, Muslims, and Hindus now living in the American heartland as well as in the big cities. Missionary strategy must now take into account the presence of other religions everywhere and the self-confident activism of other religions both in their own homelands and in ours.

 The third changing condition missionary strategists face is the problem of missionary access to those who most need the gospel. Prior to the mid-twentieth century, most of the world was accessible to Christian missionaries. The closing of China after the Communist takeover in 1949 was only the beginning of a process that accelerated in the decades to come. As non-Western nations gained their independence from colonial rule in the decades after World War II, many chose to restrict or prohibit missionary activity. The spread of communism closed off the Soviet bloc from external Christian witness, and Islamic countries in particular shut their doors to overt Christian missionaries. The unreached people groups that remain unengaged with the gospel live mostly in places where the government will not allow missionaries per se to work.

At the same time God is raising up Christians around the world with a vision for finishing the task of the Great Commission. In the face of increasing opposition, the gospel is advancing in places where it has never been heard before. The gospel is more truly global now than it has ever been in history, and it is advancing like never before. That advance will simply be under

---

[1] "Buddhist chaplain is Army first," accessed April 5, 2013, http://usatoday30.usatoday.com/news/military/2009-09-08-buddhist-chaplain_N.htm.

conditions and in ways that are unlike what the church experienced in the days of Western global dominance and Western state sponsorship. This chapter will examine some of the key issues that face the mission of the global body of Christ in the twenty-first century.

DEFINING THE TASK—1: WHAT IS THE MISSION OF THE CHURCH?

During the Great Century of Christian missions (1792–1910), most Christians considered this question to be unnecessary. The mission of the church was obvious: to Christianize the world. In practice this often meant Westernizing the world in the process. In the early twentieth century, with the rise of theological liberalism in the major denominations and in most of academia, the fundamental consensus of the nineteenth century was broken, and prominent voices began to call for a new understanding of the missionary task. Greater emphasis was placed on educational, social, and medical work. In light of growing rejection of the exclusive claims of historic Christianity, evangelism was downplayed, and greater respect for local religious traditions was advocated.[2] Denominations and mission agencies that held on to the fundamentals of the historic Christian faith in this fundamentalist-modernist split naturally remained committed to evangelistic outreach. Many mainline groups continued to appoint and send both evangelical and modernist missionaries for many decades. Over time, though, those with less evangelical theological foundations quit doing mission work by and large.

In the years following World War II, the contemporary evangelical movement emerged, committed to the fundamentals of the faith but less committed than their fundamentalist forbearers to separation from secular society and from Christians who disagreed with them. The question of the relationship between evangelism and social action raised its head again within evangelical circles. Respected voices like that of John Stott advocated combining the two, while never neglecting or downplaying the primacy of evangelism.[3] In the early years of the twenty-first century, evangelical advocates of "missional" Christianity have seen

---

[2] See, for example, William Ernest Hocking's pivotal publication, *Rethinking Missions—a Layman's Enquiry after One Hundred Years* (New York: Harper & Bros., 1932).
[3] John Stott, *Christian Mission in the Modern World* (Downers Grove: IVP, 2008).

the mission of the church as equally encompassing everything the Bible commands Christians to do, with special emphasis on engaging society, doing justice, creating culture, and performing works of mercy. Are all of these equally and independently valid as expressions of the mission of the church? As church attendance and missions giving shrink in the post-Christian West and as significant voices within the evangelical community offer differing visions of the nature of Christian mission, how should Christians and churches prioritize their labors and their resources?

In an age when the advance of the gospel faces both unparalleled opportunity and unparalleled opposition, this question is absolutely critical. The way forward is found in the nature of the mission of God, the nature of fallen humanity, and the singular imperative of the Great Commission. The mission of God is to fill the earth with the knowledge of his glory as the waters cover the sea and specifically to do so by calling a people for himself out of every tribe, tongue, people, and nation. This redeemed people will worship him and enjoy him forever. Because the Bible is clear that there is no salvation apart from hearing and believing the gospel of Jesus Christ and that people cannot hear it and believe it without someone telling it to them, the priority of proclaiming the gospel is intrinsic to the mission of God. The mission of God's people nests within that mission. The biblical picture of humanity is realistic about the horrors of ignorance, disease, and poverty, but it does not locate the root of humanity's woes in any of these things. The fundamental problem facing every human being is sin: guilt before a holy God and corruption in every aspect of our nature. Even the most educated, healthy, well-fed unbelievers on earth still face eternity under the wrath of God for their sin. Such people have many needs, and all of them should elicit compassion from Christians, but their greatest need is salvation in Jesus Christ. Finally there is one and only one imperative in the Great Commission as recorded in Matthew's Gospel, and that is to make disciples. Making disciples necessarily involves proclaiming the gospel and calling for a response, as there is no other way to become a disciple. This priority is confirmed by the references in Luke and Acts to proclaiming the good news and to being Jesus' witnesses. Those disciples, in turn, will obey all Jesus commanded, including loving their neighbors as themselves. Prioritizing making disciples and then teaching those disciples to obey everything Jesus commanded will thus preserve the imperative of advancing the gospel and will simultaneously increase the number of those who will feed the hungry, heal the sick, and do all the other things disciples do.

This may well be the most important issue facing the missionary enterprise in the twenty-first century. Mission strategy must reflect the love of Christ. Followers of Jesus should never be able to live in the face of human suffering without doing something about it. However, they must also keep what is less obvious clearly in view: the worst possible human suffering is separation from God. Disciples of Jesus should always act like disciples of Jesus wherever they live, but they can never lose sight of the priority of making more disciples, specifically out of every people group on earth.[4]

DEFINING THE TASK—2: MISSIONS RESEARCH

In the Great Commission, God gave the basic task: to make disciples. He also gave the scope of that task: all people groups on earth. But what does this mean? Since Ralph Winter brought the significance of unreached people groups to the attention of the evangelical world at the Lausanne Conference in 1974, people-group research has blossomed in the evangelical missionary community. This research faces a number of unhelpful temptations. One such temptation is to expend a lot of time and energy wrangling over the precise definition of a people group. For a cultural anthropologist, such discussions may be inevitable, but for Christian missionaries the unhindered spread of the gospel is the main issue at stake. A people group is a group of people who think of themselves as "us" versus everyone else, based on kinship, language, religion, culture, historical experience, geography, or whatever else goes into their sense of identity. For gospel purposes it is the largest group of such people through whom the gospel can spread without encountering a significant barrier to its progress. The people-group strategy of

---

[4] For an extensive discussion of this subject, see Kevin DeYoung and Greg Gilbert, *What Is the Mission of the Church?* (Wheaton: Crossway, 2011).

missions entails planting churches within every people group that will evangelize and reproduce within that group. Where a barrier is encountered to the continued spread of the gospel, cross-cultural missions are then necessary. The definition of "people group" has to focus on the significance of ethno-linguistic and cultural differences to the spread of the gospel and nothing else.

Another temptation is to draw lines more sharply between people groups than is warranted by reality. The Western mind often desires mathematical precision in all of its distinctions, but human reality is usually not that neat. Some people, particularly in cities, may have multiple identities. A government official in a city within the 10/40 Window once described the ethnic makeup of his city as 70 percent People X and 50 percent People Y, with the rest of the population divided between Peoples Z, Q, and R! Oddly enough, he was probably right. Again, remembering the missiological and strategic dimensions of people-group research will be useful in deciding where to draw solid lines, where to draw dotted lines, and where to be content with pure ambiguity.

Another temptation is to forget that a people-group approach to missions is designed to make us inclusive and not exclusive in our gospel witness. The point is not to decide what people we care about and what people we don't care about, nor is it to reinforce barriers between different people groups themselves. The point is to make sure no group of people is neglected, ignored, or left out of hearing the gospel in a way they can understand. The gospel breaks down barriers between former enemies. A church-planting approach which reinforces those barriers is fundamentally in opposition to the gospel itself. At the same time, no one should have to learn another language or join another people group in order to hear the gospel and follow Jesus. Missionaries have to make choices about which language they will learn and which people they will get to know. Given the finite nature of both time and energy, that necessarily means choosing to focus on some people and not on others. Still, Christian workers need to cultivate a love that clears the barriers that exist between people groups in their field of service, and they need to share the gospel with anyone, from any people group, as God provides the opportunity.

Another temptation in people-group research is to accept information uncritically. Majority people groups almost always overestimate their own numbers and underestimate the populations of minority groups. They also tend to assume a greater degree of assimilation of minority groups than those groups themselves acknowledge. Rival people groups may easily give inaccurate information about one another. Missionaries often accept the perspective of their local friends without checking to see how accurate those perspectives are. Perhaps the greatest temptation for missionaries and for those who send them is to accept unverified or inflated statistics about converts to Christianity. We want such reports to be true, so we easily accept rumor as fact. Local sources know what we want to hear so they sometimes tell us what will make us happy. The missionary may feel pressure to report results that will please sending churches and supporters back home. Whatever the cause, God is not honored by inflated reports. The cause of the gospel is best served by careful research and critical analysis, and it is better to report only what can be verified than to risk the sins of pride and dishonesty.

People-group research is a critical issue facing the missionary enterprise in the twenty-first century. The church needs to know where and how to deploy its resources. Growing cooperation and information sharing between mission agencies is providing an ever-clearer picture of the global gospel situation. The research must continue, soberly and carefully, to make sure the job is done wisely.[5]

CONTEXTUALIZATION

Contextualization is the word we use to describe the process of proclaiming the gospel and living as the church in a modern cultural context. Every twenty-first-century Christian does it. No one today lives in a first-century Palestinian cultural context, so every modern Christian contextualizes the gospel and the church in a cultural setting fundamentally different from the world of the Bible. However, most people don't realize they are doing it. They read their own experience into the text of Scripture, and what comes out at the other end is a blend of biblical

---

[5] For an excellent example of careful research clearly presented, see the IMB's research website, http://public.imb.org/globalresearch/Pages/default.aspx.

teaching and their own cultural norms and practices. This is as true of people in traditional "Christian" cultures as it is on the front lines of the advance of the gospel. Often those who grew up in a traditional church setting subconsciously equate their own practices with biblical Christianity, even in matters of style and extrabiblical form. Because contextualization is a necessary part of every Christian's life, it is essential that they realize they are doing it and that they think through carefully how it should be done in faithfulness to the Word of God.

Two dangers face every Christian in the matter of contextualization. One is the danger, already mentioned, of identifying tradition with Scripture. This can occur for those who never leave their own cultural context. Traditionalism can happen as easily in Protestant Christianity as in Roman Catholicism. Believers can unconsciously assume that the style of building they grew up with, the hymnal they used as children, or the exact order of service they have always known are all part of biblical Christianity even though Scripture allows a level of freedom in each of these areas. After all, New Testament believers met in first-century Mediterranean homes, not church buildings; they sang hymns in a musical style totally different from ours, and they probably followed a pattern of worship modeled after the liturgy of the synagogue service. Among cross-cultural missionaries this tendency is seen when foreign workers reproduce their own home culture in the life of the church, even in areas not directly addressed by Scripture. This can be seen in English Gothic church buildings in the middle of South Asia or in American hymns that are translated into the local language and whose musical style sounds totally out of place in a Middle Eastern setting.

The other danger is to assume that the nonnegotiable core of Christian truth is something less than everything the Bible teaches or commands. Among those who remain in their home culture, this can be seen in attempts to make the gospel more user-friendly that end up leaving out the uncomfortable parts, like the pervasive depravity of sin, repentance as an essential component of saving faith, or radical discipleship as the norm of what it means to be a Christian. It also shows up in churches that neglect aspects of God's design for the church that grate against the values of popular culture, such as church discipline. On the mission field this tendency expresses itself in uncritically adopting practices or cultural forms that actually contradict some aspect of biblical teaching or in failing to address worldview issues that end up reinterpreting biblical teaching in unbiblical ways. The result, in either setting, is syncretism: the blending of biblical Christianity with elements of the local culture or religion that are fundamentally incompatible with the gospel.

The question in every age is this: what is nonnegotiable and what is flexible in our expressions of the gospel and the church? In the early twenty-first century, this is a hot issue. Reacting against the perceived cultural imperialism of nineteenth-century missions, some missionaries today are experimenting with contextualization models that push the envelope of previous mission practice. In particular, the insider-movement approach takes its starting point from Charles Kraft's conviction that cultural forms are intrinsically neutral, including religious forms. Thus, this perspective views nonbiblical religions as potential vehicles for expressing biblical faith, viewing religious labels as matters of communal identity rather than spiritual allegiance. Thus, one can be a faithful, saved follower of Jesus while remaining self-identified as a Muslim and continuing to practice the pillars of Islam. Is this within the boundaries set by Scripture?

This issue has generated intense controversy in the contemporary missions community, and it shows no signs of abating. Time and space do not permit a nuanced consideration of the arguments for and against insider movements.[6] However, the authors of this book offer some critical points that we regard as definitive against the practice. First, culture is not neutral. Culture is a human product, and it expresses both our creation in the image of God and our fall into sin. It is anything but neutral.

Second, the Bible was written in a context of religious pluralism, and it nowhere regards other religions as potential vehicles for worshipping the true God. It always, without exception, regards other religions as acts of rebellion against the true God. The book of Hebrews even warns against sliding back into Judaism, the only world religion other than Christianity that is based on

---

[6] For more information, see Sam Schlorff, *Missiological Models in Ministry to Muslims* (Middle East Resources, 2006).

genuine revelation from God. Third, words and practices carry multiple levels of meaning, and it is dishonest to pick the levels we want and to pretend the others aren't there. It may be true that one level of meaning of "Muslim" is membership in a community, but another inseparable level has theological content—content that includes an explicit denial of the Trinity, the deity of Christ, and the possibility of substitutionary atonement. It is dishonest for someone who believes in the Trinity, the deity of Christ, and substitutionary atonement to claim the label "Muslim." Fourth, religious words and religious practices carry emotional and spiritual baggage. Words and practices taken from a non-Christian religion carry connotations that may contradict biblical truth to someone who grew up in that non-Christian setting. For these reasons, among others, the insider-movement approach falls outside the boundaries of legitimate contextualization.

The issue of contextualization remains significant and contested. Both missionaries and local believers in every setting need to think it through carefully. They need to examine everything in the light of Scripture to avoid the twin errors of traditionalism and syncretism.

ACCESS

Most unreached people groups are unreached for a reason. They are not easy to access. For some the difficulty is physical, but for most they are hard to reach because of governmental restrictions on missionary activity, religious and social opposition to the gospel, or a combination of both. Most unreached people groups live in countries that do not grant missionary visas or that restrict the ability of missionaries to share the gospel with non-Christians. For years most mission agencies allowed those restrictions to limit the scope of their evangelistic activity. In recent decades, however, mission leaders have concluded that no human government has the right to veto the command of the King of kings. Today the cutting edge of the advance of the gospel among unreached people groups uses creative access strategies.

The idea is not new. If anything, the idea of the missionary visa is new. While there have been missionaries throughout the ages whose only vocation was their mission work, there have also been other believers who have used their business enterprises or other secular skills as a conduit for taking the gospel to those who have never heard. The advance of Nestorian Christianity across Asia in the Middle Ages owed as much to Nestorian merchants as it did to professional missionaries. J. Christy Wilson Jr. popularized the idea with his book *Today's Tentmakers*,[7] based on his own experience working in Afghanistan after World War II. The past few decades, however, have seen a proliferation of creative-access gospel workers who are using nontraditional means to get the gospel to those who have never heard.

Creative-access platforms can take a number of different shapes. Some are little more than paper companies created for the purpose of applying for a business visa but then doing little actual business. Such platforms usually do not last long, as hostile governments quickly see through the pretense. Other platforms can either be nonprofit or for-profit in nature. Much early creative access work in the modern era fell in the nonprofit category. Missionaries gravitate naturally toward relieving human need so many set up human needs, relief and development, medical, and educational service companies to establish their presence in places where they could not go as missionaries per se. There are many places in the world where such service is welcome and where this approach is still viable. Many other countries, however, became suspicious of international nonprofit organizations (nongovernmental organizations, or NGOs for short), as they recognized the missionary intention behind many of them and as they also grew to fear that they were fronts for the CIA or other Western intelligence agencies. In many countries NGO work is either forbidden or severely restricted. This left the sphere of for-profit work. Two options are open to a Christian who wants to use for-profit work as a platform for Christian witness in a restricted-access country. One is to find a job with an existing company that is willing to hire you and is not hostile to your evangelistic intentions. The other is to set up a for-profit company, either in the country where you want to work or in your home country with a branch in the country where you want to work. This overall approach, using for-profit

---

[7] J. Christy Wilson Jr., *Today's Tentmakers* (Wheaton: Tyndale, 1979).

business as a platform for taking the gospel where Christ is not yet known, is known as Business as Mission, or BAM for short.

There are certain pitfalls to the BAM approach. One is that it is hard to start a successful business anywhere. A high percentage of new business start-ups fail in the United States; in a foreign context it is only more difficult. A second pitfall is that new business startups usually require a significant outlay of capital in order to begin. Even the best businesses take time before they begin to show a profit. Eventually a successful business becomes self-sustaining, but in the beginning BAM is expensive. Third, not many missionaries have the skills or the inclination to run a business well. A poorly run business platform will not present a good witness to the people of the host country, and it will not provide access for the workers for long.

On the other hand, there are significant advantages to BAM. A well-run, profitable business enterprise can provide a secure foundation for residence, even in otherwise-closed countries. A secular occupation also provides the worker with a nonthreatening identity in the community that often opens more doors for witness than an overt missionary role. Furthermore, people practicing a secular occupation have natural access to the local people with whom they work, people who might otherwise be inaccessible to the gospel. A good creative access platform not only provides access to live in the country but also provides relational access to people for the sake of sharing the gospel.

Years of experience with creative-access approaches to missions have taught several valuable lessons. First, the platform must have integrity. It must do what it says it does and do it well. This is both for the sake of the reputation of the gospel and for the sake of the longevity of the platform. Second, a worker's platform must fit that person. It must be something he is capable of doing with excellence, and it really should be something he enjoys doing. Otherwise it will have no credibility at all in the eyes of the host country. Third, a good platform should maximize contact with people. A platform job done alone in a cubicle or office with little contact with the people you are trying to reach is not helpful. Fourth, a good platform requires hard work at the platform itself. If the worker views it as a nuisance or a distraction from the "real" work of missions, it will be only a source

of frustration. The worker must come with a realistic understanding of work involved and with a serious commitment to do
that work. Fifth, however, a good platform is always in danger of
becoming an end in itself. If workers find themselves not sharing
the gospel or discipling new believers at all, either because they
are too busy or because they want to protect the platform, it has
become a roadblock rather than a conduit for gospel ministry.
Sixth, platform work requires people with genuine dual compe-
tence. They must be competent at sharing the gospel, discipling
believers, and training leaders. They must also be competent at
their secular skill. For this reason high school and college students who are considering a call to missions should seriously
consider concrete academic and experiential training in a secular occupation they enjoy as well as biblical and theological
training. God is using business people, doctors, nurses, lawyers,
sports coaches, engineers, agriculturalists, English teachers,
information technology experts, travel agents, and any number
of other professions to take the gospel to the unreached.

Most of the remaining task of engaging unreached people
groups will require creative-access strategies. BAM is currently
one of the most helpful of those strategies. The years ahead will
require continued creative thought to push through the remaining barriers to global evangelism.[8]

MISSIONS FROM RECENT MISSION FIELDS

God did not restrict the Great Commission to the Western
church. He gave it to his entire body. One of the most exciting
phenomena of recent years has been the growing involvement
of churches in recent mission fields in the task of taking the
gospel to those who have never heard. These younger churches
recognize from Scripture that they also have an obligation to
share Jesus to the ends of the earth. This trend is encouraging.
It is a sign of spiritual maturity on the part of churches that have
only recently come into being. It greatly increases the global
gospel workforce. It also mobilizes Christian workers who have
less of a sense of entitlement than many Western missionaries,
more experience in suffering for the gospel, and an easier time

---

[8] An excellent resource on the subjects of tent making and BAM is Patrick Lai, *Tent Making*
(Waynesboro, GA: Authentic Media, 2005).

relating to new believers in difficult situations. God is raising up new missionaries from Latin America, Africa, and Asia at an unprecedented rate, and they are already having an impact on reaching the lost for Christ around the world.

However, challenges go along with this opportunity. The first challenge is training these new missionaries. Culture shock and the difficulty of cross-cultural communication happen to everyone, not only to Americans. Contextualization presents a challenge to everyone, regardless of that person's nationality. New missionaries from recent mission fields need to be trained well in the Bible and theology; they also need to be trained in missiology and cross-cultural communication. Second, those missionaries need to be sent and supported. Many of the areas from which these missionaries come lack effective mission agencies. The sort of support structures that work well in Europe and North America may not work in other contexts. Third, an international Christian workforce that is growing in national diversity presents new challenges in cooperation on the mission field. Each missionary brings his own culture with him to the mission field, and these cultural differences between Christian workers can be as challenging as cultural differences between missionaries and their host cultures.

The internationalization of Christian mission is here to stay. It is a glorious thing. It displays the wisdom of God and the power of the gospel. It accelerates the advance of the good news around the world. It should be encouraged and nurtured. This means missionaries in all mission fields, both old and new, should devote energy to encouraging a mission vision among their new brothers and sisters and to creating structures for training and sending missionaries from the four corners of the earth to the four corners of the earth. It also means Western missionaries, in humility, need to explore ways to facilitate these new missionaries from recent mission fields and to partner with them and work cooperatively alongside them.

USE OF INFORMATION TECHNOLOGY

Information technology has developed at a dramatic pace in recent decades, and that pace shows no signs of slowing down. There are now ways of getting the gospel, the text of Scripture, and helpful discipleship and leadership training materials into people's hands in remote places that no one could have imagined only a few years ago. Also, ways exist of interacting with people across the globe that are private and secure. Print, radio, and television are still useful media for getting the gospel into people's lives, but new options seem to emerge on a regular basis. As this book is being written in 2013, Christian communicators are sharing the gospel using interactive websites and chat rooms in local languages as well as via social media such as Facebook and Twitter. Audio and video resources can be downloaded from the Internet in any language Christian workers have engaged, and it can be done from anywhere and made available anywhere the government has not succeeded in blocking it effectively. Satellite television goes around local censorship with the same materials. The ubiquity of personal computers, tablets, and smart phones make it difficult for governments to know and control what comes across their borders, and large amounts of text can fit into a small memory device. Such is the rapid pace of technological development that this brief list will probably seem humorously outdated in only a few years. (Anyone remember the eight-track tape?) Internet access and basic IT tools are far more widespread than the gospel at this point and can be found in some highly unlikely places. The point is that Christian communicators need to stay on the cutting edge of communications technology, and they need to use new tools quickly to get the good news to as many people as possible.

URBANIZATION

One final trend in twenty-first-century missions is the growth of urban populations. Globally speaking, more people are now living in urban areas than ever before in history. *Urbanization* is a term that describes both the expansion of existing cities and the movement of people from rural to urban contexts. Both facets of meaning have important implications for Christian missions. Urbanization has slowed in the developed world (North America and Europe, for example), but it is continuing at a rapid pace in much of the global South (Asia, Africa, and Latin and South America).

First, when people move from place to place, there is often an opportunity for them to hear the gospel more openly. They are away from their families and religious influences and are experiencing new cultures and lifestyles. After a window of time, however, rural-to-urban migrants frequently cluster with others of like faith or culture, resulting in a hardening of their hearts against spiritual change. A second important implication of migration is what is known as "diaspora" missions. A diaspora is essentially a scattering of people to new places. As immigration (both rural and urban) increases, individuals and families from unreached peoples are moving to areas with more Christian and missionary presence. Most of these immigrants end up in cities.

While migration presents a great opportunity in missions, cities also add a significant challenge for missionaries. The issue is that, while people groups retain many of their core values and faith in a city, "urbanness" adds an entirely new layer to culture. Cities tend to be places of high population density, a fast-paced lifestyle, great diversity, and creativity. One only has to look at cities like Atlanta or Miami, both of which are different from their surrounding rural areas, to see that city residents are culturally different from others from a relatively close geographic area. For example, if a family from one people group moves to a European city, they will maintain some cultural distinctives while taking on others from their new home. Missionaries must consider both to effectively plan strategies for evangelism and church planting.

Urban areas also present social ministry challenges that are different from rural areas. Health and development needs take on a different character in cities. In the countryside those in poverty can often provide some of their basic necessities through small-scale agriculture, but that option is not available to the urban poor packed into slums and shanties. The anonymity of a large city makes social problems like crime, prostitution, slavery, and other crises seem much more common and easier to live with. Urban missionaries must be careful not to be overwhelmed with the need in crowded places.

Finally, church planting takes on unique characteristics in urban contexts. The cultural diversity and variety of people groups living in close proximity to one another make planting new churches inherently more complicated. At the same time, the opportunity to reach out to a diverse population adds real beauty to the task. Property costs are generally much higher in cities than in rural areas, making creativity in finding meeting places especially important. House churches and small-group-focused churches tend to be prevalent in unreached cities as opposed to traditional church buildings.

Missions is inherently a complicated work, but that work is made more challenging when faced with the complexity of urban contexts. The trends discussed in this section are but the beginning of issues facing urban ministry. At the same time they reflect the dynamic nature of engaging cities and peoples with the gospel. In one sense church planting and the growing presence of diaspora peoples are broad missiological trends. But among these opportunities urban centers present challenges that demand significant thought and research. Growing interest in reaching cities and urban populations will provide avenues for further discussion as the global church strives to fulfill the Great Commission among all the peoples of the world.

To start engaging your city by building bridges, try these first steps:

- *Open your eyes.* Prayer is the vital first step in any attempt to build bridges into the community where you live. Ask God for wisdom (Jas 1:5). Pray for vision, guidance, and ministry opportunities. And pray with your eyes open. Walk around your neighborhood, praying for the people you see and into the situations you notice. Do you see a school? Pray for the teachers, children, and parents. Is there an apartment building? Ask God to give you ideas on how to reach out to all the people who live there.

  Get to know your city. When you open your eyes to building bridges and praying for wisdom, you will see the people and places of your community in a new way. What nationalities and religions are represented in your neighborhood? Are there more families with children or senior adults? Where do people tend to gather together? When? All of these factors and more will help guide you as you think about how to engage your city.

- *Open your heart.* Once you've prayed for your city and

seen your neighborhood, learn to love your city, all of it. Love what the people around you love, and you will find that relationships come more naturally. Loving the city is not always easy, especially when it is noisy, dirty, or unfriendly. God has great compassion, and so must we. Whether you are learning to love the homeless, those with HIV/AIDS, or busy professionals, you will be reflecting Christ's love when you build bridges to people who are different from you.

Opening your heart and loving your city doesn't mean accepting everything. It may be that the best way you can impact your city is by living a holy life in front of your neighbors. Read Philippians 2:12–18, where Paul encourages us to live like "stars in the world" who are "faultless in a crooked and perverse generation." You might have the most influence by being different.

- *Open your door.* Loving the city and its people will lead to giving to the city. There is no shortage of need in urban centers. First John 3:17 (HCSB) says, "If anyone has this world's goods and sees his brother in need but closes his eyes to his need—how can God's love reside in him?" That makes it pretty clear. We don't have much of an option when James says that "pure and undefiled religion before our God and Father is this: to look after orphans and widows in their distress" (Jas 1:27 HCSB).

  If you're not doing it already, you will be amazed at the number of bridges you can build by giving of yourself to the community. If, while you are praying through your city, you see a particular need, act on it. It might be as simple as joining in a soccer match at the park or as complicated as starting a clinic for pregnant teenagers.

- *Open your mouth.* This may seem obvious, but it's often overlooked: share the good news. In many cities relationships are vital to witnessing. Too often, however, believers try so hard to be good friends with their neighbors that they never share the gospel. When Peter wrote, "Always be ready to give a defense to anyone who asks you for a reason for the hope that is in you" (1 Pet 3:15 HCSB), he was talking about taking risks in order to do good. Your neighbors will ask you why you are helping them. Tell them it's because your life has been changed for the better because of Jesus Christ. If they don't ask, tell them anyway. Seed that is never sown will never bear fruit. If your community never hears that the church is doing ministry in the community because of the gospel, they will think you are only nice people. That would be a tragedy.

CONCLUSION

The global context of Christian mission is constantly changing. The danger of writing a chapter like this one is that it will be somewhat outdated by the time the book goes to print, as global conditions change and present new threats and new opportunities. The gospel does not change. The basic tasks of missions do not change. The imperative nature of the missionary mandate does not change. Blessedly, the provision of the presence of Christ through his Holy Spirit does not change. Missionary strategists need to keep their finger on the pulse of global change. They need to adapt their tactics to meet new obstacles and to take advantage of new resources, while never changing the content of the message or the direction of the mission. Missionary strategists can never rest on their laurels until Jesus returns and they cast those laurels at his feet.

RESOURCES FOR FURTHER STUDY

Ashford, Bruce, ed. *Theology and Practice of Mission.* Nashville: B&H Academic, 2011.

DeYoung, Kevin, and Greg Gilbert. *What Is the Mission of the Church?* Wheaton: Crossway, 2011.

Hesselgrave, David J. *Paradigms in Conflict.* Grand Rapids: Kregel, 2005.

Lai, Patrick. *Tentmaking: Business as Mission.* Waynesboro, GA: Authentic Media, 2005.

Nicholls, Bruce J. *Contextualization: A Theology of Gospel and Culture.* Vancouver: Regent College Publishing, 1979.

NAME INDEX

SUBJECT INDEX

SCRIPTURE INDEX